Private Gardens of England

Private Gardens of England

Penelope Hobhouse

Photographs by Hugh Palmer

Harmony / New York

Published in the United States in 1987 by Harmony
Books, a division of Crown Publishers, Inc.,
225 Park Avenue South, New York, New York 10003
and represented in Canada by the Canadian MANDA
group.

Originally published in Great Britain by
George Weidenfeld and Nicolson Limited,
91 Clapham High Street, London SW4 7TA

HARMONY and colophon are trademarks of Crown
Publishers, Inc.

Manufactured in Italy

Library of Congress Cataloging in Publication Data

Hobhouse, Penelope.
       Private Gardens of England.

       I. Gardens, English – England.   I. Palmer, Hugh.
II. Title.

SB 457.6. H63   1986   712'.6'0942   86–15018

ISBN 0–517–56267–7
10 9 8 7 6 5 4 3 2 1

First American Edition

Designed by: Helen Lewis

Endpapers: The water canal at Brockenhurst Park by
moonlight.
Half-title page: The entrance to the upper orchard at
Bramdean House.
Frontispiece: A hedge of lavender at Howick Hall.

Contents

Introduction

This is not a history book, nor have the gardens portrayed and described been chosen for their historical style or lack of it. It is primarily a celebration of the English garden and of each garden's uniqueness; it is a written and visual testimony to their quality.

In the last forty years many of the larger gardens in England have been rationalized and simplified to reduce overall maintenance. New gardens tend to be smaller. But with simplification and reduction in size and therefore of scope, more attention, not less, has been paid to style. Garden owners in the 1980s seem more aware of the importance of principles of garden design, and of matching a garden to its environment. Gardens can be richer than ever in botanical interest; yet, at the same time, fewer gardens are just plantsman's collections. Owners study the history of gardening development, then choose and adapt features from it which are appropriate to their own particular garden. Even the country cottage garden and the narrow urban town garden have become increasingly sophisticated in design and plantsmanship. This does not mean that gardens today are just a series of reproductions of historical fashions. Far from it. Just as the typical English style, as epitomized by the teachings of Sedding and Gertrude Jekyll at the turn of the century, made use of the grand Renaissance ideas of space relationships, within which exciting plant associations were planned as pictorial compositions, so by the last quarter of the twentieth century various disparate styles and ideas had synthesized to produce gardens which stand a good chance of survival. Historical styles are adapted for modern upkeep and enjoyment. With new horticultural skills, aids and techniques, including machinery, pesticides and herbicides, one person can today maintain an area where ten were needed in the past. Garden owners, with little paid labour and that often unskilled, have become increasingly involved in day to day tasks. As a result, these gardens have a personal dynamic quality which is often missing from older gardens, which may have become 'fixed' or fossilized in a set historical style.

A blend of formal tradition and exotic but controlled wilderness still expresses man's mastery over nature. Today, in search of seclusion and privacy from an increasingly invasive outer world, the garden owner needs a retreat in which to feel at ease; hence meandering paths and surprise vistas are less appealing. Although the eighteenth-century English landscape garden has been freely exported abroad as a concept – often into totally inappropriate situations – it became clear at home, even by the time its greatest exponent Capability Brown died, that the great classical parks he and others had created, philosophical and poetical expressions of the Age of Reason, would seldom satisfy the Englishman's craving for flowers and passion for collecting and arranging plants. Perhaps most important of all, the English park, where sheep and cattle grazed outside the windows, failed to satisfy a natural desire for easily accessible secluded and sheltered garden areas near the house.

In a sense gardening history repeats itself. The first paradise gardens of the Persians and the *hortus conclusus* of the Middle Ages were thought of as retreats, where real barriers kept out marauders. Renaissance gardens, classical in concept, linked geometric shapes or garden 'rooms' with the house itself; later the Baroque garden pushed out the barriers, linking house, garden and countryside together. In eighteenth-century England William Kent 'leaped the fence, and saw that all nature was a garden', and earlier gardens with inner divisions were swept away. Since then English gardening styles have see-sawed between the naturalistic and the formal. Fashions were frequently influenced by availability of plants, and the richness of new introductions from the East extended the garden to incorporate woodland suitable for these rare exotics. Here plants not architecture determine shapes, lining contoured walks. The dialogue between the plantsman who collects and the garden architect who designs continues; perhaps English gardens are so good because each owner is pulled in two directions and finds a compromise between them.

In a disordered world, gardens are increasingly seen as paradisal retreats from concrete jungles and urban sprawl. Firm architectural frameworks made by green hedges, pleached trees and geometric box-edged beds (interestingly the demand for dwarf box plants, almost non-existent twenty years ago, now constantly exceeds available supplies) express order and discipline, as well as being visual barriers that give a feeling of security. The *giardino segreto* of the Italian fifteenth and sixteenth centuries, understood in translation as a private garden rather than a secret one, expresses the idea of a place to which to withdraw. In eighteenth-century England, at the height of the development of the English landscape park, the dual meaning of 'reflection' in water and of the mind linked a Brownian lake with philosophizing. The term 'private' also has two interpretations. The gardens described are private in the sense they are not owned or shared publicly; and to each owner the garden is his own 'private' retreat where seclusion is found.

A full account of any garden must explore the owner's relationship with it. Often the garden has to fulfil a twofold purpose: to satisfy an overall aesthetic need, which will include some link with the architecture of the house; and to be a place where plants are grown successfully. In no other country have owners been so adept at combining an understanding of the *genius loci* with firm horticultural intentions. What emerges most strongly from a visit to the gardens included in this book is how each site and each style, even when historical in derivation, produces such an infinitely variable effect. The owner is the presiding spirit whose constant care and interest makes the garden live. If England has the 'best' gardening climate in the world, which makes it possible to grow plants collected from a very wide range of natural habitats, the English gardener is continually concerned with reconciling his love of plants, and the ever-growing variety available, with a sufficiently strong design structure. The process of this reconciliation, where love of plants is combined with a strong historical sense, is what the best English gardening is all about.

Some gardens have passed through the hands of successive generations of one family. At Tresco Abbey the present owner is the fifth generation to garden where success and continuity depends on horticultural dedication. At Howick Hall and at Newby two generations have shaped modern gardens round architecturally important houses dating to an earlier period. Other gardens such as Rosemoor, now a charitable trust, are the creation of the present owner, who in thirty years has assembled an important botanical collection from many parts of the world. At Levens Hall the famous topiary shapes, dating to the end of the seventeenth century, set the garden in a firm historical mould. The gardens at Hatfield House reflect an enlightened programme of restoration where history is a dominant feature, the great house absolutely requiring an appropriate period garden to frame it. Smaller gardens combine botanical collecting with a sense of scale and design. Great amateur gardeners such as E.A.Bowles and Canon Ellacombe have worthy successors in modern gardeners such as Lady Scott (Valerie Finnis), Christopher Lloyd and John Codrington. At The Dower House Lady Scott has a collection of alpines in raised beds; she propagates and selects new hybrids, while over a wall the woodland garden made by her husband Sir David reflects Robinsonian style and an interest in the more unusual shrubs.

In the 1980s there is a growing awareness of how native English flowers can contribute to the garden and how easily colonies of the rarer ones can disappear with urban or factory spread. Many private gardens now have meadows where native flora seed and butterflies are encouraged. Christopher Lloyd's mother was a pioneer in the field, and the meadow at Great Dixter, not mown until late in the summer, has been an inspiration to many other gardeners. At Stone Cottage John Codrington mixes native wild flowers with plants collected on foreign travels; plants seed to make unexpected effects. Gertrude Jekyll and William Robinson would have approved the carefully chosen colour schemes at Kemerton Priory or the 'natural' water planting at Hodnet Hall. At Renishaw Hall Sir George Sitwell made an Italian Renaissance garden in the first quarter of this century; at Brockenhurst Park a water canal, terraces and a green theatre evoke an Italian atmosphere of simplicity and restraint. Sir Geoffrey Jellicoe's designs for Sutton Place, still not completed, seek to embrace the whole development of Western civilization, the gardens round the great Tudor house reflecting

John Codrington's garden at Stone Cottage.

the ecletic art collection inside. A section – Monet's garden – based on flower and colour schemes at Giverny, inextricably links painting and gardening: Monet planted his garden in order to paint it later. 'Here you find lush profusion, organized anarchy, riotous colour and a celebration of simple cottage plants, but all displayed within a symmetrical frame-work.'

Many garden owners are quite ready to share their gardens, within limits, with an increasingly keen and knowledgeable public. Indeed many find their visitors horticulturally stimulating. Garden visiting has become a national pastime – and it is with gratitude that this book is dedicated to the owners who not only give such pleasure to many millions each year by allowing them to share in such a variety of beauty, but also set a standard of imaginative gardening which remains the best in the world.

If there is heaven on earth, it is here, it is here, it is here.
(Inscription outside an Indian Mogul garden of the sixteenth century)

This book could not have been written and illustrated without the unfailing help and courtesy of the owners. Their inspiration and expert knowledge have been a constant source in broadening my own horticultural horizons. I hope the book adequately expresses my gratitude and admiration.

Author's acknowledgments

I am very grateful to Michael Dover at Weidenfeld and Nicolson for asking me to write this book, to Barbara Mellor and Penny David, without whom it would never have reached its final form, to Helen Lewis for designing it with such care and imagination, and to Anthony Lord for correcting the biological nomenclature.

This book is dedicated to my grandchildren, Eleanor and Arthur.

Photographer's acknowledgments

I would like to thank the garden owners for their kindness and forbearance throughout a year of repeated photographic onslaughts. Thanks also to Michael Dover, Barbara Mellor, Helen Lewis and Pat White, and to Abe Seltzer and Ken Ohara in New York.

Trewithen

near Truro, Cornwall
(Mr and Mrs Michael Galsworthy)

SET IN A windswept Cornish landscape, the elegant eighteenth-century stone house at Trewithen now looks out on perhaps the most beautiful woodland garden in England. At Trewithen the twentieth-century garden has been designed as a fitting frame for the house rather than as a separate entity and the resultant coherence is completely satisfying. House and garden seem perfectly attuned and linked together, fitting snugly into the greater landscape as the garden merges into shelter belts on its boundaries.

As new exotics from all over the world, but particularly from Asia and the southern hemisphere, were introduced in rapidly increasing numbers during the nineteenth century and the first quarter of the twentieth, many of the greatest woodland gardens began just as a collection of trees and shrubs; there was often little expression of 'style' and minimum attention was paid to a fitting relationship with an existing house. The overall unity of design between the house, the surrounding gardens and the landscape beyond was ignored. As trees and shrubs matured each specimen demanded space to realize its full potential. Paths or rides through woodland glades were cut to conform to the spread and canopies of plants; the woodland became a plantsman's museum where plants were admired and identified rather than contributing to any design pattern. In Cornwall and other favoured west-coast areas collecting became ever more tempting, and if any formal lines such as hedges or walls were introduced, it was generally to provide sheltered microclimates for specimen plants rather than as a planned architectural contribution.

Not so at Trewithen. Major George Johnstone MVO, who inherited the property in 1905, found virtually no garden. When he died in 1960 the gardens held not only one of the best collections of tender woodland plants in the country but also were so planned as to enhance and frame the house. Still eighteenth-century in spirit, garden and house are linked with each other to give a unity and coherence of design seldom realized in the twentieth century. To the south of the house, where two-hundred-year-old beech trees grew almost to the windows, Major Johnstone pushed out a great lawn on the flat hilltop, extending it to more than 200 yards (180 metres) with sweeping wings of mixed rare tree and shrub planting. Near the house the grass matches the width of the façade, with its central block and symmetrical wings, but it gradually narrows

In the sheltered quarry known as the Cockpit, azaleas, meconopsis and primulas thrive.

and tapers into woods at the far end. The view from the house down the garden is progressively more informal; the vista back from the furthest end shows the house anchored to the grassy site, its classical proportions cleanly framed by planting.

Today this planting is mature, the central grass an open sunlit glade. The giant Himalayan pink tulip tree (*Magnolia campbellii mollicomata*) now opens its lily-shaped buds in February and March, but Major Johnstone waited twenty years for it to flower; near it *Corylopsis platypetala* flowers in April, and a tall Chilean nothofagus, *Nothofagus procera*, was planted as a 6-inch (15-centimetre) seedling in 1923. Across the lawn on the east side the rare *Rehderodendron macrocarpum*, with white flowers in May, was first discovered on Mount Omei in western China in 1931 and now produces its own seed, the only specimen in cultivation to do this regularly. It grows above bushy specimens of *Magnolia kobus stellata* and is backed by the coloured barks of graceful birch trees. The large tender evergreen *Reevesia*

A winding path leads through the woodland.

pubescens resembles a bay and has creamy-white fragrant corymbs in July. It faces a specimen Kashmir cypress which has survived 10°C of frost in 1979, and 7°C in 1985, and the willow-leaved magnolia, *Magnolia salicifolia*, with lemon-scented bark and fragrant white strap-like flowers. This is a calcifuge magnolia which flowers in the first few years. The splendid red-berried *Viburnum betulifolium* at the east end of the lawn was one of 'Chinese' Wilson's plants. It takes many years to give its maximum performance. Beside it the leaves of *Fothergilla major* and *Acer triflorum* turn brilliant red in autumn.

Trewithen, 10 miles (16 kilometres) from Cornwall's south coast, was built on a flat hilltop for Philip Hawkins in 1720. Its name means 'the house in the spinney', so probably natural woodland of scrub oak, some beech and gorse would have already existed to give wind protection. Philip's cousin and heir, Thomas, was responsible for much of the tree planting that followed, writing at the age of twenty-one *On the Care and Cultivation of Trees*. A contemporary plan shows woods to the south and south-west of the house, protecting it from the prevailing wind, and broad avenues radiating from the house to north and east. On the south-east, where a ha-ha still marks the garden boundary, earth-moving operations altered and lowered land contours. Traces of the avenues still remain: stag-headed tree specimens, their tips pinched out after planting to promote sturdy growth on the windswept site. The only garden was a walled enclosure to the east, probably for herb beds. Ilex groves, a feature in the park today, were planted to the north of the house during the long minority of the nine-year-old heir, grandson of Thomas, whose father managed the estate from 1829, after the death of his elder brother. The acorns were sent from his own Bignor Park in Sussex. Christopher Hawkins lived until 1903 and left Trewithen, which he had probably never visited, to his sister's son, who died within a year. The new heir, aged twenty-two, was the eldest son, George Horace Johnstone, grandfather of Mr Michael Galsworthy, the present owner. He was to make the garden.

Perhaps Trewithen was fortunate to avoid Victorian garden development. Without a legacy of Italianate parterres and terraces (Nesfield, in fact, worked for Lord Falmouth, a neighbour at Tregothnan, during the 1860s), the front lawns were uncluttered and the only noticeable change since the eighteenth-century

Camellia 'Donation', one of the many camellias that flourish at Trewithen.

layout had been a thickening of the woods with cherry laurel, the extra shelter proving of great assistance in establishing the new young plants when gardening began. The beech woods had flourished and, in George Johnstone's words, 'It was necessary to take an axe and claim some air and light from amongst the trees'. A hundred *Rhododendron arboreum* were ordered and planted; 'these coming early "pinched" the best places', and a few survive, marking the foundations of this great garden. During the 1914–18 war three hundred beech trees were requisitioned for trench-props, and their felling allowed George Johnstone to plan and develop the great open glade on the south side of the house. Where trees had grown for more than two centuries a rich acid overlay on the basically clayey loam and shale provided perfect conditions for many of the exotics then being introduced. Bays of laurel provided screens for individual plant specimens, and further tree clearances to the south-west allowed planting space while retaining overhead canopies and the woodland character. Near the house tall screens of *Griselinia littoralis* shelter a hedge of the tender Chilean *Myrtus lechlerana*, with copper-coloured young foliage and fragrant flowers in May. More hedges of laurel and *Crinodendron hookerianum* criss-cross lower garden areas; planting in an old quarry, named the

OPPOSITE
The eighteenth-century house is glimpsed from the end of the long vista. To the left is a magnificent giant Himalayan pink tulip tree (*Magnolia campbellii mollicomata*).

15

Cockpit, is protected by stone banks. Japanese azaleas, meconopsis and primulas make a patterned carpet which can be looked down upon. More subtly *Philesia magellanica*, a dwarf evergreen, produces crimson tubular flower-bells in August, the flowers almost hidden among the foliage. Individual specimens of *Drimys winteri*, *Eucryphia cordifolia* (now 72 feet or 21 metres high – recognized as the tallest in Europe) and *E. moorei* thrive in sheltered corners and have grown to tree size. Two much-prized plants of *Laurelia serrata*, introduced from Chile in the 1840s, have foliage which is aromatic when bruised. The tender Chilean hazel, *Gevuina avellana*, has handsome polished pinnate leaves. Winding paths among thick rich planting direct and lead the visitor sometimes beside the original ha-ha, now used for composting leaves, at others on the outer perimeter of the garden permitting views across the countryside, surprising vistas to the outside world.

Many of the trees and shrubs in the glade and in the rest of the garden were grown from seed introduced during the early years of the century and the plant-hunting expeditions of the 1920s. Major Johnstone's neighbour, J.C. Williams at Caerhays, gave financial backing to George Forrest, and seedlings from his expeditions to China found their way to Trewithen. In 1913 Forrest first brought back *Rhododendron sinogrande* and a fine specimen flourishes in the Trewithen woods, its flowers hanging in creamy-white trusses in April.

R. macabeanum, considered the best rhododendron of all, was introduced from Manipur in 1928 by Frank Kingdon Ward, and bears its bell-shaped purple-blotched yellow flowers near by.

Major Johnstone became well known for his hybridization of rhododendrons, and after a hunting accident in 1932 became interested in breeding daffodils. His search for a narcissus with a pink trumpet was finally rewarded by 'Chelsea China' and 'Grace Moffat', the latter named for his secretary. The desirable *Camellia × williamsii* 'Donation' was a gift to Trewithen from Borde Hill, and became the parent plant to all future generations. The *williamsii* hybrids, first raised at Caerhays from a cross made from Forrest's *C. saluenensis* and *C. japonica*, are free-flowering and hardy, suitable for many gardens colder than Trewithen.

The woodland garden covers 28 acres (some 11.3 hectares); its favoured climate and rich planting giving pleasure and horticultural interest to many. The small eighteenth-century walled garden through which the wood is reached has a different flavour. There, formal rose beds, a lily-pool, a wisteria-clad pergola and planting against warm brick walls all make a more intimate atmosphere. Even here rare climbers distract: mutisias, trachelospermum, berberidopsis and twining schisandra curtain walls. The magnificent wall shrub, *Ceanothus arboreus* 'Trewithen Blue', with panicles of deep blue flowers, originated in this garden. This is a garden to return to after the excitements beyond have been discovered; the pergola offers shade above inviting seats.

Major Johnstone waited many years to see some of the plants reach their peak. He died in 1962, but before his death Trewithen had become internationally known for its collection. Planting was continued by his widow Alison, for whom he named his own rhododendron hybrid 'Alison Johnstone', by his daughter Elizabeth, and, since 1978, under the supervision of his grandson, Mr Michael Galsworthy. Where gales have brought down trees (for instance, in 1979) new planting begins. In the latest area a large stone urn stands

BELOW AND OPPOSITE
The atmosphere of the walled garden near the house, with formal beds and borders, offers a complete contrast to the woodland planting.

where in the eighteenth century there was a statue of the goddess Pomona. Then it was the centre of a 'pleasing labyrinth', described in a contemporary diary.

Seeds still come to Trewithen from the wild. Most recently seed was retrieved in Mexico of the rare *Magnolia dealbata*, only known because it was illustrated and described during Cortez's conquest, growing in an Aztec herbal garden at Huaxtepec. When they germinate and grow at Trewithen they will make a fitting addition to a garden whose late owner wrote a scholarly monograph on the Asiatic magnolias.

New planting at Trewithen, as in the early years of the garden's development, is done for the enjoyment of future generations. This is what real gardening is about. Mr and Mrs Galsworthy and the head gardener, Mr Michael Taylor, (awarded the Waley Medal for the cultivation of rhododendrons by the Royal Horticultural Society in 1975) plant for posterity.

Tresco Abbey

Isles of Scilly
(Mr Robert and Lady Emma Dorrien-Smith)

THE GARDENS at Tresco Abbey are not only exciting to botanists and knowledgeable plantsmen. They have a special 'painterly' quality which stimulates an aesthetic response quite different from the normal experience in English gardens. Surrounding blue sea and sky and the intense flower colouring of the open terraces provide unadulterated hue contrasts – colours only dimmed when bright sunlight and heat haze temporarily reduce the glare. The saturated grey tones which turn many of the mainland gardens into subtle exercises in softly blending flower and foliage colour are absent. At Tresco colours remain distinct, contrasts positive. The leaves of agave, aloe, opuntia and yucca, all of sword-like architectural quality, are sharply defined in a landscape where walls are draped with fleshy rosettes of aeoniums, Canary Island relatives of the alpine houseleek, and other members of the *Crassulaceae* which thrive in pockets of earth between the stones. In season soaring vertical stems of giant furcraea and puya become dominant focal points.

In comparison, walks in woodland on the lower levels seem intensely green. In the dense shade of tall metrosideros species and fine old Monterey cypresses, and beside groves of orange-barked *Luma apiculata* (syn. *Myrtus a.*) from New Zealand, a long path traverses the garden from east to west. *Eucalyptus globulus* (Tasmanian blue gum), the rare *Calodendron capense* (cape chestnut) from South Africa, aromatic-leaved camphor trees and podocarpus all tower above olearias and other tender shrubs to conceal cool cross-paths. Dark and sombre from below, *Metrosideros excelsa* (syn. *M. tomentosa*), with streamers of aerial roots in some cases reaching the ground, is the New Zealand Christmas tree. In July at Tresco its brilliant crimson bottle-brush flowers smother the branches, visible three miles away at St Mary's and startlingly exotic from the sky. The more modest-sized rata, *M. robusta*, flowers a

few weeks earlier, its clustered stamens a more coppery red.

Still in this lower garden, hedging of aromatic bay and, to the east, tall *Quercus ilex* make screens to shelter New Zealand tree ferns, lower-growing ground-covering ferns from Chile (*Blechnum chilense*) and silver-leaved tussocks of *Astelia nervosa* and *A. cunninghamii*. Under the sweeping umbrella foliage of the arboreal ferns including *Cyathea dealbata* (the ponga), black-stemmed *C. medullaris*, and *Dicksonia antarctica* on their sturdy trunks, *Woodwardia radicans* (the walking fern, whose arching boldly divided fronds have tip buds which easily root in adjacent soil) has spread to make thick clumps. Beyond, to the west, rustling bamboos provide hidden alleys for exploration, extending green tones and textures.

When Augustus Smith first came to Tresco in 1834 there was little vegetation on the island. Old Abbey ruins dating back to the twelfth century provided several walled enclosures where he began his gardening, while building the new Abbey in the local granite on a rocky outcrop marking the eastern boundary of today's garden. His garden developed across the treeless south-facing slope, terraces linked by steep steps into an almost geometric grid system. By 1855 the 17 acres (almost 7 hectares) which comprise the main area today had already developed a Mediterranean flavour with succulents, agaves and hard-leaved salt-resistant plants which flourished in the open site. By 1871, the year before his death, he was able to describe his mesembryanthemums, many sent to him from Kew by Sir William Hooker in 1849, 'the large purple being already one grand blaze of beauty'. At first many of his plants were from South Africa; later they came from Australia and New Zealand. In 1866 a parcel dispatched from Kew to Tresco contained two *Furcraea longaeva*, the spectacular agave-like Mexican plant which bears a flower-

stalk 20 feet (6 metres) high after ten to twenty years. The descendants still thrive in the garden; in a 'furcraea' year the flower-spikes are yellow waterfalls outlined against the blue sky through June and July. After flowering, little bulblets are distributed and root in the garden. Gradually Augustus Smith learned which plants would thrive and what conditions he could offer new introductions. Temperatures at Tresco seldom fall below freezing, although 24°F (−4°C) has been experienced. Nor do they rise above an uncommon 82°F (28°C). Although rainfall is low, hardly more than 34 inches (86 centimetres), humidity is high, and even in periods of extreme drought heavy dews are precipitated. Salt winds, with gusts up

to 110 mph, were then the greatest hazard, and remain so. Augustus Smith, from the outset, identified garden areas with countries: Australia, higher and lower Australia, Mexico and South Africa, and Cyprus. Today this topographical arrangement still indicates aspects and microclimatic conditions to be found in the areas of the garden that approximate to conditions associated with the 'wild' in different world climates.

Augustus Smith started to plant trees experimentally on the woodland drive behind the garden slope and on the western ridge above. By 1872, at his death, his nephew and heir Thomas Algernon Dorrien-Smith was able to select two low-rainfall trees, the Monterey

In the ruins of St Nicholas's Benedictine Priory climbing plants festoon the stone walls and succulents have seeded in cracks.

19

pine and cypress, (*Pinus radiata* and *Cupressus macrocarpa*) for further major windbreaks. A hundred years later, the pines, shallow-rooted by necessity in the almost bare rock, are now regularly replaced with bishop pine (*Pinus muricata*) when they fall. Major Arthur succeeded his father in 1918; under his care plants and seeds from New Zealand and the Chatham Islands enriched the collection. His son, Commander Thomas Dorrien-Smith, lived until 1973, his contribution to the gardens lying in the exciting emphasis on South African *Proteaceae*, plants which challenged even the skills of hot-house experts at Kew. These are generalizations; in fact this remarkable family produces dedicated horticulturists whose comprehensive individual skills and knowledge have ensured the garden's survival and continuous progress. The plant catalogue is worth studying not only for the accurate botanical nomenclature and some indication of a plant's site in the garden, but also because it is a record of the year in which a plant was first introduced to Tresco.

Another source of historical record are the beautiful flower paintings made by Frances Le Marchant, Augustus Smith's sister, of garden scenes and particularly of plants in the garden as they first came into bloom. The first flowers are painted in January 1873: they include *Pittosporum tobira*, the sweetly scented white-flowered evergreen shrub; an acacia; and *Hakea suaveolens* planted on the east rockery. In 1874 a furcraea flowers and is painted, and later this event is reported in *The Gardener's Chronicle*. There are forty-four paintings in all. Painting number 44 includes *Dianella tasmanica*, sent by Kew in 1872, bearing its turquoise-blue berries in 1879. Today this grassy-leaved plant grows almost by the new entrance, where the axis of the garden leads up to the Neptune statue.

The drive, the main approach from the rest of the island, now runs through dense woodland, where pines and cypresses, thickened with self-seeding tree clethras, *Clethra arborea* from Madeira, and the rare Tasmanian evergreen *Anopterus glandulosus*, which carries lily-of-the-valley racemes of white flowers in early spring. Above, over the north-facing ridge, acacias have also multiplied in full sun, and twenty-six different species flourish in the woods and garden, most flowering during the winter months. *Brachyglottis repanda* (the rangiora), an evergreen shrub from the North Island of New Zealand, which has soft green leaves (used by Maoris for writing messages) and panicles of ivory flowers, has naturalized beneath the woodland canopy, a neighbour for the African sparmannia, with rough-textured hairy leaves and white flowers, a familiar conservatory plant on the mainland.

From the wood an archway by the Abbey points a route into the garden and rockeries beyond, where, in April, primrose-yellow-flowered brooms, including *Cytisus fragrans* from south Europe and *C. stenopetalus magnifoliosus* (syn. *C. maderensis m.*), and coronilla mingle with the green-flowered aeoniums, and scent the air. Above the arch there is a tall bush of *Banksia serrata* with silvery-grey flowers – a tender Australian member of the *Proteaceae*. This family is also represented at Tresco by hakeas and the more familiar grevilleas, which are often found in favoured gardens on the mainland. Along the top terrace there are colonies of South African *Proteaceae*, leucadendrons and proteas, backed by large tree heaths with scented flowers in spring. The notable silver tree, *Leucadendron argenteum*, its leaves shimmering in the sunlight on the top terrace by the Neptune steps, flowered for the first time in 1985. Near by, more sober green-leaved leucadendrons, their flowers sur-

The spectacular flower-spike of a *Furcraea longaeva* is a focal point.

rounded by translucent bracts, and *Banksia grandis* and scarlet-flowered *B. coccinea*, brought back from Australia by Commander Tom Dorrien-Smith, father of the present owner, all thrive, proving that Tresco's long hours of sunlight, low night temperatures, and good drainage yet adequate moisture suit these plants.

The focal point or axis of the garden is the steep, almost centrally placed stairway known as the Lighthouse Walk which cuts abruptly straight up the slope to the statue of Neptune. At right-angles to it, paths run along the contours at spaced levels. From the Abbey courtyard, steps ascend to Neptune, or drop down to the sheltered green valley behind the 40-foot (12-metre) ilex hedge which shelters the garden from east winds. Today most visitors enter from below, where formal bedding-out traditionally flanks the central path. Shrubberies to right and left are tempting; an excursion east brings one to a circle of exotic palms and on to the old Abbey ruins

where plants climb and tumble over low walls. Blue-flowered *Convolvulus sabatius* (syn. *C. mauritanicus*) is hardly recognizable in its vigorous growth to eyes attuned to mainland gardens, where it is nurtured through cold spells and given a specially well-drained site. Near a large specimen of thorny-stemmed *Caesalpinia japonica*, dripping yellow racemes in May, a strange desert succulent *Dasylirion acrotrichum* has fallen over, its main stem now supported by granite pillars. A Brazilian *Bomarea caldasii* climbs and winds through shrubs, showing off its orange and yellow flower-heads. A relation of alstroemeria, it can be grown at the base of warm walls in the milder counties; a hybrid, *B. × cantabrigiensis*, has pinkish green flowers and is hardier. The climbing rata (*Metrosideros carminea*) is supported by its natural New Zealand host, the cabbage tree (*Cordyline australis*).

Reaching the east end of the Middle Terrace, follow the path westward as it opens out in full sun, where blue-flowered echiums – both of them tree forms from the Canaries, self-hybridized in the garden, and the monocarpic elephant trunk (*Echium pininana*), which seeds freely in mild west-coast gardens, make a mist of blending blues in May. Flower-spikes are recognizable by their resemblance to viper's bugloss. Other sun-loving flowers – arctotis, osteospermum, gazania, lantana and pelargoniums – sprawl horizontally in drifts and drape themselves vertically over walls as patches of vivid colour. Later agapanthus, watsonias and amaryllis contribute, and colonies of nerine, both *Nerine bowdenii* and *N. sarniensis* flower on sloping banks until November. Near by, *Beschorneria yuccoides* has arching spikes of coral-pink, and from pink translucent bracts droop green flower-bells. Its sword-like leaves of blue-green are soft, not sharp and fierce like those of a yucca, and make a rosette 2 feet (60 centimetres) high and wide. These plants become weeds at Tresco, seeding in every available crack in stonework as well as in soil. A stone pergola is roofed by a Burmese honeysuckle (*Lonicera hildebrandiana*) with exotic scented flowers in August. Above, a twining *Muehlenbeckia complexa* seems to strangle a host ilex, its black wiry stems making an impenetrable mat. In August on the lower level *Bursaria spinosa* is covered in creamy-white flowers, and is now 12 feet (3.6 metres) high and wide, with vicious spiny branches. This Australian tree was introduced to Great Britain in 1793, and will thrive against a warm wall in gardens colder than Tresco.

On the top terrace pines hang over the path providing shade for banks of tightly packed fasicularia between tree heaths, callistemons, grevilleas and olearias. The South African *Erica formosa* has green-tipped tubular red flowers. *Dryandra formosa*, a member of the *Proteaceae*, and *Acacia riceana* both have yellow flowers in April and both come from Australia, but are totally dissimilar in form and flower. From the steep slope the view is over the dense green canopy of the lower garden with its contrast in atmosphere and jungle growth.

The Tresco Abbey gardens contain a plant collection unique in the British Isles; indeed many plants found there are hardy nowhere else. Sub-tropical plants are those which cannot survive extremes of heat or cold, and the gardens provide this temperate climate. This does not mean that all the genera are unfamiliar and confusing. In fact many of the plants, if not identified with botanical exactitude, can be 'recognized' by family characteristics. The serious student and casual visitor alike can enjoy and name plants, but at different levels of achievement. Sometimes the profusion is almost daunting; the orderly mind craves group planting not for visual satisfaction but for simpler classification. Maybe, as Sir Thomas Hanbury once said about his own garden, La Mortola on the Italian Riviera, it is not a truly benevolent act to daunt British gardeners with such a bewildering list of exotic plants. But a visit to Tresco is not just to view a botanical collection; it is a rich, varied and atmospheric experience. Lasting memories contain strong 'colour' pictures immediately evocative of scents of flowers and leaves, and of the contrast between bright sunlight and cool shady walks.

On the Middle Terrace dwarf pale blue agapanthus grow round the edge of the pool. Above on the pergola the Burmese honeysuckle, *Lonicera hildebrandiana*, flowers in August.

OPPOSITE ABOVE
In the lower garden below the stone terraces tree ferns flourish.

OPPOSITE BELOW
Desert succulents and tropical jungle plants thrive beside each other in the garden.

Ince Castle

Saltash, Devon
(Patricia, Viscountess Boyd of Merton)

EVERYTHING is theatrical at Ince. The approach is confusing, through narrow winding lanes where the faintest glimpses of distant water just prepare the visitor for the final drama of the site. Seated on a wooded promontory, this unusual brick 'fortified' house built some time in the seventeenth century commands a view east and south over the spreading estuary of the Tamar to green slopes and woods beyond. Up the long west avenue with a tight perspective between two lines of stone pines (*Pinus pinea*) contained by clipped beech hedges, one emerges onto a forecourt dominated by the square brick house. Symmetrical towers were originally square fortified blocks at the four corners but, altered in the eighteenth century, now have pyramid-shaped roofs clad with tiles. Very steep broad granite steps lead up to the first-floor apartments, and fuchsia and valerian grow haphazardly in the cracks.

Almost an island (from which it derives its name *innis* or *ince*), the promontory provides a flat-topped windswept site for this unusual house. When it was first built, the approach would have been mainly by boat up the Lynher

RIGHT
Stone pines, clipped beech and ribbons of daffodils line the avenue approach to the fortified house at Ince. Symmetry and formality contrast with the wild windswept landscape which sweeps down to the Lynher estuary, preparing the eye for the sheltered garden enclosures and the rich planting beyond.

FAR RIGHT
Aromatic silver-leaved santolina spills over the edge of paving and cobbles. Stone finials and ornamental pots planted with agapanthus formalize a garden area with a central sundial.

river (where a pier is still in use) and it is certain that the pinkish-grey bricks, probably of Dutch make, which give it such a distinctive flavour in a landscape where local stone is used almost exclusively for walls and buildings, were floated to the shore below. Ince and its gardens are swept by strong gales, the only natural protection being woodland to the north, where in an enclosed bowl rhododendrons, camellias and other exotics thrive. Almost on bare rock, the thin earth remains poor and shallow, and much of Lady Patricia's gardening success has depended on raising beds to give plants more root space and on adding nutrient-rich and moisture-retentive topsoil. The force of the wind and its potential damage have been tamed by walls and planting, and the garden, now maturing rapidly after twenty-five years, shows how important initial preparation is to gardening efforts. The high light intensity, relative humidity and good drainage provided by so many raised beds in full exposure to the sun has allowed experiments

with the more exotic semi-tropical plants, many of which came as slips, seed or cuttings from the island of Tresco, and from neighbouring gardens in the warm south-west.

To the left or north of the house one quarter of the almost square forecourt is filled with a many-branched Turkey oak (*Quercus cerris*), which now lies partly on its side to reveal an intricate and contorted pattern of branches, a feature which makes a lasting impression, especially before leaves emerge in late spring. In April the edges of the drive are yellow ribbons of narcissi under the greyish-green umbrella heads of the Mediterranean pines. To the right and south a weeping *Hoheria sexstylosa* and a blue-leaved Atlantic cedar will eventually give volume to match the oak. A west-facing wall provides a warm site for climbing roses, ceanothus, abelias, the difficult *Lobelia tupa*, the silvery *Dorycnium hirsutum*, with brownish pink pea-flowers and mahogany seed-pods, and aromatic-leaved *Myrtus communis*, which bears its pink-white flowers in

The view over the sunken Italian garden from the terrace incorporates the wider Devon landscape beyond.

late summer, followed by black fruit, if a site suits it.

Lord and Lady Boyd came here in 1960 and restored the house and fundamentally reconstructed the garden. Now walled enclosures to the south and south-west provide shelter for Mediterranean-type plants which take advantage of the strong light and few frosts (which, when they come, drain away down to the exposed shores). On the southern side a paved courtyard, once enclosed by tall yew hedges, is open-sided to the landscape, allowing the eye to sweep over smooth lawn and a sunken formally patterned flower-garden to the blue waters and gentle Devon hills beyond. Round the walls on two sides 6-foot (1.8-metre) wide raised beds house a collection of tender climbers, shrubs and perennials, and thymes creep through the stonework, softening the harsh expanse of horizontal surface. Against the house vast *Magnolia grandiflora* bushes flower in spite of having to be severely cut back to allow light to the narrow windows, and in a sheltered angle the Asiatic evergreen magnolia, *M. delavayi*, is making good progress, although the severe winter of 1984–5 took its toll. The climbing evergreen *Stauntonia hexaphylla* has heavily scented white flowers in late spring, and sometimes bears its purple-tinged fruits in this favoured garden. *Vestia lycioides* with yellow tubular flowers, *Cestrum parqui* with vespertine musk-scented flowers, and the New Zealand kowhai (*Sophora tetraptera*) all enjoy the warmth, and osteospermum species and hybrids have a long flowering season. The bright blue *Salvia guaranitica*, the velvet-flowered *Salvia leucantha* and purple-crimson *S. involucrata* are all spectacular here. Not all the planting, however, is of plants which need special shelter and aspect; Lady Patricia uses the architectural blue-green leaves of *Euphorbia characias wulfenii*, silvery *Artemisia arborescens*, daphnes and the Mediterranean bush *Bupleurum fruticosum* to good effect, thickening up groupings of more vulnerable plants which may show damage in a severe winter.

In the formal garden which lies to the south, paving of slate and cobbles radiates from a central sundial, copying in essence the design of the hanging garden in the Renaissance Piccolomini Palace at Pienza, which Rossellino designed for a pastoral antiquarian pope to incorporate the fine views of south Tuscany across the valley. The garden layout at Pienza is in fact a later adaptation, but it captures the vision of the great Humanist philosophers: thus from the amenity and shelter of a carefully contrived and architectural garden, with raised beds and a sense of enclosed space, the eye travels towards a panoramic view. At Ince much of this atmosphere is evoked: overflowing flower-beds edged with stone kerbs are filled with scented flowers and foliage plants, many of which represent the Mediterranean *maquis* of cistus, broom and myrtle and which delight in the heat. Seclusion, security and solitude prevail, yet the garden in the foreground is linked with the drama of water, land and sky beyond. Other Italian touches are the specially designed stone finials and a dovecote with pointed roof, in which local and exotic shells decorate the walls. These elements make vertical accents, formalizing the free planting which partly disguises the geometric layout. Although the atmosphere is Italian, planting is eclectic; shrub roses and symmetrically placed bushes of *Magnolia kobus stellata* make a structure where tender evergreen correas, leptospermums and grevilleas from New Zealand and Australia, the rare Chilean guava, *Myrtus ugni*, with edible mahogany-red berries, azara species and the hairy-leaved herbaceous *Francoa sonchifolia* also from Chile, Mexican salvias and hebes, now often garden hybrids, mingle above bulbs of watsonias from South Africa. The grassy-leaved turquoise-berried *Dianella tasmanica* from Tasmania fruits here. Many low-growing plants have grey or silver leaves, which add a richness of colour and texture. Phlomis, helichrysum and fern-leaved dicentras thrive where drainage is sharp. At the bottom of this garden a water-canal is aligned on the dovecote and a long low seat invites a view back towards the castle framed against the northern sky.

The remains of a lime avenue underplanted with spring bulbs and later with a froth of Queen Anne's lace divide this garden area from the west, inviting a walk in shade to new walled compartments which lie snugly against the outer stone walls of the kitchen garden behind. Beyond, a swimming-pool area is hidden from view where it will receive the full strength of the sun. The lime trees provide necessary wind protection from the south-west, and stress the straight lines and right angles which hold together the design of this part of the garden, a complete contrast to the informality to the north and east. One of the garden enclosures, reached through an ivy-clad arch from the forecourt, is planted with flowers and leaves in white and cream only, while a rectangular compartment hidden beyond holds a collection of plants with purple, grey

and golden leaves and flowers of strong 'hot' yellow, orange, scarlet and crimson, especially chosen for their late summer performance and as a contrast to the pale pinks, yellows and blues of the Italian garden.

In the white garden raised beds round the edges overflow with philadelphus, deutzias, libertias and, for late summer, the little white-flowered *Aster divaricatus* with black wiry stems and a floppy habit. In shade a large specimen of *Rhamnus alaternus* 'Argenteovariegata' is ghostly and shimmering. More than in most 'white' gardens, variegated cream/white and green leaves blend; there seem to be no flowers in solid almost 'laundry'-white, which can be heavy and too dominant. The garden area with strong colours to the south depends equally on the use of leaf and flower colours. Purple sword-like leaves of New Zealand flax, *Phormium tenax* 'Purpureum' and some of the brightly coloured smaller garden cultivars in this genus, are always striking, and *Pittosporum tenuifolium* 'Purpureum' has more glossy crinkled foliage. Golden creeping Jenny (*Lysimachia nummularia* 'Aurea') and the elegant shrub *Physocarpus opulifolius* 'Luteus' give contrast. *Crocosmia* 'Lucifer' with scarlet flowers and *C.* 'Solfatare' with bronze foliage and sulphur flowers all contribute to the riot of summer colour.

On the east front of the house all formality has gone; a wide undulating border backs the outstretched wall of the southern courtyard, and island beds in the lawn reduce the severity of the wind, narrowing the prospect across the waters to glimpses at eye-level over a ha-ha. From the first-floor windows the view is still wide and open. Informality increases to the north as in a sloping bowl sheltered by woods of lime, oak, ash and sycamore a site is provided for groves of acers, camellias, rhododendrons, South American myrtles and New Zealand olearias, which thrive where light and shade and a moist root-run of acid soil provide ideal conditions for growth. Plantings of these evergreen shrubs partly surround an open glade with a central water feature. Once this was a bowling-green, but now moisture allows Robinsonian natural planting where giant kingcups, irises, primulas, astilbes and ferns jostle each other on the swamp edge, and a pump keeps the area suitably flooded. Pausing here it is still possible to feel a strong sense of design unusual in a Cornish woodland garden, where overhead canopies and rounded bush shapes usually dictate the curves of meandering pathways. Trees have been felled to allow

glimpses into the darker wood and other sunlit glades beyond, and the whole area is a pictorial essay in alternating light and shade, its patterns constantly changing as rough winds blow from the north and east. With the future in mind new tree planting has not been neglected: the Californian redwood (*Sequoia sempervirens*), groups of *Cercidiphyllum japonicum*, Chusan palms (*Trachycarpus fortunei*), and the uncommon *Tetracentron sinense*, discovered by Augustine Henry and introduced from western China by Ernest Wilson in 1901, are all growing away above clumps of good foliage shrubs such as elaeagnus, *Eupatorium ligustrinum*, apple-leaved

Griselinia littoralis, osmanthus and rustling bamboos which provide a windbreak for young trees when they are at their most vulnerable. This is a garden area for spring and early summer flowers, but its patterns and textures of leaf in the later season make it quiet and attractive to the discerning in search of subtle effects of differing green tones. By late summer brighter hues return with orange- and red-capsuled fruit of euonymus species and the startling scarlet leaves of the American tupelo (*Nyssa sylvatica*), with dense pyramidal growth. Near by the Chinese *N. sinensis* will be as striking, but needs time to develop.

Hydrangeas and vertical leaves of New Zealand flax frame the dovecote.

OPPOSITE ABOVE
In the formal garden to the south of the house patterned paths of slate and cobbles divide beds where Mediterranean-type plants thrive in the mild climate.

OPPOSITE BELOW
Daffodils are naturalized along the drive.

Penheale Manor

near Launceston, Cornwall
(Mrs Norman Colville)

THE APPROACH TO Penheale Manor is normally from Launceston, winding over a bleak
windswept plateau where oak and ash are
shaped by salt-laden Atlantic winds. Finally the
road drops down below the eastern slopes of a
steep ridge into a sheltered wooded valley,
where the granite house and terraced and
walled garden enclosures lie protected against
the hillside. A lime avenue leads from Eglo-
skerry village to the north entrance of the

manor, where a mid-seventeenth-century
gatehouse closes in the almost square forecourt
of the original façade. Both above and below
the house more geometric enclosures are
shaped by walls and terraces, their outlines little
changed over centuries, and a broad walk,
dating to Elizabethan times, lies beneath the
main retaining wall of the house, and runs
along the length of the lower garden. A central
vista cut through the woodland in the valley

Below the granite steps a
large clump of royal fern
(*Osmunda regalis*) grows at
the water's edge.

allows a glimpse of distant open moorland, a part of Dartmoor stretching to Devon in the east.

Dating from the late sixteenth century, the building was much altered over successive centuries and in fact was almost derelict when 'discovered' by Colonel Norman Colville just after the First World War. Edwin Lutyens (later Sir Edwin) was still working at the great fortress of Castle Drogo on the eastern side of Dartmoor and was called in to restore and enlarge the house. Few architects have so respected tradition without sacrificing their creative power. As Ralph Edwards wrote in 1925, soon after Lutyens' work at Penheale was completed, 'We feel that, if its builders were alive, thus they would have chosen to enlarge it; so perfectly has he interpreted the spirit of the place. The new and the old are readily distinguished, and each gains from the proximity of the other.' Sixty years later we can echo these words. Lutyens seems to have captured and distilled the architectural style of this isolated Cornish manor, and romanticized its ruggedness without in any way diminishing its essential austerity.

When it came to designing the garden at Penheale, both Colonel Colville and Lutyens again worked to 'improve' while retaining the original and quite functional character; house and garden remain inextricably linked both architecturally and in spirit. The formal garden frames and extends the function of the house so that together they make a completely integrated unit. Although rich planting softens the lines of steep granite steps and distracts from the geometric layout, the design is deliberately austere, in keeping with the spirit of the house and the remote wild landscape in which it is hidden. In the wood there is a similar feeling of secrecy and remoteness. In spring, in the shelter of the wooded valley, flowering exotics offer an exciting contrast to the rough exposure of windswept fields beyond.

To the east, formal gardens almost encircle the house; to the west, woodland shrubs thrive under the canopies of old oaks. In both areas the rich planting, now more than half a century old, takes natural advantage of the differing aspects. Colonel Colville immediately appreciated how the existing walled and terraced levels which fitted round the old house could be exploited to make a 'new' formal garden looking back in style to the period when the house was built. Lutyens proposed firm structured designs to be fitted on to the existing horizontal levels, which, in essence, had been carved out of the hillside perhaps three hundred years earlier. Colonel Colville asked Lutyens to call in Gertrude Jekyll (in 1920 she would have been almost eighty) to help him with the plans and plants for the formal gardens. Although she never visited Penheale, the existing garden, of partly walled enclosures and terraces, would have appealed to her designer's sense. Perhaps her most successful gardens were those where she was able to 'furnish' a structured architectural framework with her informal planting. She loved to soften hard masonry with soft flowing lines of plants, and compose her series of carefully balanced garden pictures so that each unfolded as the viewer moved between different garden compartments. The harsh white granite of which Penheale's walls and steps were composed, the latter almost uncomfortably steep, was very different from the warm soft tones of her native Surrey stone, yet she would have appreciated how house and garden were linked together to survive the battering of the Atlantic gales from the west and south. Terraces and steps were strictly functional, for adjusting levels, and the steepness of the east-facing slope ensured wind protection from the west.

Some of her plans for the gardens survive and much was executed just as she and Lutyens proposed, but as Colonel Colville's own gardening knowledge and interest grew he added tender shrubs and climbers and, in particular, the collection of rhododendrons and camellias in the woodland. These, as they matured, brought Penheale to other gardeners' notice. Nevertheless, Miss Jekyll's influence has ensured that the garden today, unlike any other of the great Cornish 'plant' gardens, retains its formal aspect, with broad herbaceous borders to give colour and interest in summer after spring-flowering trees and shrubs are over. Lutyens' layout on the lower east terrace, with its axis on semicircular curved granite steps which gave a view to the south, below a gateway, to a pond surrounded by dense tree planting, was not completed. In fact Colonel Colville designed his own complicated yew 'frames' where geometric enclosures now provide sheltered inner garden areas. Formal blocks of yew hedging are interspersed with small secret garden rooms, where different plant or colour themes (and, in one, a swimming-pool) lie concealed. The pattern is asymmetrical, and most easily understood from the house windows above. Today the yew has grown wide, so dense and thick that the wind bounces off the vertical surfaces to

create turbulence and funnels of air of gale-
force strength.

In the upper walled gardens to the west Miss
Jekyll drew out a design for a sunken rose
garden, each bed enclosed in box hedging, and
a wall border. A large ilex, which has now
gone, shaded the south-west corner. The beds
are much as she drew them, although those
nearest the house, in front of a wall where the
old architecture merged with the 'new', have,
since the ilex tree was felled, been restructured
and planted with sun-loving crinums. Plants
we see today are probably the choice of
Colonel Colville, who developed a love and
appreciation of woodland trees and shrubs. In
the border camellias, corylopsis, *Magnolia*
hypoleuca, *Stewartia sinensis*, *Rhododendron mu-*
cronatum 'Lilacinum', a cultivar with soft-lilac
flowers in May, and other shrubs have now
grown large. Against the north-facing wall the
Chilean *Lapageria rosea* thrives in cool moist
soil; at its feet is another Chilean, the desirable
small *Philesia magellanica* with wiry stems and
crimson flowers in August. Beside them, to
delight the botanist, the bigeneric hybrid of
these two evergreens raised by Veitch's nursery
in 1870, × *Philageria veitchii*, scrambles and
bears rose-purple flowers in late summer. A
second enclosure on a higher level above the
front courtyard is a formal rose garden, a raised
bed against its south-facing wall providing a
sheltered well-drained site for tender shrubs.

Many of the other great Cornish gardens are situated on the south coast, almost at sea-level. With mild winter temperatures and a long growing season they provide perfect sites for many exotics. But for any coastal garden the greatest hazard is wind and, in this respect, Penheale has a natural advantage. Almost on the north coast, the garden, although 450 feet (135 metres) above sea-level, lies in a comparatively sheltered valley. The growing season starts late but in an average year will continue well into December and the relatively cold winters without warm intermission make some genera that need a 'resting' period easier to grow here than in the warmer gardens of the south-west coastal region. The high rainfall of 46 inches (117 cm) leads to fast growth, and the general humidity provides perfect conditions for magnolias, rhododendrons and camellias which grow in the natural woodland of oak at the western end of the garden. The soil is acid but shallow – virtually shale from rocks close to the surface – and except in the woodland, where it is more silty, cultivation has to be started with a pickaxe rather than a spade. Thus in a year of drought such as 1976 many shallow-rooting plants suffer badly, and losses at Penheale also increased in the two dry summers of 1983 and 1984.

The entrance archway of the gatehouse frames the doorway of the main building at the end of a paved path. Through this, on the inner south side, a gallery raised on granite pillars resembles an Italian loggia, and is festooned with roses and tender climbing plants. A yellow-flowering Banksian rose covers one south-facing wall and the rare *Dendromecon rigida* from California, with narrow glaucous leaves and poppy-like buttercup-yellow flowers, performs on another. A twining 'gazania', the daisy-flowered *Mutisia oligodon*, grows up a pillar, its suckering base developing into a thicket of stems. Introduced from Chile by Harold Comber in 1927, it bears its salmon-pink flowers intermittently all through the summer, and here at Penheale continues to flower almost until Christmas. In the narrow bed at the base of the pillars spreading ceratostigma and perovskia, both with blue flowers in late summer, and the tender woody *Salvia microphylla* (syn. *S. grahamii*), crimson-flowered with fresh green leaves, survive even a severe winter. Across the courtyard and flanking the steep granite steps which lead up to the formal rose garden, massed planting of the creeping form of Forrest's rhododendron, *Rhododendron forrestii repens*, is unusual and

In one of the narrow inner yew enclosures planting is simple.

bears its scarlet bell-shaped flowers in April. In a shady corner, *Crinodendron hookerianum*, with long-stalked crimson lanterns, thrives in the acid soil.

Colonel Colville, always a collector of beautiful and rare objects, used his well-developed artistic sense in planning his garden colours and plant juxtapositions. The garden at Penheale reflects his wider interests. At first, near the house, architecture and formality dominate, yet at the same time are subtly softened and invigorated by the uncommon and tender plants which seem carefully placed to arrest and distract from the pure geometry. In the woodland, his assemblage of 'collectors' plants' are arranged so that soft colours blend in gentle progression, each garden picture carefully contrived as paths wind through the glades. In his lifetime, with his head gardener, Penheale became known for rhododendron and camellia hybrids, but perhaps his most striking legacy to the gardens surrounding this remote house is the disciplined moderation with which they were planned. At the same time as being a plantsman he knew when to resist further garden planting, leaving the view southwards over the big pond, shaded by dense planting of trees, as an uncluttered foreground to pale rhododendron flower colour beyond the dark water. Few other such knowledgeable gardeners could have resisted the temptation to 'improve' the prospect. Penheale retains its remote and rather austere atmosphere; set in a wild windswept landscape, the house and gardens are inward-looking in conception, a refuge from the world outside which – except for one vista to the moors beyond the lower valley to the east – is deliberately excluded.

ABOVE
Thick yew hedges are a perfect background for overflowing borders.

LEFT
The rare *Dendromecon rigida* has narrow glaucous leaves and bright yellow poppy flowers. It thrives against the sheltered loggia.

FAR LEFT
A view across the pond from the rhododendron wood to the curved granite steps and formal garden enclosures.

Rosemoor

Torrington, Devon
(Lady Anne Palmer and The Rosemoor Garden Trust)

ALTHOUGH many think of Lady Anne Palmer as pre-eminently a dendrologist (after all she is now Chairman of the International Dendrological Society, and for seven years organized many of its outstandingly successful tours abroad), her knowledge and the garden she has made at Rosemoor belie any suggestion that her interests do not cover a broader spectrum of gardening. Today it becomes obvious immediately on arrival that in the years since 1959 when she first began serious gardening she has built up an outstanding and interesting collection not only of rare trees. She has steadily and unostentatiously gathered together many uncommon smaller shrubs, bulbs and perennials. Indeed, now that the garden, as a charitable trust, also incorporates a successful nursery

Near the house curving island beds are packed with plants of botanical and gardening interest.

area, where the plants for sale are almost all produced by the 'home-team', it is only necessary to glance at the admirable list of plants available to realize that not only tree seedlings but some of the smaller plants in the nursery are unlikely to be found elsewhere in commerce.

Rosemoor lies facing south almost at the bottom of a steep-sided valley above the river Torridge near Torrington in north Devon. Woodland, mainly of coppiced oak, Scots pine, Douglas fir, *Abies alba*, alder, ash, birch and beech, shelters the garden to the north and east. Across the river valley the hillside rises steeply and the Forestry Commission plants oaks and blocks of quick-growing commercial softwoods. Situated 100 feet (30 metres) above sea-level with a rainfall of 40 inches (101 centimetres) annually, the garden is climatically favoured, but early mild springs are deceptive and rising sap often receives a severe setback from sharp late frosts, which can be very damaging to young plants and may destroy precocious flower-blooms overnight. The soil is basically a heavy clay with a range of acidity from pH 5 to as high as 8. Alluvial soil is brought up from the river bed when possible and mulches of leaf mould, chopped up as well as gathered by machine, are used to prevent drying out in summer. All compost used in the nursery is also made in the garden. Gardening techniques are practical and labour-saving; while upkeep is impeccable, the survival of the collection depends on keeping down labour costs as well as making the nursery garden a viable commercial enterprise.

In 1923 the house was merely a family fishing lodge. Much of Lady Anne's childhood was spent in New Zealand. Married in 1947, she returned with her husband and family to live permanently at Rosemoor but did not become interested in gardening until 1958. Then, recuperating from measles in Algeciras, she met Captain Collingwood Ingram. 'Cherry' Ingram, as he was called, was at this time nearly eighty (he died in 1980 aged a hundred), and the greatest authority on the history of the Japanese cherry, and the main species and numerous cultivars of garden origin which were grown at that time in the British Isles. His book *Ornamental Cherries* (1948) is still a standard work. However, in his garden at Benenden in Kent, he assembled, besides cherries, an historic collection of plants, mainly grown from his own seed collected in the wild. It seems that his influence on Lady Anne's future gardening development was enormous. Thrown in at the deep end, through him she met people at the top in the horticultural world and started to develop the gardens at Rosemoor. His influence as well as his knowledge

extended far beyond the genus *Prunus*. From the outset, planting in the garden was serious and scientific; each plant being efficiently labelled with its name, country of origin and date of planting. This documentation ensures that the collection at Rosemoor, where so many plants have come straight from the wild, is of exceptional botanical *and* horticultural interest. Today new trees from seed collected by Lady Anne herself, Roy Lancaster and Keith Rushforth, and from Kew and Wakehurst plant-hunting expeditions, continue to enrich the garden, and importantly are occasionally available in the selling bays. Her own seed also goes to Kew, Wakehurst and numerous other botanic gardens and private collections,

In the foreground a broad mass of the umbrella plant (*Darmera peltata* syn. *Peltiphyllum peltatum*) is planted at the water's edge. The tree beyond is the tupelo, *Nyssa sylvatica*, the leaves of which colour vividly in autumn.

carrying on the best of gardening traditions.

In the garden itself there was early planting of prunus specimens. A fine *Prunus* 'Kursar', one of Captain Ingram's own hybrids, with deep pink flowers borne just as the reddish-bronze young leaves appear in March, is draped with *Lonicera × americana*, a vigorous July-flowering honeysuckle. A sucker from his own Benenden tree of the Fuji cherry, *Prunus incisa*, has grown large; it bears pinkish-white blossom also in March. In a warm bed outside French windows at the base of the house walls *Cistus* 'Anne Palmer', a pink-flowered hybrid with sage-green crinkled leaves, was raised by Collingwood Ingram. As some of the hanging woodland behind the house was cleared, groves of other prunus were planted to cover the lower slopes behind and

east of the house. The Korean Hill cherry, *Prunus serrulata pubescens*, flowers later. Hill cherry *P. s. spontanea* has grey bark and bronze young foliage and Sargent's cherry (*P. sargentii*), with pink flowers and chestnut bark, has brilliant autumn colouring.

In 1959 the garden area was much smaller, but it had a few good trees which remain part of its structure: a *Libocedrus decurrens* planted near the house in 1912, a large walnut, two tulip trees and some fine oaks in the fields beyond its perimeter are now part of an expanding arboretum. Garden expansion began near the house, where a series of informally shaped beds have planting in three layers. Today tree canopies protect and shade lower-growing shrubs, and spreading perennials and bulbs make drifts between the taller plants. In

Prunus 'Taoyama Zakura' has a spreading habit and bears fragrant semi-double blush-pink flowers, backed by coppery-tinted young foliage shoots.

OPPOSITE

Against the house wisteria, clematis and ceanothus provide a curtained backdrop for tender rhaphiolepis, pittosporum and variegated myrtles.

39

On the northern slopes above Pfitzer's juniper, flowering cherries are grouped for spring performance.

such as the creeping dogwood (*Cornus canadensis*), meconopsis, euphorbias in quantity and the little *Hacquetia epipactis* with golden-yellow flowers in spring thrive in the well-mulched soil.

By the water an American swamp cypress (*Taxodium distichum*) is beautiful with pale green frond-like leaves in spring and bronze autumn colour – one of the conifers which drops its leaves. Ferns such as *Blechnum chilense* and drifts of hostas, astilbes and rodgersias dominated by giant gunnera pattern the pond edge with rich textures all summer and with flowers in season. The stems of *Salix fargesii* glow reddish-brown all winter. East, above the drive, *Pyrus nivalis* draws the eye in spring, and a grove of birch with shining pink and cream bark catches the afternoon sun. Leaving other genera clumps for exploration another time, the return towards the house passes many specimen pines, their green and grey outlines stabilizing and giving structure to a garden landscape, with large spreading clumps of the Pfitzer juniper planted at intervals along the lower slopes above. On an old tennis court a collection of dwarf conifers is interesting to a specialist, and sloping banks in full sun provide ideal growing conditions for brooms and cistus, towered over by eucalyptus, the leaves of which fill the air with fragrance.

North and east of the house more beds, some raised and containing special soil mixtures for growing alpines and other plants which require good drainage, are surrounded by winding gravel paths. In one corner sheltered by old garden walls a collection of tender plants, many collected on expeditions with the International Dendrological Society, are given a favoured site. From New Zealand the dwarf conifer *Dacrydium laxifolium*, known as mountain rimu, was grown from seed collected on a wind-swept hillside. A leathery-leaved monotypic genus *Pachystegia insignis*, with white daisy-flowers carried on stiff stalks, is rare in gardens. These and a group of celmisias, and viciously spiked wild Spaniard (*Aciphylla colensoi*) cover a wide range of botanical interest from this country alone. Watsonias, itea, *Phlomis fruticosa* 'Angustifolia', cestrum, and autumn-flowering *Alstroemeria pulchella* from Brazil make this an area to visit in late summer, while nearby beds of mixed day-lilies provide summer colour and one area is dominated by *Prunus serrula* with striped mahogany bark. In spring the tree peony, *Paeonia* 'Joseph Rock Variety', has white papery flowers, stained maroon-purple inside the petals, and pale

beds by the house pink-flowered *Rhaphiolepis* × *delacourii* flowers in front of *Ceanothus impressus* 'Puget Blue' and beside *Viburnum carlesii* 'Diana', a variegated myrtle and a dwarf pittosporum, *Pittosporum tenuifolium* 'Tom Thumb'. To the south sweeping island beds, set in mown grass, frame views to a pond, its sides planted with large-leaved water-plants. Shrubs with golden and variegated leaves, such as *Sambucus racemosa* 'Plumosa Aurea', *Physocarpus opulifolius*, the elegant eye-catching bamboo *Arundinaria viridistriata* and the horizontal-branching *Cornus controversa* 'Variegata', give interest as leaves unfurl in spring and complement blue-flowered *Rhododendron augustinii* and other similar hybrids. The uncommon *Trochodendron aralioides* and *Stewartia monodelpha*, both from Japan, a fine early-flowering *Magnolia campbellii* and a specimen *Arbutus menziesii*, the latter grown from seed, are all botanically stimulating as well as first-class garden plants. Beneath them smaller plants lavender-flowered *Anemone nemorosa* 'Robinsoniana' grows densely below shrubs.

As the slope steepens, beds are terraced with stone from the river quarries, and smaller woodland plants cover the ground where the soil is acid. Gaultherias, vacciniums, epimedium with bronze-tinted leaves flourish between hollies, viburnums and pieris. Lady Anne is interested in hollies and now has a good collection of more than a hundred. Among them are the Canary Island holly, *Ilex perado platyphylla*, broad-leaved *I. latifolia* and *I. × koehneana*, a hybrid of the latter, and *I. aquifolium*, with purplish young shoots and toothed leaves. In a sheltered corner a bramble from northern China, *Rubus lineatus* has rambling stems covered with silky down and leaves arranged like those of a horse chestnut. Japanese azaleas line a pathway winding round the slope where *Narcissus cyclamineus*, grown from seed from Sir Eric Savill, have naturalized.

The area of garden is now approximately 11 acres (about 4.5 hectares), of which the arboretum on the slopes to the north and in the outer field occupies a good third. Such distinction is in fact misleading because, except for the most recent planting of collections of sorbus, nothofagus and zelkova, garden and trees flow together as a unit and do not demand separate 'botanical' visits. Although most important genera are grown in groups together throughout the garden, Rosemoor still seems pleasantly informal in atmosphere, and not a collector's museum. The National Collection of cornus is now in the garden; conditions suit most of the Asiatic species, but Lady Anne feels that even favoured sites on the lower south-west-facing slopes may not have enough hot sun in summer for *Cornus florida* and many of its cultivars raised in America.

Even now she is disarmingly modest about her garden; a perfectionist, perhaps, she seldom considers that it looks at its best. Not only a plantswoman, Lady Anne cares for each specimen, and each plant or group of plants is given a site as exactly suited to its requirements as possible. Perhaps this explains some of the garden atmosphere. Without formality of design, plant and site groupings nevertheless seem so appropriate that an outsider, even a non-specialist, moves logically from area to area without feeling jarred by changes of theme. The garden at Rosemoor combines botanical interest with a display of good gardening technique and a sensitive appreciation of the quality of plants. Not only is the garden of importance in the development of twentieth-century English gardening, but it also provides much pleasure and stimulation to an increasingly large number of visitors.

BELOW LEFT
A pair of white-flowered rugosa roses (*Rosa rugosa* 'Alba') lead into a wide lawn.

BELOW RIGHT
A group of orange-flowered *Lilium tigrinum* behind hypericum in the border.

The Gables

Stoke-sub-Hamdon, Somerset
(Mrs Kenneth Beaumont)

THE GARDEN at Stoke-sub-Hamdon lies behind the seventeenth-century house which faces on to the village street. Like Montacute House near by, it is built of the golden Ham stone quarried from the high cone-shaped hill which lies just south of the village. Against the low wall and mullioned windows overlapping bushes of herringbone *Cotoneaster horizontalis* are draped in slanting patterns, leaves and berries scarlet for long autumn months. Behind the house the garden is almost 2 acres (0.8 hectare) in extent, and although modern housing estates threaten the boundaries, the atmosphere remains remote and secret. Tall trees, once planted for wind-protection, especially to the east, seem to encircle and shield the house and garden. One vista alone remains: the hill and the monument on its summit are glimpsed between the branches of an old cedar and the feathery grey foliage of *Chamaecyparis lawsoniana* 'Triompf van Boskoop'.

In 1904 Gertrude Jekyll wrote: 'In the teaching and practice of good gardening the fact can never be too persistently urged nor too trustfully accepted, that the best effects are accomplished by the simplest means. The garden artist or artist gardener is ever searching for these simple pictures; generally the happy combination of some two kinds of flowers that bloom at the same time, and that make either kindly harmonies or becoming contrasts.' Mrs Beaumont's garden seems a remarkable collection of these 'simple' garden pictures; the whole effect breathes with some extraordinary and magical excellence which is seldom achieved and certainly cannot be arrived at by consulting a rule book.

Dr and Mrs Beaumont have lived at The Gables for twenty-five years. When they came there were a few trees and an Edwardian rock garden where raised beds were encircled by winding paths. Some old apple trees and two ancient espaliers showed where the kitchen garden had once been. Stone pillars come

probably from the ancient castle and priory at Stoke, and the lowest part of the garden concealed the monks' bath-house, natural springs providing water still in modern times. Walls surround the garden, and others remaining from old buildings divide it into sections. Today the planting is thick – some would say crowded – but so placed and contrived that open sunlit lawns give way to dark glades in pleasing succession. Yet 'contrived' is too strong a word to describe the planting here. Mrs Beaumont seems to have some instinctive feeling for wise plant and colour juxtaposition. In the garden each path or turning reveals tempting views, through shady undergrowth under canopies of tall trees, to some new patch of open lawn where dense planting conceals the edges. A patch of flower or leaf colour on one side is repeated again at the end of a vista, so that each garden area has a unity and purpose of its own, yet leads and flows into some new theme. In fact Mrs Beaumont's themes are practical ones; she grows and encourages her plants in the conditions which suit them, never struggling to create artificial effects. Often the garden scenes are created by light and shade, where plant groups gradually merge from sun into shadow round the base of a tree. A drift of blue-flowered brunnera becomes luminous as the light fades on the fringe of dense planting; red tulips, eye-catching in sunlight, mellow and darken under the edge of tree or shrub canopies. Gleaming yellow flowers lighten a dark corner, and trees and shrubs with gold foliage are contrasted against the background of heavy architectural evergreens. Mrs Beaumont denies careful colour grouping, her modesty almost a fault as her garden inspires a new gardening generation who strive to emulate and capture something of her talent.

The garden entrance is through a side yard, where a tall *Photinia serrulata*, a bright golden and green-leaved elaeagnus, and a thriving buckthorn, *Rhamnus alaterna* 'Argenteo-

Plants scramble and intertwine: above a seat *Buddleja alternifolia* with mauve flower-sprays becomes a host to climbing *Actinidia kolomikta*, with leaves variegated in pink and cream.

In spring bulbs are grouped in the beds where the leaves of later-flowering hardy perennials are just emerging.

variegata', grow above glossy *Acanthus mollis*. A doorway opens on to a lawn at the back of the house where, to the east, a long narrow path edged with massed sprawling plants leads to the distant end of the garden and the shelter trees at the boundary wall by the monks' ablutions. Although the garden is informal in atmosphere, this path acts as an axis. All other garden areas lead off it, except for the south-west lawn which fits round the corner of the house. In winter the garden layout is clear and decisive; in summer it is totally obscured by dense foliage and overhead canopies.

At first Mrs Beaumont planted the borders edging the path with yellow-flowered shrubs and lower-growing perennials. Between them drifts of yellow and cream tulips extended the colour scheme. Golden-leaved privet (*Ligustrum ovalifolium* 'Aureum') and *Thuja occidentalis* 'Ellwangeriana Aurea' are now large plants, but other colours since introduced are

framed against them. The purple-leaved sage, potentillas – attractive in winter with cinnamon-brown stems – and grey-foliaged bushes now mingle with euphorbias and *Alchemilla mollis*. The tall grey-leaved *Euphorbia characias* 'Lambrook Gold' came from Lambrook Manor, only a few miles away. It has lime-yellow flower-bracts on tall spikes. Hostas, some bred by Eric Smith, include *H.* 'Hadspen Heron' and *Hosta* × *tardiana* 'Hadspen Blue'; deeper in the wood glaucous-leaved *H. sieboldiana* has grown into a wide clump. Where vegetables used to grow a new formal rose garden has recently been made. Pink, flame-coloured and red roses are under-planted with tulips in massed colours. Stone paving divides the beds, but already other plants are beginning to soften hard lines. Creeping scented thymes, blue-flowered *Delphinium tatsienense*, silvery-leaved artemisias, liriope, carpeting ajuga and small trailing campanulas have all been planted. Against a wall *Azara dentata* and a large *Hedera canariensis* 'Gloire de Marengo' are mixed with a climbing rose from behind the 10-foot (3-metre) wall. A large specimen *Eucalyptus gunnii* survives severe winters and a tulip tree (*Liriodendron tulipifera*) near by is making good progress. One of the triumphs in the garden is a huge bush of silver-leaved *Elaeagnus umbellata parviflora*. This form from the Himalayas has creamy fragrant but inconspicuous flowers carried at the end of May. In autumn the fruits are cyclamen-tinted and, untouched by the birds, stay on the bush until Christmas.

At the far end of the path the open lawn is dominated by the cedar, a spreading *Acer platanoides* 'Drummondii', two pyramidal hornbeams, a yellow-berried sorbus and a closely planted group of birch and liquidambar, all of which protect and shelter the garden from the east. A well-shaped *Magnolia kobus* × *loebneri* 'Leonard Messel', originating from the gardens at Nymans, has flowers tinted pink in April. Elsewhere in the garden *M.* × *soulangiana* 'Lennei' opens rose-purple flowers a few weeks earlier. *Osmanthus delavayi*

is 12 feet (3.6 metres) tall, a dark evergreen mass except when covered in scented white flowers in April. Under it hellebores, epimedium, cyclamen, *Tiarella cordifolia* and lamium carpet the earth. The old rock garden overflows with good planting. A large cotinus sprawls over the stonework, and pink tulips make drifts between purple-leaved berberis, pink-flowered *Daphne* × *burkwoodii* 'Somerset' and the marbled foliage of *Arum italicum* 'Pictum'.

A fern-leaved beech spreads over an outhouse, and a magnificent old laburnum has fallen sideways but, its trunk almost horizontal, continues to flower each May. Just to the south-east of the house high walls protect an area in full sun, where a large romneya suckers in a warm flower-bed. Shallow steps drop down to a paved sitting area. Here the colouring is pale, with pastel-tinted flowers and silver-leaved bushes and low-growing creepers: *Buddleja alternifolia*, tree peonies, grey-leaved phlomis, spreading *Alstroemeria ligtu* hybrids, and a clump of lavender-flowered *Aster* × *frikartii* 'Mönch', the best of these seedling hybrids. Against the wall *Azara microphylla* scents the air with vanilla in early spring.

BELOW LEFT
The variegated native flag iris, *Iris pseudacorus* 'Variegatus', thrives where soil is moist.

BELOW RIGHT
Planting areas flow into each other, and stone and gravel paths link the garden divisions, which are accentuated by the dense shade cast by tall trees alternating with open sunlit lawns.

Everywhere plants mingle and intertwine; many pleasing associations come, Mrs Beaumont says, from some chance seeding – what Gertrude Jekyll would have called 'happy garden accidents'. All the plants have natural flowing shapes; Mrs Beaumont apologizes for not being a severe pruner, nor indeed a gardener who controls and disciplines. Yet there are no weeds, except for those plants which, thriving under her care, spread and seed to make new groups and carpet the ground where there is space. In this way many plants are repeated round the garden: alchemillas, hardy cyclamen, euphorbias, hellebores and lamiums, their seeds carried by wind and the birds who are provided with plentiful baths and drinking bowls. A 3-inch (7.5-centimetre) seedling of a Portugal laurel, rescued from the rockery, now stands 17 feet (5 metres) high, making a fine feature on the corner of the main path. One of her finest magnolias, the sweetly scented *Magnolia wilsonii* with pendent cupped flowers in June, seeds freely, the young plants now elsewhere in the garden or given to friends. A fine specimen crab, *Malus* 'Dartmouth', and some tall 'John Downie' give heavy crops of golden-red fruit. A seedling of the Cockspur thorn (*Crataegus crus-galli*) at The Gables is treasured in the National Trust gardens at Tintinhull; this small ornamental tree from North America has vivid autumn colour and scarlet fruits. Corner bushes of the tiered *Viburnum plicatum* 'Lanarth' are also repeated in the garden, all suckers taken from Mrs Beaumont's first plant, now nearly twenty years old. Yellow and orange-flowered Welsh poppies (*Meconopsis cambrica*) are sprinkled through the flower-beds.

The soil is light, part of a ridge of almost neutral greensand which runs up through the south part of Somerset. Easily worked and friable, it also provides good drainage. Most

Plants in the garden always seem perfectly adapted to their site and their neighbours. Mrs Beaumont has a gift for apt plant association.

trees grow quickly; in fact, the *Cedrus deodora*, now 30 feet (9 metres) high, was planted only fifteen years ago. The dense tree and shrub canopies keep areas cool and moist in periods of drought, and provide a natural leaf mulch in autumn. Sedge peat from the moors in north Somerset and home-made compost help retain moisture. Weeding is all done by hand and weedkillers are never used, although flame-guns keep the paths clean and roses are sprayed with fungicide against blackspot, a hazard in the clean west-country air. The lawns, not inconsiderable in area, are still mown weekly with a hand-mowing machine.

Some of the secret of the garden's special atmosphere must lie in Mrs Beaumont's total involvement. She knows her plants and watches them change through the seasons. As Miss Jekyll said, 'To achieve anything beyond the ordinary commonplace mixture ... needs years of observation and considerable knowledge of plants and their ways as individuals.' Mrs Beaumont brings dedication as well as discrimination to a remarkable garden.

A Victorian rockery has been turned into a flowering wilderness.

Chilcombe

near Bridport, Dorset
(Mr and Mrs John Hubbard)

'ALL GARDENS and what they grow are a product not just of generalized trends but of the fascinating local combinations of aspect, soil, exposure, and shelter which tend to modify or exaggerate the bigger facts.' So writes Allen Paterson in his introduction to *The Gardens of Dorset, Hampshire and the Isle of Wight*, in the Batsford series of *The Gardens of Britain* (1978). Chilcombe, near the exposed coast, benefits from many localized factors. Lying under the ridge of a wooded hill only a mile from the south Dorset coast, the house has an incomparable view to the south-east over rolling chalk downland, but fortunately wood and garden lie where the chalk dips and a deep layer of sandy soil provides easily worked texture and perfect drainage.

Climatically this part of west Dorset is within the January isotherm with average mean temperatures of 42°F (6°C). Rainfall tends to be low, perhaps 28 inches (71 centimetres), but humidity is high, and natural springs in the wooded hill behind the house run constantly, providing not only an essential water supply but also a pleasant murmur from a Portland stone shell fountain, and keeping the air cool and fresh. As in all sea-coast gardens, wind is the great enemy; much more so than the occasional severe frost, which at Chilcombe rolls away down the falling hillside. Great elms used to shelter the garden from prevailing southerly winds, and in their place the Hubbards have planted mixed almost indigenous trees, similar to those in the wood above, which as they mature will blend into the Dorset landscape. Horse chestnuts, introduced by the Romans (whose traces are everywhere in this county), poplars, lime, ash and beech, and more recently silver lime (*Tilia tomentosa*) will take up two acres (0.8 hectare) and besides providing a windbreak will eventually make a woodland canopy for native undergrowth and wild flowers. Inside the walled garden small enclosures, made mostly with different sorts of

hedging or stone walls, provide pockets of favourable microclimates where tender plants succeed. Many of these, including felicias, diascias, malvastrums, salvias and verbenas, all of which can be termed 'in and out' plants in most gardens, survive the usually mild winter conditions.

The northern approach to Chilcombe is over open downland, the road dropping to a sheltered farm courtyard with fig trees and a climbing hydrangea on the walls. The old farm buildings house John Hubbard's studio. From here the visitor proceeds on foot, making a choice between a gateway leading to a border and lawn at the south-east front, and a narrower entrance to a paved courtyard at the side of the house. Beds bordering the lawn are edged with London pride, and to the south-west a gate into a field is framed by *Rosa* 'Frühlingsgold'. In June pink roses and blue flowers predominate: a large bush of 'Constance Spry' is tied back against the house wall into an evergreen ceanothus, and the narrow bed is filled with bright blue anchusa and small violas. On either side of the front steps a pair of *Ceanothus* 'Gloire de Versailles' and rosemary bushes give formality and contribute more blue flowers in season. Tall hollyhocks tower behind caryopteris. Smaller rare plants reveal the Hubbards' interest. A blue pea, *Lathyrus sativus*, climbs into a vine; *Phlox* 'Chattahoochee', *Nepeta nervosa, Calamintha nepetoides*, euphorbias and blue-leaved *Hosta × tardiana* all thrive.

John and Caryl Hubbard came to Chilcombe in 1969, moving only from across the valley. The house front faces the steeply falling slope; terraces contained by low walls, espalier fruit trees, a cross-axis of a double hedge, and a higher wall at the garden perimeter all hold the garden design together and anchor the tall house into its site. The house sits on the widest terrace where the green lawn welcomes the visitor to the front door. Below a stone wall a

A hybrid Wichuriana rose, 'May Queen', with semi–double lilac-pink flowers, falls over a shady wall between the upper courtyard, where creeping thyme, fennel and *Stachys olympicum* seed freely, and a sitting area by the fountain.

pair of dark old Irish yews frame descending steps, leading to the hidden garden below. The scale of this enclosed garden is small, matching the house with its geometric layout, and reminiscent of a perfectly designed needlework sampler, where working in one plane the seamstress can achieve only a horizontal network.

In 1618 William Lawson published *A New Orchard and Garden*. In it he recommends the garden layout for the smaller manor house and larger farmstead. Divided into six equal parts, a rectangular garden included areas for decorative topiary, espaliers, fruit trees, a knot garden and two sections divided into vegetable beds. A clergyman, Lawson had strict views as to the respective responsibility of farmer and housewife. The orchard and fruit remained the man's concern; the wife managed the flower and kitchen gardens. Concession to garden fashion was minimal, yet a desire for plants to be ornamental as well as useful had reached a relatively humble level of society. Not until Loudon in the early nineteenth century did another garden writer so explicitly describe gardening suitable to rank and means.

Although probably built towards the end of the seventeenth century as a substantial farmhouse, when the Hubbards came Chilcombe still had a garden very similar in basic design to Lawson's. A neglected wilderness with an infestation of perennial weeds, its layout was a firm rectangle with inner almost equal subdivisions, where an orchard, old espaliers and a cabbage patch on a sloping site were linked by primitive steps and terraces. Over almost three centuries this garden served its continuing function of supplying fruit, vegetables and herbs to the family and probably to casual farm labourers, and flowers for their enjoyment.

OPPOSITE
Cobbled paths made from
stones collected on Chesil
Beach divide one of the
inner garden areas into
geometric shapes.

RIGHT
London pride and hardy
arums (*Zantedeschia
aethiopica*) buttress the
raised pool and shell
fountain.

BELOW
Against a stone wall *Rosa*
'Wedding Day' bears
scented trusses of creamy
flowers in early July.

Before he developed as a practical gardener,
John Hubbard was already an artist, and a
painter of gardens. His wife Caryl, too, is a
distinguished figure in the art world, so that
both their working lives are intimately and
continuously involved in artistic creations.
Gardening began because the site was perfect,
and they had a walled garden enclosure which
needed to be cleaned of weeds and made to
enhance the incomparable view, rather than
remaining a foreground eyesore. Walls and
steps were in poor repair, a vegetable patch was
needed, and labour-saving flower-planting
seemed a good idea. As the undergrowth was
cleared a garden pattern emerged; an L-shaped
terrace ran below the upper outer retaining
wall, and it became obvious that the whole area

At the back of the house a conservatory looks out on another garden area where silver-leaved pears, white roses and alchemilla surround a sitting area for evening.

had once been geometrically subdivided into compartments, made by sloping banks and low walls. The Hubbards emphasized these basic shapes with espalier fruit, a long pergola, trelliswork arbours for climbing roses and honeysuckle, and formal edging plants.

Increasingly the garden was looked at with the same critical eye as would be used to appraise a painting. At first the planting was simple. Hardy cottage-garden plants were interplanted with selected shrub and climbing roses, and vegetables and fruit intermingled. Pale creamy roses such as 'Wedding Day', 'Bobbie James' and 'Francis E. Lester' festooned the high west-facing walls and clambered into old apple trees. As Lawson wrote in 1618, 'Not that we mean to perfect a distinction that ... the garden for flowers should or can be without herbs for the kitchen, or the kitchen garden should be without flowers.' Influenced by Lady Salisbury's planting schemes at Cranborne Manor, the Hubbards began to extend the cottage-garden atmosphere, adding annuals between culinary herbs, and extending their knowledge of more unusual plants which would thrive on the well-drained slopes and in protected pockets. One garden division was further divided into small beds, with cross-paths of cobbles, brought from Chesil Beach at Abbotsbury near by. Some beds were edged with box, others with golden feverfew (*Tanacetum parthenium aureum*) or lad's love (*Artemisia abrotanum*). A

preference for blue and mauve plants was extended to include the tender red-flowered sages, including *Salvia rutilans*, *S. microphylla* (syn. *S. grahamii*) and *S. m. neurepia*, besides blue-flowered *S. patens* and *S. guaranitica*. In another bed elecampane (*Inula magnifica*) and angelica tower above wildly seeding dark-leaved *Viola labradorica*. More recently the kitchen garden has been made into a patterned potager, reached by descending steps lined with regal lilies (*Lilium regale*) in pots. Standard gooseberry bushes, beds edged with alpine strawberries, lettuces and parsley are backed by Rugosa roses and tall and silver-leaved artichokes. One bed is lined with fennel, another with *Tanacetum* 'White Bonnet'. Above, two walnuts and a damson extend the utilitarian theme, but beyond, decorative honeysuckle, shrubby indigofera, a mulberry tree and a young *Robinia pseudacacia* give height and make a jungle of foliage.

A grass path runs north and south between central double borders, above the old orchard through which it continues, until the vista is finally closed by a seat against the lower garden wall, and a tall silver willow beyond. Backed by apples on a trellis frame pruned in Bouche Thomas style (fan-trained rather than horizontal), the border originally planted with shrub roses and herbaceous geraniums is now given height with giant thistles, cephalaria and crambe. An alley of mown grass edged with a tall thick hedge runs across the centre of the garden as a cross-axis. Yew, holly (both green and variegated) and green and purple beech were planted together, to give a tapestry effect where colours and textures interweave. More cross-paths are framed with Irish yews, arbours link compartments, and beds are edged with lavender and catmint. A bank of thyme leads to the steps above the potager.

Mr Hubbard sees the compartmental garden and the mass of the tall house above as a lesson in the use of volumes of space. The garden 'rooms' are an extension of the house, each open space contained by some form of hedging, firmly and geometrically orientated. Occasional vistas into the open countryside are intimate and framed. At Chilcombe pergolas and trellises sited along an axis or marking a corner, provide alternate sunlight and shadow and overhead canopies. Roses luxuriate through old apple trees, and young ornamental trees such as *Prunus* 'Tai Haku' and robinia become hosts to less vigorous twining clematis. Elements of secrecy and surprise, each area hidden and containing a different theme, make the garden seem much larger than it is.

Most of the flower colours are pale, foliage is grey and green; the heavier 'density' of purple leaves is avoided, although now the Hubbards feel they may introduce more good evergreen shrubs, making use of subtle differences in texture, shape and 'colours' of green. As he is an artist, colour language and rules are a fundamental part of Mr Hubbard's subconscious, so unlike many gardeners there is no need to spell out how colours alter and affect each other. He uses certain colour backgrounds throughout the garden, just as a theme continues in music and constantly re-emerges, because they 'work' for him and for the garden in its country setting. Blues, magentas, a double-flowered mauve geranium, plenty of grey foliage, all occur again and again, making a tapestry background against which other colours are placed. Many of his paintings are of brighter colours. In Tresco he finds the clear atmosphere, intense blue of sky and sea, and the very bright tropical flowers all of a piece, a composition; but he would never use similar pure hues at Chilcombe, where the misty atmosphere and greyer skies demand more muted tones. Instead, his bright yellows and deeper reds are revealed as separate colour incidents. Against a high west-facing wall the dark *Rosa* 'Crimson Conquest' seems mysterious, overhung by an old yew, while at its base the biennial *Salvia sclarea turkestanica* is massed for foliage and flower effects. In a leafy corner under a poplar tree, the dusky-red cupped flowers of rose 'Étoile de Hollande' shine. In the centre of the cobbled enclosure where the beds are filled with blue and mauve flowers and silvery foliage, a terracotta pot overflows with bright orange marigolds.

Above the house there is more garden. Below the hanging woods a bank of massed geranium species is allowed to spread, and the dark mourning geranium, *Geranium phaeum*, struggles for supremacy with Queen Anne's lace. Above the paved yard a shady path leads through groups of masterwort (*Astrantia major*) and sweet Cicely, (*Myrrhis odorata*), both with beautiful flower-umbels. At the back of the house a door opens to a courtyard and glass-fronted conservatory. Grey-leaved weeping pears at a high level make a background for white roses 'Yvonne Rabier' and spreading *Alchemilla mollis*, a peaceful planting to be enjoyed in the evening light. A new project is another garden on the slopes below the wood: a hedge of sea-buckthorn will contain a selection of good shrubs.

The Priory

Kemerton, near Tewkesbury, Gloucestershire

(Mr and The Hon. Mrs Peter Healing)

TOWARDS the end of the 1939–45 war, Mr Peter Healing found himself in Germany, with access to only one book. William Robinson wrote *The English Flower Garden* in 1883, but it was re-issued again and again for the next fifty years. The chapter 'Colour in the Flower Garden' especially took Mr Healing's attention. 'Splendid harmonies of rich and brilliant colour, and proper sequences of such harmonies, should be the rule; there should be large effects, each well-studied and well-placed, varying in different portions of the garden scheme. One very common fault is a want of simplicity of intention; another, an absence of any definite plan of colouring ... it is important ... that the mass of each colour

should be large enough to have a certain dignity, but not so large as to be wearisome; ... in Sunny Places warm colours should preponderate; the yellow colour of sunlight brings them together and adds to their glowing effect ... a Shady Border ... seems best suited for the cooler more delicate colours ... One or two colours, used temperately, and with careful judgement, will produce nobler and richer results than many colours purposely contrasted, or wantonly jumbled.'

The garden Mr Healing made when he returned to England might have exacted warm praise from Mr Robinson.

The four-acre (1.6 hectare) garden at The Priory lies on the south-facing slopes of Bredon Hill, 250 feet (76 metres) above sea-level, and with views across the Bristol Channel to the Welsh hills. In the 1940s there were few trees to give character to the garden; the only existing features were three herbaceous borders. Two, viewed from the west windows of the house ran north and south; the third, a large yew marking its corner below the old priory ruins, lay just above the house. Walnuts, maples and mulberries were quickly planted; the borders, still basically in the same positions, were planned in a series of colour harmonies for July until late summer. A dark yew hedge became the background foil for the main border, its southern end, with clipped extending buttresses, concealing a new garden area where today, geared for performance in June and July, gentle grey-foliaged plants with pale flower-colouring spill over a central paved path.

Mr Healing arrived home with his garden plans drawn out in Indian ink on parchment. The three main borders still have the same harmonizing colour schemes as in the original designs, but over the years many of the plants have changed. In the beginning the plants were what Mr Healing calls 'ordinary'. In 1945 it was difficult to find many species or cultivars, including a number of those mentioned in Robinson's book, and substitutes were accepted until nurserymen could build up post-war stocks, or nursery beds at The Priory would yield sufficient plants to make the firm groups necessary for good border design. Seeds were searched out from abroad: gardening friends love to exchange rarities. Plants were chosen because they would satisfy the overall planning requirements which seemed the first essential. Interestingly, today, when nurserymen find it uneconomic to compete with containerized plants in the modern garden centre, it is to private gardens such as The Priory that they usually turn in search of obscure or difficult plants. Mr Healing is a collector of fine plants; he propagates six thousand a year and sells them to his garden visitors. Many are quality plants which will not survive ordinary garden-centre treatment, are slow and difficult to produce, are not reliably hardy, and perhaps have a limited 'up-market' appeal. From California, a silvery-foliaged shrubby lupin (*Lupinus albifrons*) with blue-violet racemes, can be grown easily from seed but is temperamental and needs care in the early stages. Also from California another grey-leaved shrub, *Corethroyne californica* is a treasured rarity. *Senecio appendiculatus* and *S. heritieri* (now more correctly *Pericallis lanata*), both from the Canary Islands, have toothed leaves covered densely with tomentum, and flowers of white/crimson and crimson respectively. *Lobelia tupa*, first introduced from Chile in 1824, has red-brown tubular flowers carried, if soil is rich and moist, on 6-foot (1.8-metre) stems above long downy leaves. There is a wide range of salvias, both woody and herbaceous, penstemons of particularly good 'blue' strains, and many rare kniphofias include *K. snowdenii* with flower-spikes of coral and scarlet.

The main border, 60 yards (55 metres) long and today 18 feet (5.4 metres) wide, set against the dark yew hedge, starts at the southern end with pale silvery foliage plants; flowers in white (creamy tints, not eye-catching 'flat' whites), pale pink or yellow pastel tints are of gentle colouring. Stronger yellows such as that of the flat-plated flowers of *Achillea* 'Coronation Gold' build up to the rusty oranges and reds of daisy-flowered helianthus and to the deeper scarlet of *Lobelia* 'Dark Crusader'. An almost centrally placed *Cotinus coggygria* 'Foliis Purpureis' marks the climax of deep rich colouring: further to the north hues fade again to pale misty tones and relieving grey foliage. Not only colour interests Mr Healing: contrasts between leaf shapes and plant forms all contribute to make a balanced composition. Architectural sword-like leaves of phormiums, crocosmia and kniphofia set off and accentuate the more lax curving shapes of mounded bushes or clumps.

The second, much shorter border is nearer the house. It appears as a foreground to the carefully orchestrated richness of the main border behind it. Flower colours are pink, mauve and purple, and the lavender-blue flowers of forms of *Aster × frikartii* and *A. sedifolius* (*A. acris*), the latter now uncommon

but worth finding. Groups of white roses, creamy-flowered *Artemisia lactiflora* and white Japanese anemone are permanent, white and pink dahlias and scented tobacco plants (including the tall stately *Nicotiana sylvestris*) are annual additions. Grey- and silver-leaved plants are distributed throughout. Artemisias, helichrysums and perovskias weave a tapestry background which cools and brightens the predominantly pale flower colouring.

The third border at The Priory, with origins dating to Mr Healing's first garden plans, is the cross-border under the ruin. He describes its conception: it 'would be for every shade of red. It would never become garish or too strong, as there are so many really dark reds and bronze flowers and foliage to choose from and these would absorb the heat of the scarlets.'

In the bed scarlet *Dahlia* 'Bishop of Llandaff', with elegant bronze leaves, *Penstemon* 'Firebird', annual *Nicotiana* 'Dark Red', low-growing *Iresine herbstii* and startling red-stemmed ruby chard are assembled in decisive groups for mid- and late-summer display. 'Old

red roses, penstemons, monardas backed by purple-leaved nut and the darkest cotinus, should make the border overflow like a cornucopia.' Peter Healing's own description conveys its spirit.

The June garden tucked behind the thick yew hedge was not part of the early layout. Twin borders are planned to bridge the gap between spring and summer flowering: here annuals and tender bedding plants augment the schemes, coming to their best after June and keeping the garden in beauty and display until the first frosts. Most of the plants are permanent features, and the planting is mixed. Shrubs give height and form, perennials and bulbs seasonal foliage and flower, and tall grasses have arching rustling stems. This tightly packed enclosed garden, one of the most satisfying garden 'pictures' in a known modern garden, represents all that is best in English gardening tradition. William Robinson would echo the praise. 'The gardener should follow the true artist, however modestly, in his love for things as they are, in delight in natural form and beauty of flower and tree, if . . . our gardens are ever to be pictures. The gardener has not the strenuous work of eye and hand that the artist has, but he has plenty of good work to do – to choose from ten thousand beautiful living things; to study their nature and adapt them to his soil and climate; to get the full expression of their beauty; to grow and place them well and in right relation to other things, which is a life-study in itself.' *Acer griseum* with peeling bark, a Judas tree, golden-leaved *Gleditsia triacanthos* 'Sunburst', philadelphus with heavy-scented fragrance and *Buddleja alternifolia* give height and increase the feeling of privacy.

This is not all at Kemerton; a rose pergola marks an axis leading to a stream garden at the north-east boundary, and beyond the house to the south-east a sunken area contains a lily-pond. On paving, ornamental pots contain lilies and strongly scented daturas; raised banks are partly built in dry-walling to provide homes for smaller plants, alpine types which need free drainage for their roots. Violas, *Omphalodes luciliae* and *Campanula betulifolia* thrive here, many grown from seed. In shade hostas, ferns, meconopsis and giant lilies look exotic. By the front door a raised bed against the house wall is annually 'bedded out' with tender plants overwintered in the greenhouse. A plantsman will delight in *Cassia corymbosa*, bearing yellow pea-flowers all summer, *Rehmannia angulata* with cherry-red foxglove-like tubes of flower,

The pergola leading down to the herbaceous borders. Roses and vines alternate on the pillars.

Salvia leucantha with velvety violet-coloured flowers and, falling over the stone edges, silver-leaved *Lotus berthelotii*, with lobster-scarlet flowers in summer.

The garden developed by the Healings is now forty years old. The soil, with a pH of 7–8, is a sticky clay. It was difficult at first, but its texture has been so improved by humus-forming organic mulches of horse manure or mushroom compost that digging is now never considered necessary. The thick mulches are simply hoed into the soil surface. There is little weeding, as germinating weed seeds are controlled by mulch and close planting. Mr Healing does all the propagating. He, his wife and the gardener, who comes for four days a week, keep the garden spruce and cope with increasing numbers of interested visitors. The latter find their way to a selling area in a courtyard but, below, orchid houses and a path to the kitchen garden lined with more good plants remain more private.

Mr Healing seems to have mastered the mystery of colour behaviour; his beds and borders are an inspiration to the gardener and the artist. As such the garden is recorded photographically and on canvas; future generations can refer to its schemes. More complicated in essence is his personal plant collection. This depends on vigilance, day-to-day skills and Mr Healing's own instinct for a 'quality' plant. William Robinson wrote, 'Select only good plants; throw away weedy kinds, there is no scarcity of the best.' Who decides and evaluates 'the best'? Gardeners such as Peter Healing are teachers as well as creators.

OPPOSITE
From the old priory ruins a stone archway looks out towards golden-leaved privet and a mulberry behind the red border.

Essex House

Badminton, Gloucestershire
(Mr and Mrs James Lees-Milne)

OPPOSITE
Daffodils and wood
anemones are naturalized
in the grass under the great
cedars.

BELOW
Clipped shapes hold the
design together at Essex
House, and contrast with
free-growing plants which
cascade over the edges of
beds.

SYLVIA CROWE once wrote that all great gardens of the world have a unity both of execution and conception which shows that they were created in singleness of thought. The garden at Essex House, although hardly more than half an acre (0.2 hectare) in extent, expresses this unique quality. The house, built in 1680 at the gates of Badminton Park, now has a garden entirely appropriate to its period.

A seventeenth-century garden layout was geometric and ordered. Divided into compartments by masonry or by 'walls' of living plants, the garden became a series of outdoor rooms, linked by directional paths and steps which adjusted horizontal levels. Statues in marble and stone and topiary urns, vases and more fanciful sculptured shapes marked corners and emphasized the strong architectural quality of this rigid framework. Parterres were laid out like patterned carpets, each 'room' with different furnishings. Even a garden for quite a small manor house would have had some, if not all, of these features and Mrs James Lees-Milne, who has lived at Essex House since 1975, has a strict historical sense. She is well known (as Alvilde Lees-Milne) as a garden writer, and as co-editor of *The Englishman's Garden* (1982) and *The Englishwoman's Garden* (1980).

The house was built for Mary Capel, daughter of the Earl of Essex and widow of the first Duke of Beaufort. She was renowned in her own time for her interest in gardening and the acquisition of exotics, which she kept at Badminton 'in a wonderful deal of Health, Order and Decency'. Thus wrote Stephen Switzer in 1715, in *The Nobleman, Gentleman and Gard'ner's Recreation*, adding that 'excepting the times of her Devotions ... Gard'ning took up two Thirds of her time'. The Dowager Duchess was also a patron of botanical painters, and liked her own collection of plants recorded. Above the doorway facing the village street a coat-of-arms of Somerset impaling Capel is carved in stone, and the name Essex House implies her connection. She would be pleased with her successor.

Mr James Lees-Milne, who has completely remade the garden in the last ten years, has combined her architectural experience with a very varied and comprehensive knowledge of plants. House and garden are closely linked and each area of the garden, although separate, seems to follow logically. Entrances, pathways and steps adjusting levels are framed invitingly by ornamental pots. But like the Duchess she loves to collect 'quality' plants and skilfully deploys them without interrupting the overall concept. At Essex House the scale is small and only the perimeter walls are even head-high; instead of continuous solid lines to separate each distinct garden area, Mrs Lees-Milne has used clipped plant shapes and textures arranged

A pattern of box and clipped hollies gives the garden its distinctive architectural quality.

in regular repetitive formulas to indicate inner boundaries. Elsewhere a pergola marks a garden division and low box hedging defines planting areas.

Mrs Lees-Milne spent many of her formative gardening years in France. She made a garden in the early 1950s overlooking the sea at Roquebrune, not far from Lawrence Johnson's garden at Serre de la Madonne. Unlike English Restoration gardens, where planting possibilities were limited by availability, these twentieth-century Mediterranean gardens can be filled to overflowing with exotics from all over the world. In such a favourable climatic setting a successful garden design needs to have a compelling sense of order and architecture. In her next garden, which she made in the 1960s at Alderley Grange, on a sheltered west-facing ridge of the Cotswolds, she again resisted the collector's impulses and the plantsman's enthusiasm which can so easily destroy both any

sense of framework and that coherent unity which Dame Sylvia Crowe describes. There, inside an old walled garden, she made separate garden areas, a herb garden with box-edged beds, a pleached lime palisade and a collection of shrub roses, and the walls were clothed with luxuriant climbers. Simple plants mingled with the more exotic; the profusion of planting was tempered with architectural austerity. It is Mrs Lees-Milne's disciplined attitude to her garden-making, combined with her knowledge of plants and her aesthetic feeling for the blending of colours and identification of textures, which make her gardening style so satisfactory.

The garden at Essex House stretches mainly southwards behind the house, which is separated from the village street to the north only by a narrow strip of walled garden. To the east, trees in the park of Badminton House provide shelter from the cold winds but the site, 600 feet (180 metres) above sea-level and with an alkaline soil, remains inhospitable. The garden is dominated by three substantial and beautiful cedars of Lebanon which, almost marking three points of an equal-sided triangle, stand on the raised bank to the south. When Mr and Mrs Lees-Milne came in 1975 the only other garden features worth preserving were an old tapestry hedge of mixed yew and box which, with a stone wall, marked the western boundary of the garden, and a hedge of golden privet on the street.

Today the garden is tightly packed with plants; the 'bones' which make its framework are in different evergreens. Plain green and variegated boxwood and holly, yew, Portugal laurel, osmanthus clipped into regular ball shapes, textured pyramidal conifers and the soft grey-green of the great cedar trees give a wide range of foliage colour and texture, which extends to give winter interest. The three cedars remain dominant, their dark mass beyond the open lawn a perfect essay in garden structuring, providing contrast of light and shade and architectural balance. It would be nice to think they were planted by the first Duchess, but they are not so old.

The maximum use is made of plants with strong upright forms, so increasing the actual numbers of plants which can be fitted in; geometric patterns, paths and steps are emphasized and outlined by topiary evergreens on standard trunks beneath which box bushes or flowering plants find space to spread. Walls are curtained with intertwining climbers while a palisade above the sunken east garden provides a frame for flowers and foliage. Raised beds allow downward-trailing plants to cover vertical stonework. Beds and borders viewed from the front are also backed with narrow paths from which new depths and planes of planting are revealed.

Climbing schizophragma and hydrangea cling in deep shade on the north face of the house above a pair of variegated box pyramids, which, in elegant glazed green pots from Serre de la Madonne, frame the front door. Shrubs with scented leaves or flowers are gathered here, each in season a welcome to passing visitors or returning owners. An incense rose, *Rosa primula*, invites one to crush the aromatic leaves. The air is scented with the lily-of-the-valley flowers of *Mahonia japonica* in mid-winter, and by mid-April with the white flowers of *Osmanthus × burkwoodii*. Small alchemillas, campanulas and geraniums fall over the edges of the stone path. Already a note of formality softened by profusion of planting

gives a foretaste of garden planting round the corner to the west.

Strengthened and thickened by glossy-leaved *Prunus lusitanica*, the old hedge of yew and box remains. In the corner immediately facing it a semicircle of dwarf box makes a pattern repeated throughout the garden. In the opposite corner *Magnolia × soulangiana* is similarly framed. On the pink-washed wall of the house a *Wisteria sinensis* is intertwined with clematis, *Clematis macropetala* for its rich blue flowers in spring and 'Perle d'Azur' for summer. In an angle of the house sheltered walls are covered in clematis, jasmine and roses. A paved yard provides space for sitting. Low-growing flowering shrubs include cistus, hebe, and shrub roses, all interplanted with bulbs, annuals and perennials chosen for fragrance of leaf or flower and for soft colouring. Scented white *Narcissus* 'Thalia', creeping campanulas, annual pink and white lavateras and petunias, spreading *Alstroemeria ligtu* hybrids, golden marjoram and pink-flowered hardy geraniums spill and press over each other. A now-rare rose, 'Rose de Resht', introduced by Miss Nancy Lindsay, bears neat rosettes of dark crimson-pink flowers all summer. It is unlisted in catalogues, but Graham Stuart Thomas describes it as probably some sort of autumn damask. The

Beyond the cedars formal evergreens and a weeping prunus are planted at the edge of the path.

The scale of planting at
Essex House is small.

Welsh poppy (*Meconopsis cambrica*) seeds
everywhere. The tender glaucous-leaved
Melianthus major from South Africa is brought
in each winter but quickly grows to make an
imposing sculptured mound each season. In
pots lime-green *Euphorbia myrsinites* and trailing *Convolvulus sabatius* (syn. *C. mauritanicus*)
give height, and standard honeysuckles frame
steps which lead on to a central axial path,
flanked with pyramids of variegated box,
which carries the eye and directs the feet across
the main lawn and to the cedars beyond.

Here in 1975 there was what Mrs Lees–Milne
has described 'as a curious arrangement of
paving stones with straggly helianthemums'.
This has been transformed by formal treatment, and now, although its area is small, it
makes a dramatic impact. Low box hedges
surround beds crossed by the main pathway. In

Elegant wooden Versailles
containers overflowing
with plants are
architectural features.

each section further sub-divisions are made by curving wings of golden-leaved box. In a pair of copper tubs and marking the four outer corners, standard clipped balls of variegated holly give height and accent. Creeping thymes emit scent when trodden upon and silvery-leaved *Tanacetum haradjanii* and blue-foliaged acaena glow even in winter. In spring small tulip species and alliums give colour.

Looking south from the house two pale grey-leaved weeping pears (*Pyrus salicifolia* 'Pendula') are symmetrically placed at the southern corners of the lawn, contrasting with and lightening the dark effects of cedars beyond. In front of the pears, standard 'Little White Pet' roses rise in a sea of white petunias to flower from June until late autumn, and the beds are hedged again with boxwood. On the opposite corners of the grass *Amelanchier canadensis* casts light shade. To the west by the boundary hedge *Acer pseudoplatanus* 'Brilliant-issimum' produces its shrimp-pink leaves in spring. A line of Jackman's rue (*Ruta graveolens* 'Jackman's Blue') runs below. On the east side of this lawn Mrs Lees-Milne made a conventional border into a raised bed where steps framed with box bushes lead to a painted seat. Hidden paths run along it, allowing planting in the narrow back border, while in front standard rose bushes of pink-flowered 'The Fairy' once again establish a formal rhythm, and hold together the profusion of shrubs, perennials and annuals. Trellis above the fence provides a climbing frame for roses, clematis and honey-suckle.

From the lawn curving box invites one up steps to the shadows under the cedars. A statue of Apollo is draped with ivy, his plinth surrounded with the spreading evergreen *Euphorbia amygdaloides robbiae*, which thrives in shade and dry soil. From here looking south towards the garden boundary more good shrubs and shrub roses come into view, the golden-leaved *Robinia pseudacacia* 'Frisia' immediately standing out among more sober-leaved neighbours. Here the grass is less mani-cured, providing satisfying contrast with smooth lawns below. Daffodils and small cyclamen are spreading under the trees. A functional gravel path has a line of alternating feathery junipers and clipped osmanthus on one side.

To the east down steps a new garden area appears with a centrally placed formal pool. Again free plant shapes are tamed by architec-tural verticals of slim *Prunus* 'Amanogawa', a pair of which flanks a seat, and rows of standard

roses are underplanted with rosemary and scented tobacco plants. More box pyramids define the shape of pool and beds. At the shadiest end, where the soil is damp, hostas, *Iris sibirica* and variegated comfrey (*Symphytum* × *uplandicum* 'Variegatum') thrive near yellow-flowered *Primula florindae* and a golden-green *Gleditsia triacanthos* 'Sunburst'. To the north, where the aspect is more open and sunny, silver artemisias, variegated *Buddleja* 'Harlequin', *Weigela florida* 'Variegata' and variegated ivies stand out between solid bushes of evergreen choisya.

In the upper garden moisture-loving grasses grow in shallow water at the edge of the lily pond.

65

Barnsley House

Barnsley, near Cirencester, Gloucestershire
(Mrs David Verey)

BARNSLEY HOUSE, on the outskirts of the village only a few miles east of Cirencester, was built in 1697. Although alterations and additions have since partly changed its aspect, it is the seventeenth century which has perhaps most influenced the development of its modern garden. Mr and Mrs David Verey, who inherited the house and its three and a half acres (some 1.5 hectares) in 1951, have both played a part in its transformation from the conventional English lawns and herbaceous borders which Mr Verey's mother had tended. At first their children were young and needed lawns for cricket, so borders were grassed over and the garden waited, poised, as it were, to become one of the most intriguing and charming gardens of the second half of the twentieth century.

Mr Verey himself was an architect with a strong interest in design and a training in the use of three-dimensional space; his wife Rosemary is a plantswoman, in the sense of being a lover of flowers rather than a competitive collector, and above all an academic and literary gardener who interprets garden space in terms of garden history. Mrs Verey's own collection of garden literature includes early herbals which explain how plants were used rather than their ornamental value in a garden, knot and parterre pattern books which have influenced her in establishing her own geometric compositions, philosophical and poetical works which influenced or described the emergence of the Landscape Movement in the eighteenth century, and dictionaries and histories relating how plants were discovered and introduced and their first influence on garden design in England. But even before acquiring her library, a gradual process, she was reading classic contemporary teaching books on garden planning and plants. Russell Page's *Education of a Gardener*, Vita Sackville-West's *Garden Book*, and the writings of Christopher Lloyd and Graham Stuart Thomas are among the books which she enjoyed and used as 'tools' in her creation at Barnsley.

The gardens as they have developed in the last twenty years reflect the Vereys' partnership: an overall pattern of straight directional paths framed by pleached lime trees, a laburnum tunnel, and the original 'avenue' of Irish yews stretching at a right angle from the house to a view in a perimeter wall, with a series of cross-axes to reveal views or distant vistas and focal points, which occupies and dominates the east and south. Each turn and view makes use of linear perspective; each narrowing perspective is centred and 'stopped' by some architectural feature – a temple, fountain or sundial. To the perceptive historian garden scenes are revealed which seem to have been taken straight from some seventeenth-century gardening manual: a knot garden of interlacing tightly clipped evergreens making a horizontal pattern between low hedges of rosemary, and a herb border where diamond-shaped box-edged beds contain different culinary and medicinal plants grown in the seventeenth century. Outside the walled garden area a French-style *potager*, where all is geometry and fruit trees are clipped in goblet and espalier shapes, is in fact inspired by William Lawson's *Country Housewife's Garden*, first published in 1618. Narrow brick paths in differing patterns mark out a horizontal grid system with a central curved area, and the fruit trees give height and vertical accent.

A 'wilderness', where planned paths – tightly mown between rougher-textured grass full of bulbs in spring – guide the feet to ornaments and specimen trees (seventeenth-century still in inspiration), is planted with more recently introduced exotics. Batty Langley, writing as late as 1728, speaks of 'rural walks between groves and thickets' and marks the gradual transition in thought between the disciplined geometric layouts surrounding Tudor, Jacobean and Carolean houses and the dawning of the new Landscape Movement of the eighteenth century.

In 1962, when gardening at Barnsley was getting under way, the Vereys heard that a fine Tuscan Doric temple built in 1787 at nearby Fairford Park was about to be demolished. They rescued and reassembled it. Now the temple stands against the east wall at the bottom of the garden, dominating a view westward to a modern fountain by Simon Verity against the farthest garden boundary wall. Surrounded by paving, it looks out across a pond through open ornamental gates, appearing from afar to float like the Music Temple at High Wycombe: an amazingly successful planning feat in a garden of such modest proportions.

Near the Wilderness at the other end of the garden a stone Gothic summerhouse was built in 1762, after the house had become the rectory. Then its construction would have been in the forefront of fashionable taste, rare in a provincial Cotswold village far from the mainstream of architectural thought. It sits, embowered with trees and bushes, at an angle to the house and lawn, facing another addition to the architectural richness at Barnsley, a castellated veranda with stone columns built on to the south-west end of the house in 1830. The incumbent, the Rev. Richard Musgrave, also enlarged the house with a top storey and altered the windows to make it seem more Tudor in style, which accounts for some confusion today to a casual visitor. Fortunately past history at Barnsley House and the modern garden's unfolding are fully documented for future scholars.

Part of the charm and stimulation of these gardens lies in their power to please without any appreciation of details of historical style. In fact it is possible to enjoy Barnsley without any pre-knowledge of design or of plants and gardening techniques. The garden, richly planted, almost overflowing with scented flowers in gentle colours, seems of one piece with the house; each separate garden area flows into another without abrupt transition. Each inviting path or vista reveals some new focal point, or delays the garden visitor with some planting association which needs closer examination.

The approach from the main road is past limes and chestnuts under which aconites flower in mid-winter. The house stands on a steep slope above terraces, where staccato Lawson cypresses (*Chamaecyparis lawsoniana* 'Ellwoodii') give emphasis against a retaining

wall, with low mounds of silvery santolina and stonework draped with herringbone *Cotoneaster horizontalis*. The shade-loving *Parthenocissus henryana* with pink-veined leaves clings against the house. Away to the west past an old robinia a blue Atlantic cedar stands on the lawn above the bank where a Victorian rector had earlier planted a sweep of trees to thicken the western boundary of the garden. The Gothic summerhouse is glimpsed and paths invite exploration of the Wilderness and appreciation of 'modern' tree planting, which includes a wellingtonia, metasequoia, a ginkgo, a fine tulip tree and smaller ornamentals for foliage fruit and form. Among these, prunus flower in spring, grey-foliaged sorbus unfurl pale leaves in May, a catalpa flowers in summer, and *Sorbus sargentiana* and *S.* 'Embley', both with striking glowing red leaves in autumn, bear clusters of red and orange fruit respectively. Paths open out on to a more manicured lawn, fenced in at the eastern corner by an L-shaped bed of Rugosa roses which divides this part of the garden from the geometry and straight lines beyond.

By the veranda the knot garden, its design outlined in box and germander (*Teucrium chamaedrys*) on a bed of gravel, has a central bush of the evergreen small-leaved *Phillyrea angustifolia*, pruned to match the pudding shapes of symmetrically placed hummocks of silver-leaved *Santolina incana*. On the outer corners, between rosemary bushes, spirals of variegated holly are clipped into firm lines. Everywhere, by steps, framing doorways and lining pathways, stone and earthenware pots overflow with planting mixtures. More holly spirals and box pyramids make permanent central features while small spring bulbs and scented violas tumble over the edges in spring, to be replaced in summer with aromatic 'silvers' and tender felicias, lemon-scented verbenas and pelargoniums propagated in Mrs Verey's nursery. From a garden door Irish yews flank the central stone path where pale-flowered helianthemums open their flowers in sun.

The yews bisect a square area of lawn, where symmetrically placed outer beds flow round making enclosing wings. By the kitchen door are more pots containing plants with scented leaves, in addition to the herbs grown in the long bed cross-trellised with low box hedging, which can be brushed when passing. Against

OPPOSITE
A pleached lime walk leads into the tunnel of laburnum which is aligned on a sundial. Spherical heads of mauve alliums thrust through clumps of hostas.

In the potager Mrs Verey plants fruit, flowers and vegetables in symmetrical patterns.

ABOVE
Silvery stachys, grey
mounds of clipped
santolina and green
textured junipers are
typical of Mrs Verey's
planting juxtapositions.
Behind is the Tuscan
Doric temple from
Fairford Park.

Foxgloves and tall silver-
leaved thistles (*Onopordon
arabicum*) are allowed to
seed at will in the tightly
packed borders.

the house walls wisteria and honeysuckle,
clematis, roses, *Fremontodendron californicum*
and the purple-flowered maurandya from
Mexico grown from seed each year mix with
wall shrubs such as evergreen azara, ceanothus
and Mediterranean myrtle. A gap in the wall
leads to the greenhouses and propagating areas,
where Mrs Verey grows topiary box, holly and
phillyrea bushes to stock her nursery, besides
herbs and other seeds and cuttings from the
plants in her own garden. In the paving self-
seeding alchemilla flowers in luxuriant
profusion.

The Irish yew walk stops just short of the
first green alley, which makes a cross axis
running parallel to the lower garden walls and
is centred on the eighteenth-century temple
across the wide pool to the left. From here
Simon Verity's fountain seems far to the south-
west, snugly surrounded by large-leaved
moisture-loving plants, and overhung by
boundary trees. One water garden thus lies in
full sun, with the paved surround full of
seeding plants framing water surface and sitting area. Blue-flowered Siberian irises and
mimulus edge the water, deliberately disguis-
ing architectural lines with soft plant shapes. At
the fountain end hostas, rodgersias, ligularias
and large-leaved *Hedera colchica* are semi-
tropical in atmosphere, the area cool and
dripping. The wide grass vista joining the
contrasting water areas runs between thickly
planted borders, and occasional breaks allow
new cross-views to statues or a seat against the
wall. Towards the south-west the grassy glade
leads behind the main lawn, where shaded by
cypress and yew a bed of golden-foliaged
plants lights up a dark border. *Gleditsia triacanthos* 'Sunburst', *Lonicera nitida* 'Baggesen's
Gold' and the scented white-flowered *Philadelphus coronarius* 'Aureus' unite to make a pool of
soft colour. *Polemonium caeruleum* flowers
freely in misty blue to contrast with the pale
leaves. In an opposite bed tall spikes of *Eremurus
robustus* tower above neighbouring plants.

This first grass vista lies parallel to the most
important feature in the garden, the tunnel of
laburnum which merges into a pleached lime
walk stretching back to focus on one side of the
open paved courtyard beside the temple. A few
yards separate these two walks, but disguised
by shrubs and roses they seem more remote,
even though paths at right angles cross and join
them. Under the laburnum arbour the spherical heads of mauve alliums rise on tall stems
above hosta leaves. Golden racemes hang
down in May, but later the laburnum walk is

The sound of water splashing on the fountain, designed by Simon Verity, invites further exploration at the end of one of the cross vistas.

shady and cool, a contrast to the open lime walk. Round the base of the limes small bulbs and blue-leaved Jackman's rue give colour and interest. At the end of the lime walk beds of viola and white-flowered *Epilobium glabellum* lie in full sun. Contrast between shade and sunlight adds extra dimensions to the whole garden, already deceiving and mysterious as long perspectives disguise true distances.

Exploration of this garden is encouraged by each tempting new prospect, as each turn and corner allows some new feature to appear. Visitors treasure two aspects of its design. Firstly there is always something new to discover, some contrived viewpoint to appreciate that is easily missed on a first visit. It is a garden which stimulates thought and invites return. Secondly, and most reassuringly in spite of the complexity of design, its 'ordered disorder' seems to provide a peaceful ambience where seats deliberately placed urge rest and a pause; to prevent a hurried search for more garden delights, offering a slowing of tempo, a certain knowledge that the garden will wait. Barnsley may be a garden for both the scholar and the plant enthusiast, but beyond this it is a place in which to repose and contemplate. In fact, a garden 'where a soul's at ease'.

Sezincote

Moreton-in-Marsh, Gloucestershire
(Mr and Mrs David Peake)

IN 1795 Colonel John Cockerell, one of three brothers all with Indian or East India Company connections, bought the Cotswold estate of Sezincote from the Earl of Guildford. On his death in 1798 he left the property to his brother Charles (later Sir Charles and Member of Parliament for Evesham). He in turn employed the third brother, S.P. Cockerell (named Samuel Pepys for his great-great-uncle, and already an established architect) to build his new mansion in the Indian manner. In 1788 William Hodges had published his collection of aquatints of Indian scenery, and these were followed in 1795 by a series of prints by Thomas and William Daniell which were to prove an invaluable and stimulating source of Indian decorative detail to the Cockerell brothers. Thomas Daniell himself, newly returned from ten years in India, advised on the style of the house, and many of the garden's architectural features can be attributed to him, some being almost faithful adaptations of his Indian views. The resulting house and garden are unique, for they are not only closely integrated, as in all good design, but also perhaps the most complete Mogul landscape surviving in western Europe today.

As house and garden neared completion in 1810, Sir Charles Cockerell commissioned John Martin for ten views, in aquatint, of garden and landscape; furthermore, after 1818 views in oil were painted by Daniell himself. Both sets (Mr and Mrs Peake have all the Daniells except one) remain important records of the garden layout. Although Daniell's portrayal of recently planted trees, such as a young cedar of Lebanon (grown tall but still thriving) and weeping willow in the water garden area below the bridge, show some artistic licence, his paintings capture the spirit of this strange oriental fantasy. Today, mature trees and luxuriant shrubberies encircle and shelter the golden stone house with its turquoise copper dome (a Muslim symbol of peace and tranquillity) and the exotic Indian temples, bridges and statues which are revealed in a garden tour seem perfectly attuned to the *genius loci*, while retaining their own oriental symbolism.

A long winding avenue of evergreen and deciduous oaks leads from the Oxford road over the Indian bridge to the gravel sweep in front of the east-facing house, separated from the parkland below by a ha-ha, eighteenth-century in style but in fact only recently constructed. On the drive thick woodland prevents more than occasional brief glimpses of

Cordylines and vertical Irish yews frame the golden dome in the Mogul garden.

the house and copper dome. The latter gives no more than the first hint of the strange but coherent architectural motif in this unlikely Cotswold setting. Daniell's bridge, crossing a steep ravine to the north of the house, allows a view to sparkling water and luxuriant foliage in the valley above and below. Its style copied from the Elephanta caves at Bombay, the bridge has four octagonal columns. Below it, stepping stones lead through the clear water, which descends from the natural springs and lotus-shaped pool above. On the parapet rest four sacred bulls, and lotus flowers are moulded in stone. The bulls were originally in Coade stone, but have recently been recast in iron. Known as Nandi, the god Shiva's favourites or 'happy ones', these brahmin bulls are a recurring garden theme.

The name Sezincote comes from 'Cheisne-cote', meaning the hillside of the oaks, and besides those already passed, the English oak is a feature of this hanging landscape on the edge of the Cotswold escarpment. Behind the house the ground slopes up steeply but then curves more gently round to shield the building with protective wings, inside which to the south and north are the main garden areas. On the hill directly behind the house a tall monument celebrates Wellington's victories, and disguises a chimney from a subterranean heating chamber. The view to the east is over the Stour valley in the distance, but within the park a serpentine lake and woodland mark the boundary. Great cedars, planted at the time the house was built, dominate the view and conceal the approach drive. A dawn redwood (*Metasequoia glyptostroboides*) and new cedars have been planted in case those which are now mature fail, and in the sloping field to the south-east two wellingtonias (*Sequoiadendron giganteum*) were planted in 1965 and already make significant dark shapes. The park itself may have been inspired by Humphry Repton, who certainly visited Sezincote and praised the Indian style before 1808, when he was summoned to Brighton to discuss the Prince Regent's plans for an oriental pavilion. A sketch exists which shows his ideas for the south-east garden, and in his writings he seems to imply he advised Sir Charles, but this may only have been a casual interest. At any rate, his name can be added to the already distinguished list of garden advisers, and he may have contributed to the woodland planting which so successfully masks the north-east corner of the lake in true eighteenth-century fashion, making it appear to extend farther than it does.

Today the house and park are owned and cared for by Mr and Mrs David Peake. Mrs Peake, the daughter of Sir Cyril and Lady Kleinwort who bought the property in 1944, continues the gardening tradition, planting not only as old trees fall, but with foresight, so that new trees are already sufficiently mature in form to keep this early-nineteenth-century landscape intact as trees almost two hundred years old inevitably start to deteriorate.

Original planting by Daniell mainly consisted of an arboretum in the Thornery above and below the Indian bridge, and Martin's aquatints and his own oils are an invaluable early record. The Dugdale family, who acquired the property at the end of the nineteenth century, added much of the waterside garden planting which complements the woodland in the ravine. During the 1950s and 1960s Lady Kleinwort, with advice from Graham Stuart Thomas, expanded the planting further, introducing massed low-growing foliage plants of varying textures and shapes along the descending stream and round the pools.

The southern wing of the house curves back as an orangery built in slender stonework with carved motifs and terminates in an octagonal pavilion. This provides the setting for a flat garden area, before the ground slopes steeply up again to the south, which used to be a traditional English flower garden of rose beds and gnarled lavender bushes. In 1968 Lady Kleinwort invited Graham Stuart Thomas to design a 'Paradise' garden of water-rills, centred on the original octagonal fountain. The octagon, a recurring feature in Mogul architecture, evolved from squaring a circle to reconcile the material side of man with the spiritual. In early Persian gardens water as the source of life was fundamental to the design: on flat terrain water courses representing the four rivers of life would divide the garden by radiating from a central pool. At Sezincote a narrow canal runs north and south, while the east/west alignment is represented by a pale gravel path, which provides access to the base of the orangery pavilion steps and to the edge of the raised terrace above the gravel sweep to the east of the house. Both are bordered with sentinel Irish yews (substituted for columnar Italian cypresses which are not reliably hardy in this country), and the design is completed by symmetrically placed ornamental pots containing New Zealand cabbage trees (*Cordyline australis*) which are moved to shelter in winter. Flanking the steps to pavilion and orangery, more brahmin bulls stand guard and more

OVERLEAF LEFT ABOVE
The god Surya surveys the clear water of the upper pool. In the Thornery at Sezincote planting is naturalistic, complementing the oriental architecture.

OVERLEAF LEFT BELOW
Below the elephant bridge the water widens to surround a three-headed snake fountain.

OVERLEAF RIGHT
The curving orangery terminating in an octagon pavilion backs the new Mogul-style garden, where staccato Irish yews line a water-rill.

73

elegant containers in basketwork design are massed with tulips in spring and fuchsias in summer. Vases with similar planting frame a sitting area near a French window.

During the restoration of the orangery an old *Cassia corymbosa* and a yellow Banksian rose have survived a winter without glass. Recently there has been new planting of *Pileostegia viburnoides*, *Abutilon × suntense*, *Cestrum* 'Newellii' and *Trachelospermum jasminoides*, the latter eventually to be trained overhead to make a green canopy and fill the air with sweet scent in summer. A *Beschorneria yuccoides*, with arching pink flower-stems in June, and autumn-flowering nerines grow at the base of the back wall. Three plants of Chinese mourning cypress (*Cupressus funebris*) with soft glaucous green foliage grow in the orangery against the wall of the house. Along the front of the orangery a low wall is clothed with the small evergreen *Cotoneaster dammeri*, and the walls supporting the steps at the southern end of the water-canal which lead to a higher level are covered with golden variegated ivies and the large-leaved *Vitis coignetiae*, which colours to vivid red and orange in autumn.

To the south, on the encircling bank which curves round eastwards to the park, a copper beech dominates the view and with a neighbouring green-leaved beech hides the Indian-style stable and cottages beyond. Nearer the orangery a purple-leaved form of the smoke bush, *Cotinus coggygria* 'Notcutt's Purple', brings the eye sweeping down to the lower garden. Mrs Peake has recently planted a *Koelreuteria paniculata* to stand out among more sober planting against the hill behind. Under the skirts of the beech golden *Taxus baccata* 'Dovastonii Aurea' bushes extend their almost horizontal branches to match the contours; and other eye-catching foliage colours are contributed by a combination of a grey-leaved weeping pear and silver willow, *Salix alba argentea*, with nearby pale foliage of variegated *Cornus alba* 'Elegantissima' and golden-leaved *Robinia pseudacacia* 'Frisia'. A very large birch, an *Arbutus unedo* and more shrubs frame a rustic grotto where ferns, cyclamen and lilies of the valley intermingle. Over the brow an old mulberry sounds a more domestic note, standing above the modern tennis-court and tennis pavilion built by Sir Cyril Kleinwort in 1961, copying architectural detail from the house.

Beyond the house the north lawn has shrubbery planting to the east and, above, to the west. On the drive the modern planting is

dominated by a purple-leaved Norway maple (*Acer platanoides* 'Crimson King') and the dark filbert, (*Corylus maxima* 'Purpurea'), but these are accompanied by other good shrubs such as the evergreen *Phillyrea latifolia*, *Magnolia × soulangiana* 'Lennei' and *Viburnum opulus* 'Compactum', and by a flowering crab (*Malus floribunda*) and thorn (*Crataegus × lavallei*). On the higher slope where the Tent Room (originally Sir Charles Cockerell's bedroom) terminates the house building complex, sober aucubas and cherry laurel date from an earlier planting period.

The Thornery is reached by a curving path to allow a view of the temple pond, where clean sparkling water rises from a spring. The god Surya surveys the pool from his temple. Curved rustic arches make mossy recesses through which water trickles, before it becomes the garden stream which flows down the valley in a series of pools, cascades and narrower rills to reach the Evenlode in the lower plain. Acers, sorbus, a group of the exotic Chinese aralia (*Aralia elata* 'Variegata') with creamy variegated leaves, hydrangeas, the rare *Chusquea culeou*, a bamboo from Chile and other modern planting in this bowl complement earlier yews, up one of which vast *Rosa filipes* 'Kiftsgate' and 'Paul's Himalayan Musk' rose clamber to fill the air with scent and blossom at the end of June. A cool grey-leaved honeysuckle (*Lonicera korolkowii*) arches on the upper edge of the pond. With pink flowers in June, followed by red berries, this is perfectly sited.

Stepping stones cross the stream as it descends towards the bridge and more good shrubs, including fatshederas, golden gleditsia and an oriental plane, are grouped near perennials planted in broad masses to follow the curving banks. Grey-leaved *Hosta sieboldiana*, hemerocallis, rodgersias, brunnera, alchemilla and the skunk cabbage from America (*Lysichitum americanum*), bamboos and many other plants give foliage interest and flowers in season. *Rosa glauca* (syn. *R. rubrifolia*) is underplanted with variegated brunnera, and each separate garden picture seems part of superb planning. Above the bridge *Rhus potaninii*, a round-headed tree with pinnate leaves which colour to rich autumn shades, is outstanding and suckering progeny have been planted lower down the valley.

Below the bridge a quiet pool is dominated by a fountain where a three-headed snake twining round a post gushes water. *Primula florindae*, *Hypericum calycinum*, banks of *Viburnum davidii* with turquoise berries in autumn, Siberian iris, astilbe, and tall blue-flowered *Campanula lactiflora*, grow under cercidiphyllum, *Cornus kousa chinensis*, acers and willows in open sunny glades to the north, while the southern stream bank is in the shadow of the cedar grove mentioned earlier. A very large weeping hornbeam (*Carpinus betulus* 'Pendulus') with twisted trunk stands near *Acer griseum* with peeling glowing bark. Another pool dominated by a rocky outcrop (identifiable in Daniell's oils) allows for picturesque planting. As the valley widens the stream disappears into woodland. A modern wooden bridge with a central octagonal platform links the two banks to an island, and giant-leaved *Trachystemon orientale* and royal ferns are planted in great drifts, contrasting in shape with native flag iris spears along and inside the water's edge.

As the path winds from bank to bank the mixture of original tree planting and more recent secondary ornamentals provides a constantly changing pattern of light and shade, accompanied by the cool and refreshing sound of running water. Throughout the valley garden glimpses of oriental architectural features remind the viewer of the dominant Eastern philosophy which introduces a foreign symbolism into this water planting, giving the garden a wider spiritual significance. Perhaps the best route for the Sezincote garden visitor should be a quest upwards from the lower stream, where water, symbolizing the passage of time, is traced back to its source at the top of the garden. There the statue of Surya seems to welcome enquiry and to respond to a search for intellectual enlightenment.

Westwell Manor

Burford, Oxfordshire
(Mr and Mrs Thomas Gibson)

THE VILLAGE at Westwell seems quite unspoilt, just a cluster of Cotswold stone buildings including a small Norman church gathered round an open green and pond. It lies just below the high ridge which carries a traveller from Oxford to Burford and Cirencester. The manor itself is to the south of the green, hidden behind walls and overhung with the branches of chestnut and ash. A winding drive leads past tall yews and then between the trees to the north façade, where the final approach is flanked by a pair of walnuts and a formal 'walk' of pleached *Tilia platyphyllos*, the broad-leaved lime. In spring the grass underneath the chestnuts and a copper beech is full of aconites, crocus and daffodils, followed by a scattering of *Fritillaria meleagris* and tulips. In autumn there are drifts of pale mauve *Colchicum speciosum*. The rectangular gravel sweep is framed with strange topiary shapes in yew, and through the central archway of the adjoining barn more spiralling shapes and weird forms continue the theme.

The group of buildings consists of a central block with projecting side wings linking a high barn and other ancillaries to the main body of the house, which dates in part to 1545 and has mullioned windows and a high central gable. Over the centuries the house has been much altered, enlarged, and (in the early years of this century) reduced again to the appearance of the Tudor original. In the 1920s a central gable was added to the projecting block on the south. In 1910, when the house was acquired by Sir Sothern and Lady Holland, there was no formal garden layout except for the eighteenth-century walled enclosure which slopes up to the southern skyline, the lower south-west corner dominated by a stone dovecote, built a little earlier. A pair of symmetrically placed old yews at the outer edge of the walls frame the house from a distant southern view.

In the tradition of gifted amateurs, the Hollands designed a garden in seventeenth-century style round the house, incorporating all the existing buildings. An architectural framework stressed the unity of house and garden, and provided a setting for seemingly casual planting of hardy plants which cascaded over hard masonry lines. The garden was divided into a series of open-air rooms, made by walls and new hedges of yew and box; broad terraces at different levels were linked by stone steps and paths. Pergolas of local stone gave height, and, covered in wisteria and rambling roses, provided shady walks to contrast with the sunny garden enclosures. By using a style reminiscent of the period of the original house, the Hollands deliberately disguised the more obvious impact of later building additions and alterations. The whole complex became a cohesive unit. Today even the yew topiary, specimens specially imported from Holland before the First World War, seem to have been there as long as the house. Peacocks, finials, spirals, giant mounds and dark green 'boxes' frame doorways and views. Sir Southern and Lady Holland seem to have combined the dual roles of architects and gardeners, perfectly equipped to enrich and ornament Westwell Manor.

Mr and Mrs Thomas Gibson bought the property in 1979, and in the last few years Mrs Gibson, herself a garden designer, has not only restored much of the Hollands' layout, but has extended the architectural theme with pleached lime walks (to the north where topiary had been accidentally burned), a lime arbour framing a western view, and hornbeam blocks, designed as 'houses' on stilts as at Hidcote, in the large kitchen garden. The latter, when mature, will give three-dimensional volume where the scale of the walled enclosure seemed disproportionately empty and vast. In the rose garden a new wooden frame provides more space for climbers, and a formal walk of *Pyrus* 'Chanticleer' is a

feature to the north-east of the buildings. In a 'cutting' garden near the front gate a more rustic pergola shades a path lined with hyssop; roses and solanum twine above. Even a back drive gives a hint of architectural formality with a line of mop-headed *Robinia pseudacacia* 'Umbraculifera'.

The north façade of the house with its protruding wings lies in deep shadow. On either side of the front door are roses: double pink 'Madame Grégoire Staechelin' and white 'Madame Alfred Carrière'. To the east topiary shapes flank a vista through the open door of

the barn into an enclosed garden where more topiary sculpture towers in a simple grass setting. The main garden lies to the south. Broad terraces connected by shallow steps run parallel to the house, in front of which a paved walk leads east and west. From the garden doorway the view is framed by yew spirals, topiary introduced in the Hollands' time. A central grass path stretches 60 yards (55 metres) to the wall and the gateway on the far side of the enclosure. The central panel separates wide herbaceous borders planted in predominantly pale flower colours, with strong foliage plants

The double borders in the walled garden are centred on the house.

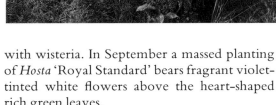

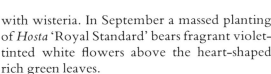

to give the scheme body. The westward view along the house terrace, through handsome wrought-iron gates in a stone wall, stops at a seat under the new lime arbour, passing first between further lavender-edged beds.

In planting Mrs Gibson emphasizes the compartmental flavour, each separate 'garden' having its own strong theme. In the area between the walls to the south-east plants with silvery foliage set off flowers in white and mauve. Standard 'Iceberg' roses, madonna and regal lilies, delphiniums with white flower-spikes, and the white-flowered form of goat's rue (*Galega officinalis* 'Alba') rise above foliage plants: hostas, anaphalis, artemisias, glaucous-leaved dianthus and santolina. In a corner *Buddleja alternifolia* makes an accent, and against the wall *Abutilon* × *suntense* is covered with violet flowers in June. Huge white-flowered trussed roses cover the house walls, and include the tender *Rosa brunonii* 'La Mortola' with delicate grey-green leaves.

The south-west walls partly enclose a herb garden, full of scented flowers and foliage. A central design of four yellow-flowered fern-leaved roses, rose 'Canary Bird', flanks a standing stone brought from a local megalithic monument years ago. Mrs Gibson never dots her plants about, but uses firm blocks of planting to make her effects, and the result is restful to the eye. Spherical heads of mauve allium grow through the purple foliage of *Salvia officinalis* 'Purpurascens'. Walls are curtained with clematis – spring-flowering *Clematis montana*, and *C.* 'Perle d'Azur' for the later summer. In a narrow bed along the house front fragrant daphnes, sarcococca, small white violas, and *Carpenteria californica* are overhung

with wisteria. In September a massed planting of *Hosta* 'Royal Standard' bears fragrant violet-tinted white flowers above the heart-shaped rich green leaves.

A yew hedge separates the terraced planting from the walled garden, where double lavender hedges enclose a row of architectural flag iris, their fading leaves disguised by flowering lavender as the summer progresses. Mrs Gibson has recently planted four weeping grey pears (*Pyrus salicifolia* 'Pendula'), each rising from a solid square of silvery-leaved cotton lavender to make a formal rhythm below the dark yew hedge. Outside to the west, below the handsome dovecote, the Hybrid Musk rose 'Buff Beauty' and the Rugosa rose 'Agnes' flank steps trimmed with daisy-flowered *Anthemis cupaniana*. Already the garden echoes Mrs Gibson's strong sense of design. Although she speaks of restoring the garden to the previous style, at the same time she formalizes colour themes, and by edging beds in stone makes the garden more manageable.

Above, the garden is simple; the planting consists only of the central double borders, the hornbeam 'houses' set round earthenware oil jars, and pink and red climbing roses against the distant walls. Beyond the south gate a green alley enclosed by a 5-foot (1.5-metre) box-wood hedge has its regularity broken by an old prunus tree. The borders are given symmetry by repetitive planting of English lavender bushes and spiky iris leaves, which hold the design together. Height is given by tall crambes, macleaya, spikes of *Eremurus robustus*, and repeated planting of blue-leaved *Rosa glauca*. The flower colouring is mainly yellow, blue and white, but there are pink roses, mauve

Stachys macrantha and plenty of textured foliage shapes, including rustling variegated grasses. As elsewhere in the garden, each planting block or drift is on a lavish scale. Interest is stimulated by rarer plants such as *Calamintha nepetoides* and *Gladiolus papilio*, with flowers marked in green and mauve. Both small-flowered lime-yellow *Nicotiana langsdorfii* and *Verbena bonariensis*, with violet-blue flowers on tall square-shaped stems, seed prolifically.

To the east of the main garden a doorway leads to a sunken stone pathway with four raised rose-beds on either side and a new wooden trellis. The old shrub roses have typical pale colours: groups of 'Madame Hardy', white with a green centre; 'Alba Maxima', a double white; 'Félicité Parmentier' and 'Complicata', with yellow-centred clear pink single flowers. They are underplanted with flowering marjoram. Beyond, a pergola

ABOVE
Lilies grow under the rose pergola next to another garden enclosure where lavender hedges and shrub roses are mingled.

Ornamental gates, lavender-edged wide stone terracing and clipped topiary peacocks frame a white seat.

of square stone pillars supports wisteria and white roses, and is underplanted with *Lilium regale*, *Galtonia candicans* and *Acidanthera murielae* (correctly *Gladiolus callianthus*) for flowering succession. Raised beds at the side are edged with catmint, and contain lime-green tobacco plants and more white roses. Everywhere yew hedges from the Hollands' time divide and frame planting schemes, yet often the vistas and gateways do not follow an axial viewpoint; rather each garden area is tightly enclosed, with a narrow path giving a secret point of access.

Against one corner of the house a mounded box shape echoes the great stone dovecote beyond. Against a warm wall, beds in gravel,

separated by curving paths, were once planted with Lady Holland's alpines; today, less formally, blue scillas flowering in spring are followed by creeping euphorbias with lime-green flower bracts. A shady pergola overhung with wisteria and the Chinese gooseberry (*Actinidia chinensis*), makes a sitting area above a water garden. A garden of 'knots' woven with box, germander, and santolina surrounding a central box pyramid reveals its intricate pattern when seen from above. The diamond shapes match neighbouring stonework. Steps lead down to water, canalized from an old pond. Rich planting of moisture-loving perennials here is less formal, and stepping stones lead to the opposite bank which

Moisture-loving plants beside the lower water garden.

rises above the stream that feeds the pool. Meconopsis, ligularia, kirengeshoma and flag iris (*Iris pseudacorus*) thrive here in spite of the alkalinity. A newly planted colony of toad lilies (*Tricyrtis formosana*) looks exotic beside a clump of grassy *Cyperus longus*.

More garden areas complete the round of the house. In terraced flower-beds, May-flowering *Paeonia lactiflora* and *Alchemilla mollis* overlook a sunken lawn and rectangular lily pond, with tobacco plants and white-flowered galtonias giving flower and scent in later summer months. Turning back towards the barn to the east of the house, stone steps lead up to the yew topiary and hedged enclosure above, and to the great barn.

There are still other areas of interest, some in the course of development. Near the lower 'cutting' flower garden shrub roses are at their best in June. In an old orchard a beech hedge surrounds a modern swimming-pool, with a pair of Moorish-style pavilions. Borders of

hardy perennials are planted with flowers of blue and cream, and with the inner lining painted black the water looks dark and mysterious. Further south a nut walk dates to the Hollands' time, but Mrs Gibson is now reopening access to it, and a winding mown path will lead down between medlars, making an alternative route to the swimming-pool. Beyond the dovecote and past a well-grown paulownia, a new orchard of half-standard crab apples, all *Malus* 'John Downie', is planted in regimented formation, equally attractive with May blossom or when bearing the golden and red late-summer fruits. Mowing here is left until mid- or late summer, and wild flowers are encouraged to seed and attract butterflies. Mr and Mrs Gibson are doing much more than breathing life into an old garden. Mrs Gibson's own vision and application have opened a new chapter at Westwell, where the architectural theme continues to expand, and is ornamented by a rich and thoughtful choice of good plants.

Heale House

Woodford, Salisbury, Hampshire

(Major David and Lady Anne Rasch)

FORTUNATELY Heale House, approached from a narrow secondary road which follows the winding Avon valley, still seems as remote as it was when the future King Charles II found a refuge here in 1651. Then, far from neighbouring large houses, yet only four miles (6.5 kilometres) north-west of Salisbury, the fugitive king rested in the house for a week before eventually embarking at Brighton and reaching safety in Normandy.

At Woodford the Avon makes a sharp right-angled bend which encloses the house and garden at Heale, extending to 8 acres (3.2 hectares). The garden setting is a natural water landscape; in the seventeenth century indigenous poplars and willows would have been the only trees in the valley, while on the high escarpment beyond the river to the south English elms would have predominated. To-day cedars, plane trees and soaring Lombardy poplars planted at the turn of the century signify garden development but blend happily into the rich pasture land, just as at ground level aconites and snowdrops, making abstract pat-

Native snowdrops, *Galanthus nivalis*, cover the sloping banks above the river Avon. In early spring snowdrops and *Cyclamen coum* make abstract patterns spreading into the water-meadows beyond the garden.

terns, creep and spread outwards, linking the wilder edge of the garden proper with the natural countryside. The high water-table and deep alluvial soil compensate for the underlying chalk, typical of the region.

From the road a poplar-lined avenue leads southwards for half a mile (0.8 kilometre), turning and dropping down from the west as the northern façade of the house is glimpsed. A cedar of Lebanon and the old yew hedges almost surrounding a gravelled square forecourt shelter the house from north-easterly gales and give it a firm architectural anchor in the landscape. Nearby *Cyclamen coum* has seeded to cover the ground under magnolias. Later, as leaves unfurl on trees, this approach gives the visitor no hint of the summer-flowering profusion of the Edwardian gardens reached through a gap in the yews on the west side of the house.

At Heale, although much has been altered over the centuries, house, garden and landscape still seem comfortably settled together and strike no jarring note. Almost completely rebuilt, the house, designed in the 1890s by Detmar Blow for the Hon. Louis Greville, still reflects the seventeenth-century style. The fine

rounded shapes of shrubs or broad-headed trees. He liked to soften the harsh edges of stonework with soft-textured plant foliage, drawing his inspiration from the greys and greens of the Italian landscape. He used pergolas to make shady cool walks to contrast with open sunlit spaces, and water in its different moods to stimulate the mind by its activity, or quieten the senses with reflective stillness.

For Heale House Peto was an inspired designer, although much of his work has been modified to suit the exigencies of a modern era, when the whole garden must be maintained by the owners, Major David and Lady Anne Rasch (a great-niece of Mr Greville) with the help of one gardener. Peto's characteristic terracing, stone balustrading and wide paving near the house give firm geometrical lines and direction to much of today's planting. The terraces to the west, linked by a broad paved central axial path, climb slowly on three separate levels, a copper pot filled with plants and framed by elaborate yew topiary making a focal point along the brow of the hill. On the lower terrace symmetrically placed water-lily ponds differ in shape from Peto's original plan. In the last few years Lady Anne has replanted an avenue of laburnums which lined the pathway of the second terrace. To frame and concentrate the view further a pair of tall pyramid-shaped trelliswork tripods edge the lower steps, their outline disguised by a luxuriant growth of rose 'Rambling Rector', clematis and honeysuckle. Modern planting perfectly complements Peto's architectural frame. Mixed borders containing shrub roses and traditional hardy plants, including the giant kale (*Crambe cordifolia*), peonies, delphiniums and day-lilies, are given 'body' with foliage plants, including the silver-leaved weeping pear (Pyrus salicifolia 'Pendula'), a purple-leaved form of *Cotinus coggygria* and golden philadelphus (*Philadelphus coronarius* 'Aureus'). To give more formality in this free planting style a pair of *Viburnum × juddii* are grown as clipped standards.

Outside Detmar Blow's new south-east drawing-room wing, a branch stream flows southwards, before turning sharply to the west to mark the edge bordering further garden levels. Here Peto paved a broad area, placing in it three large rectangular beds. Today the beds have been filled in to reduce maintenance and alchemilla, thyme, euphorbias and rue seed freely in the cracks. On the wall the evergreen *Magnolia grandiflora* is shaped to

south wing (*c.* 1640) which may have sheltered the king is all that visibly remains of a yet earlier period, and foundations of a much larger house, burnt down in 1836, lie under the gravelled forecourt to the north. By 1900 this had become the main entrance, and a new garden could be made to the south and west of the remodelled house. Here artificial water-canals, constructed much earlier for irrigating traditional water meadows, could be used as part of an overall design. Until the beginning of this century a meandering drive through the water-meadows crossed the river from the south to reach a west-facing entrance.

For this new garden Mr Greville, although himself a knowledgeable gardener, commissioned plans from Harold Peto; the first dated plan is from 1906. Peto, an architect by training and strongly influenced by Renaissance gardens of Italy, used stonework to provide an architectural frame to all planting. In his designs he loved to exploit and dramatize contrasts. As in an Italian garden of the sixteenth century, changes of level were accentuated by terracing, stone balustrading and wide steps. Vertically soaring trees contrasted with horizontal paved areas and mown grass, and with the more

OVERLEAF LEFT ABOVE AND BELOW
Roses clamber up pillars and cascade over stonework in the best tradition of English gardening.

OVERLEAF RIGHT
Stone balustrading, paving and formal water contrast with the unspoilt natural landscape of the Avon valley.

frame a pedimented doorway, and climbing roses, including pale pink 'Climbing Paul Lédé', scent the air in June. All around plants soften harsh lines of stone and a lavender hedge spills over the paving edge. Peto's formal beds are not missed and modern planting gives the whole area a sense of timeless maturity.

To the east balustraded stone steps descend grandly to the stream, evoking a Claudian landscape where the traveller embarks from a classical water gateway. Here the scale is limited and across the water a small cascade, fed from a further watercourse, tumbles and gives a constant murmur. On the banks giant-leaved *Gunnera manicata* and rodgersias contrast with the sword-like spikes of water-iris. Under a low wall supporting the paved terrace red, pink and white chaenomeles are grown as a hedge, flowering in early spring.

When Harold Peto first came to work at Heale the garden covered a larger area than it does today, and his most elaborate plan (1906) was for a rose garden on the island formed by two branching canals, the branch nearer the house turning to run westwards below further terraces, where planting was kept low. From the house the view to the south led to this layout of formal rose-beds backed by curving yew hedges. Today the island is once more a peaceful meadow, the only visible signs of previous planting being two symmetrically placed cedars between which rests a stone Italian well-head, and the line of the yew, which now grows freely although originally it was firmly clipped to mark the edge of the farther stream.

Peto's terraces to the south of the house are linked by shallow steps which lead from a broad lawn to the lower levels. On the first narrow terrace, a quiet grass walk is edged with a bed of Hybrid Musk roses. 'Penelope', 'Felicia' and 'Buff Beauty' grow on a frame to be visible from the house windows, and contain the edge of the big lawn. Carefully pruned back after the first flush of flowering in June, these roses give a repeat performance in September. Below, more roses and shrubs, underplanted with *Galega officinalis* and day-lilies, are planted in a narrow border before the lawn slopes gently down to the water's edge.

Here Peto at first made designs for a sunken garden which, never implemented, were eventually used in a new area beyond a garden wall to the west. No traces remain of any definite planting and this is now a domestic orchard, dominated by a beautiful old mulberry. A mown grass walk leads to the central

south entrance of a kitchen garden laid out in a formal pattern. Here the plan and much of the planting is recent. Sloping towards the south, the area is contained by a pergola which runs along the bottom edge of the rectangle. Originally chains garlanded with climbing roses and honeysuckle ran along this boundary walk, but Lady Anne's more architectural frame provides greater scope for luxuriant planting and emphasizes the garden division. On the other three sides this garden area is enclosed by traditional tile-topped stucco-covered walls, which provide shelter for evergreen shrubs such as ceanothus, choisya, *Garrya elliptica* and myrtle. In the centre Lady Anne designed a square lily-pond to fit between the existing eight clipped box domes. Edging the water are patterns of cobbles and smooth stone flags. Symmetrically placed tunnels of pleached fruit trees and pergolas on a central axis further divide the garden into four. On the pergolas clamber variegated jasmine, roses and a larger vine, *Vitis coignetiae*, the latter casting shade in summer and contributing fiery red leaves in autumn. Disciplined straight rows of vegetables are mixed with happily seeding violas, and groups of tulips are grown to cut for the house. It is interesting to see how Lady Anne Rasch, while adapting the garden to labour-saving techniques, yet strengthens Peto's themes in a way which is entirely in sympathy with his garden ethic. In his design for the island rose garden, pergolas firmly marked the outer boundary of the then larger garden, and the new frames in this kitchen area seem a logical innovation, providing cool walks and a delightful contrast of light and shade. At Peto's own garden, Iford Manor, domes of clipped evergreen *Phillyrea angustifolia* surround a quiet reflecting pool, and these are echoed by the juxtaposition of domed box with the new lily pond at Heale.

Peto's plans for the formal garden at Heale have only recently been discovered among old papers in the house, and may well now become the subject of serious study for those tracing the history of his development as a garden designer. Yet the gardens at Heale have long been remarkable for another garden area which lies just to the south of the partly walled kitchen enclosure. Louis Greville, for some years in the Diplomatic Service in Tokyo, brought back to Heale a plan for a Japanese garden, together with a traditional thatched tea-house and a red lacquered half-moon bridge (a copy of the Nikko bridge) actually made in Japan. Two Japanese carpenters came to assemble them on site. Beneath the tea-house two streams now run at different levels, the result of ingenious damming and tunnelling. Through the garden twisting torrents are crossed by simple rustic bridges. Informal planting of Japanese maples shades a garden where by the stream shuttlecock ferns, rodgersias, lysichitum and bog arums flourish. It is hard to know where Louis Greville's planting ends and that of Lady Anne begins. It is all moist and cool, and vistas are dominated by glimpses of scarlet lacquer and moving water, a world seemingly remote from Peto's formal terraces and the English-style planting which clothes them. Many Japanese-style gardens were made at the turn of the century, but perhaps few owners had the chance to study the real thing in its country of origin. As Lawrence Weaver wrote in 1915, 'The disposition of a few typical ornaments, of a bronze stork here and stone lantern there, does not make a Japanese garden; it only makes an English garden speak with a Japanese accent. At Heale House, however, the scheme is coherent and expressive of its owner's special knowledge and taste.' Tradition has it that this garden was constructed in 1901, and it is interesting to note that Lord Redesdale, who became an expert on bamboos during his earlier attachment to the Foreign Office in Tokyo, was making his Japanese garden at Batsford in the last years of the nineteenth century. His Elizabethan-style mansion, c1890, was designed by Ernest George and Harold Peto. In English gardening there has always been a constant exchange of ideas as well as plants between owners, who often moved in quite a small social world. Did Mr Greville know Lord Redesdale (then Algernon Bertram Freeman-Mitford) in Tokyo, and did Mr Peto borrow from Batsford the inspiration for Japanese garden-making at Heale?

Today we see magnificent London plane trees planted by Mr Greville in the outer meadows where Peto advised Lombardy poplars. Gardening, much more than architecture, calls for a fusion between the schemes of a great designer and the practical management of a talented owner, who must implement plans and tend the growing plants on which the success of a garden depends. Often planting plans are not lifted straight from the drawing-board, but themselves change as the garden is developed. At Heale House the present owners improve and adapt where eighty years ago a new garden evolved. The latest project includes a small nursery garden where visitors can purchase specimens of well-grown plants.

ABOVE
Rustic wooden planks connect the banks in the Japanese garden, where moisture-loving perennials and shuttlecock ferns are planted in drifts below Japanese maples.

In February golden aconites (*Eranthis hyemalis*) flower under the trees.

Brockenhurst Park

Hampshire

(The Hon. Mrs Denis Berry)

THERE ARE two possible approaches to Brockenhurst Park, but neither entrance drive gives a hint of the extraordinary garden landscape which lies beyond. One winds south of Brockenhurst, striking east through parkland dominated by ancient oaks. The other leaves the village through the arch of a French-style lodge gate to travel south along an avenue of horse chestnuts before joining the first. The final approach is to a square walled northern forecourt which conceals the house set at an angle across its southern corner. House and high walls are of the same brick, the whole façade, with few windows and flanking walls, giving a fortress-like effect. Dating only from 1960, the house was built on the site of the crumbling ruins of the remaining central block of a succession of buildings of varying historical periods. The substantial modern house was designed to dramatize the approach to a formal garden canal and topiary layout hidden from immediate view on the south side. The architect, Harry Graham, and his clients, the Hon. Mr and Mrs Denis Berry, maximized contrasting elements. From the forbidding and severe approach to the house façade in deep shade, a visitor moves into an entrance hall before entering a wide drawing-room where French windows look out on an open sun-filled terrace. Beyond, running south from the terrace, is a long classically proportioned water-canal. At either side green panels of grass bordered by elaborate topiary specimens are enclosed by high bay hedges. Above the hedge-line evergreen oaks (*Quercus* 'Lucombeana'), old Scots pines (*Pinus sylvestris*) and Californian redwoods (*Sequoia sempervirens*) rise to frame the view and partially shade the still water, increasing the drama. At the far end the tank broadens and a double stairway leads above a buttress and niches to a circular fountain pool in the centre of a grass stage. Round the edge clipped arches of evergreen *Quercus ilex* are flanked by more bay, together forming

The water canal, its edges softened with herringbone cotoneaster, *Cotoneaster horizontalis*, is flanked by formal clipped evergreens.

RIGHT
Solid geometric yew
shapes line the banks of the
formal water canal.

theatrical exits and entrances almost as complex as the perspectives in Palladio's Teatro
Olympico in Vicenza.

In the eighteenth century the Morants, West
Indian merchants with investments in sugar,
coffee and slaves, first acquired 150 acres (some
60 hectares) in this part of the New Forest, an
area now approximately occupied by the surrounding parkland. A Jacobean farmhouse
became the central block of an enlarged mansion on classical lines, and by acquisitions the
estate was increased to 5,000 acres (2,025
hectares). The entrance was where it is today,
but ancillary buildings and a kitchen garden
occupied a space south-east of the house, the
foundations of which formed part of the
supporting terrace of the much enlarged
formal garden made in the 1870s. At this time
the architect Thomas Henry Wyatt (1807–80)
was called in to enlarge the existing house.
Buildings influenced in style by French
châteaux rose to the east and north. Old
photographs show the completed grand

Clipped evergreens flank
pathways and frame green
alleys. By the statue
golden-leaved
Chamaecyparis pisifera
'Sulphurea' contrast with
the sober greens of ilex
and bay.

edifice; today only the ornate lodge gives a hint of the style. It is probable that John Morant himself designed the new gardens, the main outlines of which are seen today.

In the original park to the south there were already many good trees, particularly conifers, which now dominate the skyline. The soil is sandy and acid, typical of the region and ideal for these trees, which require high rainfall and humid warm summers. Early planting included five Scots pines dating from 1760, a group of *Sequoia sempervirens*, some from 1855, and six magnificent cedars of Lebanon (*Cedrus libani*) planted in 1847. Wellingtonias (*Sequoiadendron giganteum*) and a deodar (*Cedrus deodara*) also date from the period before the formal garden was made. After 1880 the garden was mainly expanded to the south and south-east, but a double avenue of lime and chestnut was aligned on a new west-facing entrance court and an avenue of lime (mixed with some already existing oak) was planted to cross the landscape to the south. Ordnance Survey maps of 1870 and 1909 show the development, and an aerial photograph of 1930 reveals the architectural garden compartments, a series of 'rooms' with clipped green hedges for walls. Steps linked levels below archways cut in hedges of bay (*Laurus nobilis*), ilex (*Quercus ilex*) and laurel (the ordinary cherry laurel, *Prunus laurocerasus*). To the east, at the end of a narrow walk, an ornamental gateway, framed with golden yew, was placed above shallow balustraded stone steps, allowing a view into the parkland beyond. A Dutch garden with ornamental summerhouse to the east had scrolls of box round a central circular pool. Statues and topiary cut in plant material, with contrasting textures and green and golden foliage, were the only garden decoration. Orange trees in octagonal-shaped tubs lined the canal edge in summer, a gravel path leading between them and the new topiary planting in front of parallel bay hedges. These specimens can be seen in early photographs, a series of alternating obelisks and domed hemispheres, now mature and vast. For the latter, golden yew was grafted on to standard green, a device much used by later landscape designers at the turn of the century, in particular by Thomas Mawson. The yew obelisks (of ordinary English yew, *Taxus baccata*) soaring upwards from solid square bases were underplanted with box. Photographs also reveal how even the bay hedging, today cut with a straight horizontal top, was originally clipped into more fanciful shapes. This section of the garden was the most

Above the water canal roses and lavender bushes scramble between vertical Irish junipers to mark the edge of the theatre stage.

ornate, but a wide bowling-green on a lower level to the east offered a restful contrast.

Gertrude Jekyll describes the garden as it was by the end of the century. In *Some English Gardens*, with illustrations by George Elgood, she praises Morant for capturing 'the spirit of the pure Italian gardens ... it is none the less beautiful because it is a garden almost without flowers, so important are its permanent forms of living green walls, with their proper enrichment of ball and spire, bracket and buttress, and so fine is the design of the actual masonry and sculpture.' Elgood's accompanying paintings (dated 1897) portray the subtlety of colouring of the clipped textured foliage. By 1907 photographs show oriental-type sculptured stone ornaments decorating the long canal, and one can speculate whether before his death in 1906 Mr Morant had come under the influence of the Far East, at a time in history when Europeans first began to assimilate the philosophical ideas implicit in Japanese garden design. Miss Jekyll would hardly have approved of this unhappy blend of different cultures.

By the 1950s the heir of John Morant, another John, reduced the house to more manageable proportions. Land was sold and finally even the remaining structure became too large for modern maintenance, and was abandoned in 1958. Much from the interior of the house and almost all the statues, fountains and steps from the gardens were dispersed. The Berrys found the house a shell, the garden a wilderness of bramble, the hedges and topiary uncut and shapeless. Even the stone parapets and kerbs surrounding garden pools had been taken. In 1960 the old house was finally demolished, and a new building was designed to serve the gardens, enough of which remained to show their unique quality. Instead of the gardens being designed round a house, to complement its style and period, the architecture became functional, to serve as a dwelling place from which to observe and absorb an exceptional landscape. On the south front all the main rooms of the house have a vista down the canal, with wings projecting forward to give maximum outlook. Like great Elizabethan houses such as Hardwick and Sutton Place, shaped bays on two floors have windows to the ground, where glass reflects sunlight and more solid masonry becomes almost invisible.

By remarkable good fortune the Berrys brought with them urns and statuary of exceptionally high quality, an inheritance from Mr Berry's family home at Dropmore. A tiered Mohammedan ablution fountain is now a feature in the stage pool, and stone cornucopia vases mark the corners of the canal. In the Dutch garden a marble Dorothea from *Don Quixote* sits in meditation; elsewhere, a stone statue of Venus capturing Cupid ornaments a sunken garden.

The story of the restoration of the garden is also an unusual one. Mrs Berry cleaned and dredged the main canal, and over the years she has skilfully directed stonework repairs. Where necessary, masons have made new cement edging; pools have again become watertight, and golden carp swim once more in the golden foliage garden. The same masons have made broad steps, already lichen-covered and ageless.

It is recorded how after the First World War it took two men five years of clipping to restore the hedges and topiary. Impatient and determined, Mrs Berry hired sixteen woodmen for six weeks. Skilled and thorough work cleared away old trees and tangles of brambles and nettles, but saved the plant 'bones' of the garden and allowed established trees to breathe again.

Emerging bramble and nettle seedlings were poisoned with SBK Brushwood Killer. Two tree surgeons tackled the main sixty trees, and finally a rabbit-proof deer fence was erected between garden and park. Over the years the basic topiary shapes have been restored, but considerably simplified, and all clipping is done annually – and economically – by a contractor. Mrs Berry does all the mowing using two sit-on 42-inch (105-centimetres) Wheelhorse machines (she keeps one as a spare in case of breakdown). The only other outside help is for eight hours a week.

Besides the trees already mentioned as being planted before the Victorian formal gardens were made, other good specimens had been added in the years up to the Second World War. A cucumber tree (*Magnolia acuminata*), 54 feet (16.5 metres) high with a bole of 9 feet 4 inches (2.8 metres), is the largest recorded in Great Britain. There is a fine cork oak (*Quercus suber*), an unusual cut-leaf lime (*Tilia platyphyllos* 'Laciniata'), *Taxodium distichum*, two *Pinus ayacahuite* in 1939, a fine female ginkgo, *Styrax japonica* and a 56-foot (17-metre) *Kalopanax pictus*. A rhododendron grove to the west of the canal recalls the end of the nineteenth century with plantings of *R. arboreum* and hybrids. Ghent azaleas since brought from Dropmore have been grouped to extend colour and scent. Already an experienced gardener, Mrs Berry was elected a member of the International Dendrology Society in the 1970s. Expeditions abroad with companions of considerable botanical knowledge have extended her interest and pleasure in good trees, to the lasting benefit of the garden at Brockenhurst. New pines, a monkey puzzle, prunus, sorbus in variety and *Picea smithiana* have been planted in the outer garden. In the formal areas walks of *Magnolia grandiflora* and camellias, and archways framed by golden-textured *Chamaecyparis pisifera* 'Filifera Aurea' and *C. lawsoniana* 'Winston Churchill' are less demanding than topiary work. In the Dutch garden the old box hedges have been removed, and soaring Italian cypresses (*Cupressus sempervirens*) mark the edges of a square, with inner

corner planting of Judas trees (*Cercis siliquastrum*) and two slow-growing Chusan palms (*Trachycarpus fortunei*). Under a giant redwood (*Sequoiadendron giganteum*) spring snowdrops and bluebells spread, and below to the north a new orchard occupies part of the eighteenth-century kitchen-garden site. There are few flowers, as in Miss Jekyll's description, but old English lavender and the pink rose 'New Dawn' scrambling over the edge of the brick parapet in front of the grass stage, between upright spires of *Juniperus communis* 'Hibernica'. By some happy accident self-sown seedlings of *Cotoneaster horizontalis* spread fan-shapes over the edges of the long canal. The dark trees rising to the skyline seem to contain the whole garden scene, adding an air of mystery and secrecy.

In the forecourt and against the house walls there are other distractions. Many botanically interesting Australasian plants thrive, to mark the friendship of Lady O'Neill of the Maine, who lives near by. Mrs Berry, with her own eye for quality plants, continually extends and alters this planting. Many specimens are of doubtful hardiness, but she likes to experiment and uses her own seed brought from expeditions abroad. Necessarily ephemeral, with many of the plants liable to damage in a severe winter, it is a stimulating area, in total contrast to the grand design beyond.

In 1904 the percipient Miss Jekyll wrote, 'The danger that awaits such a garden, now just coming to its early prime, is that the careful hand should be relaxed. It is an heritage that carries with it much responsibility; moreover, it would be ruined by the addition of any commonplace gardening.' Brockenhurst seems fortunate to have inherited a custodian of whom Miss Jekyll would have approved.

Bramdean House

Alresford, Hampshire
(Mr and Mrs Hady Wakefield)

THE GARDENS at Bramdean lie in a series of three almost square enclosures exactly aligned on the centre of the house and linked by an axial path, which leads finally to a clock-tower and gazebo at the farthest point of the garden. House and grounds lie to the north of the Winchester–Petersfield road, where it runs along a valley bottom, and old trees – ash, beech and sycamore – shelter the garden area. The main façade of the house, only a few yards from the road, is protected and hidden by a unique mounded hedge of mixed yew and box, at least 14 feet (4.2 metres) high and perhaps 10 feet (3 metres) broad at the base. Planted tightly together so that the dark sombre leaves of yew and textured paler box seem to grow miraculously as from one root-stock, this hedge is an architectural feature in its own right, its moulded contours like slumbering elephants. A pair of symmetrically placed wrought-iron armorial gates lead in to the narrow gravel sweep, and from the central front door it is possible to look through the house to the garden compartments which are laid out on the gently rising slope beyond. On the south side of the road the downland rises to the skyline, from which a glance backwards shows the house comfortably settled in its framing trees.

Built in about 1740 of mellow brick, the house today seems large and grand enough – even without later additions to the back and east – to have been given a park setting in the contemporary Landscape fashion. Fortunately, those connected with its building seem instead to have been a junior branch of the 'great' family in the village, and were happy to plan garden improvements and expansion in the style of the seventeenth century, when gardens were still enclosed spaces. The walls and hedges which divide the garden and mark its perimeters are further reinforced by almost completely encircling trees. Today, when planning permission for modern buildings is being sought by neighbours on either side, these trees ensure privacy. As a result the symmetrical garden compartments, divided primarily by walls, which make inner microclimates and welcome climbing plants, offer an example of the traditional English garden with a strong architectural and geometric framework providing the setting for imaginative planting schemes. Inside each area the themes are different, but the central part of each remains strongly defined and formal, following the axial view to the north. At the back of the house beds planted mainly with hardy perennials face each other across a grass panel; like a green corridor, this carries the eye northwards through the second and third garden 'rooms'. To the east a lawn makes a pool of light, and sloping levels are cleverly adjusted with a dry stone wall and gentle bank, so that a horizontal surface can be used for croquet. At the farther edge of this lowest garden, more sinuous beds match the canopies of large ornamental trees which give protection from east winds funnelled down the valley. Here a spreading copper beech, an American sweet buckeye (*Aesculus flava*), a blue Atlantic cedar and a group of beech give height, and more recently a golden variegated tulip tree has been planted.

Reached up a flight of stone steps and through decorative wrought-iron eighteenth-century gates, the second garden area is completely walled around, and is still used as a kitchen garden, although the central axis is edged with formal rose-beds and bedding plants in an original triangular pattern. High brick walls are buttressed with fruit, vegetables are grown in straight rows, and beds for cut flowers lie comfortably at the base of warm walls. The most northerly garden, reached through another pair of ornamental gates, was once simply an orchard, but an avenue of Irish yews now lines the central mown grass strip leading to the gazebo, and in spring daffodils make a sheet of yellow in the rough grass.

Thus the Bramdean garden provides a framework for the best of twentieth-century planting. Many traditional hardy plants are combined with the comparatively new inside a structure of open-air rooms. As Sylvia Crowe says in her classic book, *Garden Design*: 'Sissinghurst, Hidcote and Tintinhull are all variations of this theme and they all succeed because the architectural form of the enclosures is strong enough to contain the plants.' At Bramdean equally there is a balance between the firm outline of the formal rectangular enclosures and the richness of the informal planting. In the lower garden climbing plants billow and cascade to break the vertical and horizontal lines of walls, and luxuriant flowers scramble and intermingle in the borders. In contrast the central 'parterre' in the kitchen garden is designed in a series of coloured triangles, where beds of old shrub roses and winter and summer beddings, massed in single colours, establish a definite controlled pattern. Beyond, in the orchard area, spaced Irish yews re-emphasize firm garden lines and perspectives, while allowing the horizontal grass area to flow between the loosely planted apple trees (now past fruit bearing, and often hosts to vigorous roses and scented honeysuckles) and new trees and

A formal design of geometric garden compartments is softened by naturalistic planting.

Perfectly balanced borders are centred on the back of the house. In early summer flowers are mainly blue and magenta; later yellows predominate.

shrubs. The house and its three garden 'rooms' are linked together by the central directional path of mown grass, which beckons and leads from house to gazebo.

The design element at Bramdean is necessarily strong, but at the same time the siting and the mellow pink brick walls provide the perfect foil and opportunity for horticultural exuberance. Mrs Feilden found a neglected wilderness in 1944, but she appreciated the 'bones' hidden under undergrowth and brambles, and the garden we see today is a

tribute to her imaginative planting and to that of her daughter Mrs Wakefield, who continues the tradition. Although much of the planting dates back to the 1950s and 1960s (Mrs Wakefield took charge in 1975, but the old gardener remained until 1984), there is nothing dull or monotonous about the choice of plants. For the enthusiast small botanical treasures nestle between well-tried border plants, and Mrs Wakefield obviously has an eye trained to appreciate horticultural novelties as they become available. All gardeners like to experiment with colour, shape and form, thus keeping a garden dynamic and changing and preventing old gardens from acquiring a museum-like character. Equally, a garden should never be just a collection of interesting plants, but must have coherence and unity. At Bramdean the well-defined structure and the mixture of old and new in plant material seems a happy balance.

At the back of the house a round lily pond sits in a paved area, partly shaded by the wings (not part of the original building) of the house, which extend into the garden on both sides. Scented *Corylopsis pauciflora*, *Viburnum* 'Park Farm Hybrid', pyracantha clipped to outline a window, and the little *Philadelphus* 'Manteau d'Hermine' (with fragrant creamy-white double flowers), and roses on the walls are

In spring aconites and snowdrops carpet the ground under the boles of mature lime trees.

PREVIOUS PAGE ABOVE
A pink rose, *Rosa* 'Bantry Bay', drapes a pillar at the entrance to the upper orchard.

BELOW
In spring in the lower garden a fine weeping prunus, *Prunus subhirtella pendula*, is festooned with blossom.

underplanted thickly with foliage plants including hostas, ferns and bronze-toned ligularias. In June St Bernard's lily (*Anthericum liliago*) bears its white lily-flowers on tall stems. Against the north-facing wall, on the east, forsythia is tied back over a narrow bed of the perennial honesty, *Lunaria rediviva*, in which a few plants of the white-flowered biennial variegated honesty have begun to mingle. On the west wing the shell-pink climbing rose. 'Madame Grégoire Staechelin' and *Clematis* 'Hagley Hybrid' both flourish. In sun the beautiful *Codonopsis clematidea* thrives, with pale china-blue flower-bells and inner colouring of orange and maroon, and near by the smaller blue-flowered *Commelina coelestis* spreads with its tuberous rootstock.

The wide borders of mixed perennials have recently been replanted. Many of the good plants which were originally chosen by Mrs Feilden have been divided and resited. These beds, which so successfully extend the central axis of the garden, are surrounded by lawn and are thus viewed from every angle, with low-growing plants building up to height in the centre. A cross-path divides each bed into two, allowing views through to east and west and presenting an opportunity to use strong architectural plants to emphasize the corners. Each flower group is small, seldom containing more than three plants together, so that neighbouring colours, rather than remaining in distinct blocks, blend perfectly to give a tapestry effect. The beds line the central grass panel like decorative ribbons, to be seen as a part of the

overall design and not as a separate focus within it.

Many plants have strong decorative foliage, which gives body and structure to the scheme. Down the centre height is given by tall Scotch thistles, the giant kale (*Crambe cordifolia*), grey-leaved *Thalictrum speciosissimum*, and the grey-leaved comfrey (*Symphytum caucasicum*). Inulas include *Inula helenium*, the elecampane. On the outer edge, sweet peas are trained into a bird-cage shape to give architectural interest. In June the bright magenta *Geranium psilostemon*, purple Byzantine gladiolus, scarlet oriental poppies, peonies and, at the front, groups of catmint, alternate with a dark-flowered tradescantia. Galega, delphiniums and the now rare *Cicerbita plumieri* (syn. *Lactuca p.*), a member of the lettuce family, all contribute blue flowers a little later. On the corners *Clematis × eriostemon* 'Hendersonii' has soft indigo-blue flowers with twisted recurving petals in July and August. Mrs Wakefield stresses that by mid- and late summer the colour theme, mainly blue and crimson in the early summer, switches to a predominance of cool yellow, mostly contributed by representatives of the daisy-flowered *Compositae* which contribute so much to all late border effects. Groups of scented tobacco plants, mignonette and heliotrope are bedded out where space allows. To the east of the borders box topiary shapes stand in the lawn, stressing formality, before the lawn sweeps away to the trees and the garden boundary wall.

The gates above are framed with the climbing roses and clematis that curtain the warm south-facing walls. To the right a border is full of good plants: the variegated thistle (*Galactites tomentosa*), white dictamnus, the grey-leaved clematis (*C. thibetiana*), the small tender *Salvia bacheriana* (wrongly known as *S. buchananii*), white-flowered *Veratrum album*, *Senecio appendiculatus* from the Canaries, a group of the much-prized little viola, 'Irish Molly', *Cosmos atrosanguineus* and a mass of *Salvia sclarea turkestanica* flowering in July. Peonies and tobacco plants, including a clump of the tall *Nicotiana sylvestris*, all grow in profusion. To the west of the gates there is the same luxuriant planting: the rare *Allium schubertii*, its spherical flower-heads with stalks of unequal length; *Nectaroscordon bulgaricum* (syn. *Allium b.*), *Clematis recta purpurea*, the white *Abutilon* 'Veronica Tennant', the small double-flowered *Thalictrum delavayi* 'Hewitt's Double', exochorda, a pink form of the climbing *Eccremocarpus scaber*, and many other good

plants lead to a corner planting dominated by giant silver-leaved cardoons. The colour theme on this side of the garden is dominated by silver foliage, with occasional purple leaves to tone with the pink-and-white variegated climber *Actinidia kolomikta* against the wall.

The grass path, continuing beyond the gates into the kitchen garden, widens out at the centre round a sundial to make a circle thickly hedged with yew. Below this central rondel triangles of roses alternate with summer-flowering antirrhinums, while above more roses alternate with stocks and dahlias. Roses are pink, crimson, yellow and white, and the solid blocks of contrasting colour are a delibe-rate 'shock' treatment after the gently flowing lines and paler tints of flowers in the first garden enclosure. Each bed is edged with stone paving to separate and contain the plants. Behind the triangular beds scented old varieties of sweet pea, mainly the Persian *Lathyrus tuberosus*, are grown on tripods to hide the vegetable areas. Behind the top section new espalier apples serve a similar function.

Beyond the second gate the old apple orchard with its central pathway and avenue of yellow daffodils retains a formal structure, but on either side 'wilderness' planting is in natural style: flowering cherries and other good shrubs, include winter-flowering lonicera and spring-flowering *Rubus* 'Benenden'. By the gazebo a fine clump of the horizontally branched *Viburnum plicatum* 'Mariesii' is planted near a hedge of fragrant sweetbriar. There are several specimens of pink *Kolkwitzia amabilis* and on the return journey the path, which winds southwards to the east, passes shrub roses, snake-bark maple, a spindle

ABOVE LEFT AND RIGHT
Regularly spaced Irish yews and drifts of daffodils flank the wide mown path, which is aligned on the house and the gazebo to the north.

A mounded hedge of intermingled yew and box separates the gravel sweep and front door from the main road.

(*Euonymus phellomanus*) with four-lobed pink fruits in autumn, and elaeagnus. The path drops down to the secret garden area to the east of the kitchen garden wall, where in a sunny glade more shrub roses, a collection of hollies, newly planted *Ginkgo biloba*, liquidambar and a tulip tree all promise interest in maturity.

The path descends under the shade of a grove of beech and lime, where aconites have spread to carpet the ground in late winter, to emerge at the north-east corner of the lower lawn. The little daisy *Erigeron karvinskianus* (syn. *E. mucronatus*) has seeded in the dry stone wall, a remainder that at Bramdean informality and happy accident in planting enrich and human-ize a classical structured design, and contribute to the charm of the whole.

Pusey House

Oxfordshire
(Mr and Mrs Michael Hornby)

PUSEY HOUSE was built in the middle of the eighteenth century, probably to the design of John Wood the Younger. The landscape – with serpentine lake, groves of trees and an extensive view to the Berkshire downland in the south – was typically Brownian, with a decorative Chinese Chippendale bridge (almost certainly from a design by Abraham Swan published in 1757) and a classical memorial temple, placed at the western head of the lake in 1759. Groves of beech and yew hid the church across the park to the south-west. Philip Pusey (1799–1855), scholar, agriculturist and elder brother of Doctor Edward Pusey, the famous theologian and founder of the Oxford Movement, added a mansard roof and servants' bedrooms. In the garden, according to his daughter Mrs Fletcher's memoirs, he was much influenced by the German ambassador of the time, Baron de Bunsen. The lake was widened, the island decorated with a domed ironwork pergola, a sunken rose garden was made immediately to the south of the house and flower-beds and shrubberies were dotted over the main lawn, between house and lake. The landscape in the

ABOVE
In any great garden the presence of water adds an extra dimension.

OPPOSITE
The approach through the kitchen garden leads between borders in carefully graded rainbow colours.

LEFT
Under the raised terrace to the south of the house roses and lilies grow in the narrow border.

103

Viewed from the south the eighteenth-century house is framed by mature trees. Sir Geoffrey Jellicoe designed a raised terrace which links house and garden.

'dingy greys and browns of Capability Brown' had been transformed under 'Baron Bunsen's auspices' to polychrome. It is even possible that John Claudius Loudon advised, as in 1843 he was working for the Bouverie cousins at Coleshill near by.

Mr and Mrs Michael Hornby came to Pusey in 1935, and the garden today reflects fifty years of their care, knowledge and taste. Inheriting a background of beautiful trees, they swept away the Victorian shrubberies on the lawn to leave the smooth grass unadorned except for two old robinias (and today some new replacements). It slopes gently down to reeds on the lakeside, a quiet green foreground to the distant vista which remains clear of all planting.

The sunken rose garden was filled in, and with advice from Sir Geoffrey Jellicoe (then a young landscape architect) a broad terrace was constructed with widening flights of steps which fit in with the scale of the house, particularly when viewed looking back from across the park. To the east an old cedar of Lebanon and dark yews reach almost to the house, overshadowing the terrace and making a background to projecting wings of garden planting which lead down towards the bridge and lake. To the west, yews separate the house from the elegant contemporary stables with Gothic cupola, the design of which has been copied in a swimming-pool gazebo in a hidden walled enclosure between the house and kitchen garden. A curving wall leading away to the memorial temple backs the herbaceous border below the terrace.

On the terrace, planting is simple. A pair of very large Jerusalem sage (*Phlomis fruticosa*) flank the main doorway, and small plants such as *Convolvulus sabatius* (syn. *C. mauritanicus*) grow freely in the hot well-drained soil and stonework. In summer ornamental pots planted with lemon-scented verbena and daturas are placed against the house walls. Rosemary bushes make strong symmetrical mounds at the bottom of the steps and large urns overflow with the glaucous-leaved marguerite (*Argyranthemum foeniculaceum*), pelargoniums, fuchsias and petunias. To either side narrow borders are planted with clematis, roses and plants with grey leaves, including *Baptisia australis*, senecio, caryopteris, helichrysum and the floriferous daisy-flowered *Olearia* 'Waikariensis', all in soft pale colours which do not distract from the wider view across the park. On the walls ornamental vines have decorative architectural leaves which hold the design together.

The Hornbys have chosen trees to maintain and extend the pleasure grounds, both on the drives to the north of the house and in the southern parkland. Where elms have died from disease or beech trees begin to reach their natural span, as in many eighteenth-century parks, specimen trees are planted to maintain the landscape. Old oriental planes are a feature on the approach to the north-west, and another fine specimen in the southern landscape just beyond the curving lake sits beside a copper beech. To east and west many more recently planted trees and shrubs frame the open vista and are dominated by two vast cedars of Lebanon, still magnificent although beginning to lose branches and leaders. A huge ash, the more delicate flowering ash (*Fraxinus ornus*), and many groups of old yew and box trees mark earlier planting before the Hornbys' time. These make a framework for more exotic specimens introduced since the Second World War. In deep dry shade under yews the native balsam (*Impatiens parviflora*) has naturalized. A new grove of beech shelters the garden from the north-east, replacing old elms and making a green background to a collection of golden-foliage trees planted to commemorate the Hornbys' Golden Wedding day. These are sensitively hidden from immediate view by a curving hedge of photinia and the leathery-leaved *Viburnum rhytidophyllum*. Beyond a tall mulberry, plants include the pale gold-leaved

forms of catalpa, gleditsia, sentinel chamaecyparis and golden poplars, *Robinia pseudacacia* 'Frisia' and varieged hollies underplanted with yellow-flowered potentillas, euphorbias, *Cornus alba* 'Spaethii' and hypericums. Seen from the eighteenth-century bridge, willows weep over the reflecting water, hiding the termination of the lake just as Brown would have planned it.

Mrs Hornby is an artist in her own right, and arranges plant flower and foliage colours as she does paints on a canvas. She uses colour to modify or increase the feeling of distance and today's outlook from the south terrace reflects her ease in this concept. Under the boles of specimen trees shrub-beds filled with plants of textured foliage, mainly in pale receding tones, and flowers in misty blues, pale yellow or cream add dimension to the view. Round the water astilbes, rodgersias, yellow-flowered lysimachias, hostas, zantedeschias and ligularias are planted as a natural water garden in Robinsonian style, with the grey foliage of weeping pear or forms of sorbus (including *Sorbus aria* 'Majestica' and the large-leaved *S.* 'John Mitchell') as a fading backdrop. A variegated dogwood (*Cornus alternifolia* 'Argentea') stands poised with horizontal branches, like a ballet dancer. There are specimens of *Cercidiphyllum japonicum*, the swamp

Trees and evergreen shrubs provide a leafy background to a statue set among rough grass.

cypress and metasequoia. Beyond, towards the church, a tulip tree, liquidambar and a selection of maples have grown well, the latter including the peeling mahogany-barked *Acer griseum*, which grows near to *Prunus serrula* with trunk in polished rings of reddish brown. To the west a bed of mainly variegated-leaved plants is effective on the farther lake edge, partly concealed by overhanging beech, a plane tree and a vast black American walnut (*Juglans nigra*). A green-leaved *Cornus controversa* is architectural with its wedding-cake layered branches, and pale-leaved *Physocarpus opulifolius* 'Luteus' (one of the best 'golds' for keeping its colour through the summer) rise above the feathery leaves of Pfitzer's juniper. Grasses, hostas, polygonums, and the elegant Japanese *Kirengeshoma palmata* are thickly planted. In spite of the richness and variety of planting no bright advancing red or orange flower colour disturbs the main composition which represents the view southwards from house and terrace. This vista remains dominated by the high downs many miles away, framed and emphasized by the parkland planting.

This description of the pleasure grounds sets the house and more intimate garden into the wider landscape, but it is perhaps the long herbaceous or mixed border which makes Pusey a Mecca for garden visitors. Each section of plant grouping in the border, in the small walled enclosure known as Lady Emily's garden, on the house terrace and below it, and in the double mixed borders which lead the public in from the stable yard, is a carefully planned exercise in colour arrangement. Here Mrs Hornby sets a standard of composition which will help aspiring gardeners to relate their gardening skills to a wider aesthetic sense. Although the actual planting areas are still large, any section of each border, bed or wall planting could be an individual scheme for a much smaller garden.

The entrance borders unfold their 'rainbow' colour scheme as the spectator advances along it. Arranged in a strict order, the first section moves from dark and bright red flower colour to more crimson shades containing blue pigment; then bluish pinks, then blues followed by yellow and blue again. In the far corner and gateway, the flowers are white, the foliage silvery, and golden hops make a frame. In earlier years Mrs Hornby used the pure hues of the spectrum, allowing a strict progression of orange, red, violet, blue and white to dominate. Now orange is banned to a further garden area near the 'golden' garden, and the

colour scheme is quieter as she makes use of modified, toned-down flower shades. The result is a perfect exercise in the harmony of analogous colours, with nothing to jar or surprise.

At the gateway the view opens to water and parkland, and curving borders backed by a stone wall stretch to left and right. Here again colour schemes are carefully thought out, while wall shrubs, climbing roses and twining clematis give vertical height and extra body to more ephemeral herbaceous plant material. Primarily designed for 'high summer' effects, taller crambes, galegas (both white and blue), delphiniums, the delicate *Salvia haematodes* and thalictrum give colour earlier. Aconitum, creamy feathery plumes of *Artemisia lactiflora*, macleaya, spires of blue-flowered *Veronica virginica* and dahlias in strong colour groups dominate the later summer. Shrubs such as *Ceanothus* 'Gloire de Versailles', the tender *Buddleja crispa*, with silvery felted foliage and lilac flowers sheltered by the warm wall, and clematis make pockets of colour at the back. At the front annuals such as scented nicotiana, clary (*Salvia horminum*) and clumps of laundry-white *Lavatera* 'Mont Blanc' are interplanted with groups of more permanent perennials. Violet-flowered *Salvia* 'Superba' and *Aster × frikartii* 'Mönch', with lavender-blue daisy-flowers, contrast with the lemon-yellow of *Anthemis tinctoria* 'E. C. Buxton' and the silvery-leaved *Achillea* 'Moonlight', while the brighter gleaming golden-yellow of *A.* 'Coronation Gold' makes a strong eye-catching bank of colour behind. Mrs Hornby plants in interlocking drifts rather than blocks, so that each colour touches more than one neighbour and the effect is closer to a woven

From the raised terrace at
the back of the house there
are wide views into the
parkland. The Chinese
Chippendale bridge is a
focal point.

texture than to an artist's two-dimensional canvas.

To the west a wall opening invites exploration to a hidden compartment, Lady Emily's garden. Warm pink brick walls are festooned with honeysuckles, climbing roses and clematis such as the dark *Clematis* 'Royal Velours', blue *C*. 'Comtesse de Bouchard', large white 'Marie Boisselot' and the delicate pink-flowered 'Étoile Rose' which is so difficult to propagate. Wall-shrubs include *Ceanothus impressus* and in shade a magnificent *Hydrangea sargentiana*. On a central frame roses such as 'Parade', 'Pink Perpétue' and 'Lady Waterlow' make a canopy, while formal rose-beds contain the salmon-pink bush rose 'Violinista Costa'. In beds cut in the lawn penstemon, peonies and herbaceous clematis, including both *C. heracleifolia* 'Wyevale' and *C.h.* 'Davidiana' are lavishly planted, and small violas such as the clear blue *Viola* 'Lorna' thrive under taller plants. In two beds a mass of *Alstroemeria ligtu* hybrids

blend pinkish-orange flower-heads with the wide blue bells of *Platycodon grandiflorus* 'Mariesii'. Pushing through their foliage, tall stems bear spherical allium heads in deep mauve. On the hottest wall *Ceanothus* 'Trewithen Blue' appears to do well in spite of several severe winters.

Beyond the house terrace is a shrub rose garden where the 'olds' are augmented by modern roses such as 'Aloha', 'Ballerina', 'Cerise Bouquet', 'Constance Spry' and 'Fritz Nobis', all with flowers in pinks and mauve tints, and underplanted with carpeting foliage groups. Hybrid Musk roses which flower again after their first flush in June ensure interest in late summer. The scented sweet woodruff (*Galium odoratum*), lamium, acaena, euphorbias of many different sorts, *Brunnera macrophylla*, herbaceous geraniums and the invasive dark-leaved *Viola labradorica* provide variety. In the shadiest beds Lenten and Corsican hellebores open the season in spring.

Sutton Place

Guildford, Surrey
(The Sutton Place Heritage Trust)

SUTTON PLACE was acquired by Mr Stanley Seeger in 1980; it was established as a Charitable Trust in 1982.

The house was built soon after 1523 by Sir Richard Weston, and represents the most complete example in England of the transitional style of domestic architecture between the Medieval and the Renaissance. Weston had attended Henry VIII on his historic visit to the Field of the Cloth of Gold and had then visited some of the châteaux on the Loire. Today,

although the great house continues to dominate the landscape, the gardens around it are a modern creation. When Sir Geoffrey Jellicoe was first asked by Mr Seeger to design the gardens they together foresaw a long period of gradual development. At Sutton, except for the remains of great lime avenues to the north of the house, virtually no garden remained of a definite historical style. Yet in Sir Geoffrey's own words, 'The creation of a new garden in an old setting is not unlike the painting of a

Clipped yews, planted in Lady Northcliffe's time at Sutton Place, still dominate the southern view.

portrait on and within a canvas and frame that already exist. Sometimes the frame can be such as to dominate the painting; at others it may scarcely exist. At all times however it is the sitter and his/her unspoken feelings that are paramount, and these the artist will endeavour to penetrate, understand, portray and integrate with the setting.'

The house's new use as a centre for an eclectic collection of paintings, tapestries and sculpture from different periods of history could be complemented by a garden which might equally represent the civilization and development of man, and, beyond that, capture the spirit of man's aspirations. Sir Geoffrey feels that the objective in landscape design is not to smother history but to build on it. Sutton Place offered a unique opportunity of linking together a sixteenth-century house, the formality of Renaissance landscape, the naturalism of the eighteenth-century park *and*, most unusually, the 'unseen', or elements of fantasy which exist in the mind or even the subconscious. Together, as plans for the garden developed, Mr Seeger and Sir Geoffrey allowed a greater and allegorical concept to emerge. The lake landscape to the north represents Creation, the gardens round the house the Life of Man. Reached through a dark wood at the culmination of a garden tour, Ben Nicholson's Wall represents Aspiration. The garden today tells the story of man's evolution and gradual civilization and his search for fulfilment.

At the time it was built the house was set in a hunting park crossed by a traditional grand avenue of limes aligned on the gatehouse which enclosed the northern forecourt. Vast walled gardens stretched to the west but there seem to have been no pleasure gardens – the outdoor 'rooms' formed of living green hedges or protective walls that were so essential a feature of Elizabethan and Jacobean garden architecture. In the eighteenth century Capability Brown was asked to design the park, but when he proposed the destruction of the main lime avenue his advice was declined. At much the same time the early gatehouse was demolished. In the early years of this century Lady Northcliffe designed new formal gardens on the south front. A directional avenue of Irish yew matched and extended the lime avenue already existing on the north, and a broad terrace and walk defined a cross-axis. Beyond the grass terrace, sentry yew cones led the eye to woodland on the steep ridge above the valley of the river Wey. Yew hedging further

The circle of moss under the great plane tree in the secret garden interlocks with wild flowers and rough grass.

OPPOSITE
Pleached limes to the east lead to the giant classical vases of different sizes, used deliberately to confuse perspective.

In 1980 only a few lime trees to the north indicated the line of the sixteenth-century avenue. Today fifty Turkey oaks reconfirm the 'closed' structure aligned on box-edged beds which mark the foundations and shape of the original gatehouse connecting the two wings of the house. Beyond, new blocks of informal woodland are composed of native trees and shrubs, a return to the indigenous forest from which the great park was first carved out. The new lake to the north, half a mile long and shaped as a fish, is the start of the allegory linking man with his origins. The spoil was used to create smooth grassy hummocks: the largest of these represents man, and smaller contoured shapes woman and their union, the child, symbolizing the mystery of procreation and the birth of civilization. On this site it was intended to place a gigantic Henry Moore bronze, but as yet plans for this monument have not come to fruition.

To the east of the house two walled enclosures now complete the symmetry, matching the sixteenth-century walls to the west. In the first a pleasure garden, separated from the house by a moat, represents paradise. Between flower-beds and lawns, curling paths, based on the spiralling shapes of Tudor chimneys, link arbours curtained with climbers and roses, designed temptingly for rest and enjoyment. At either side tunnels of intertwined laburnum and honeysuckle provide shady walks for contemplation. Central fountains and trickling masks set into the high brick walls fill the air with the music of water. The moat is crossed by hazardous stepping stones: paradise is never easy of access. In the garden colour, scent and the murmur of water present a vision of heaven brought to earth, encircling walls giving protection from a hostile outside world. Small trees and shrub roses give undulating height over carpets of spring bulbs and low-growing perennials which ensure a succession of flowering. All through the garden Lady Jellicoe has chosen the plants to interpret each theme.

Beyond an old yew hedge lies the secret garden, a further enclosure at the heart of the allegory of man's development. Grilled *claire-voyées* cut in the brick walls allow views to the outer woodland, a reminder that even in an escape of the mind the real world is not far away. Mr Seeger wanted flowers he remembered in a book from his childhood; he gave the book to Lady Jellicoe; she found the plants and turned the dream or fantasy into reality. Now the garden is a contrived wilderness

contained and formalized the immediate landscape backing rectangular flower-beds on the new avenue axis. One rectangle was an orchard, and an avenue of Japanese cherries (now beginning to deteriorate) completed the planting. Inspired by Sir Richard Weston's visit to the Field of the Cloth of Gold, daffodils were planted to make a golden carpet in spring. Lady Northcliffe also commissioned plans from Gertrude Jekyll for a south-facing border against the sixteenth-century garden walls which extended westwards from the house. It is Lady Northcliffe's ironwork Tudor roses which decorate the gate leading to the first of the walled gardens. Gertrude Jekyll designed the lily pond and Dutch garden where the final surprise awaits discovery today.

The lily pond, designed by Gertrude Jekyll in the early years of this century, now reflects Ben Nicholson's wall of white marble.

where moss, ferns and wild flowers evoke a child's imagination. A circle of moss below the canopy of a great plane tree interlocks with a wider circular lawn, surrounded by thickets where privet, holly and even the trunk of a dead elm provide inner planting glades for hart's tongue fern, primroses and bluebells. This secret garden may be part of the broad allegory, but it also fits aptly into the historical context. In *Of Gardens* (1625) Francis Bacon wrote of the essential 'heath' which should complement the luxuriant pleasure gardens. 'Some thickets made only of sweetbriar and

honeysuckle, and some wild vine amongst; and the ground set with violets, strawberries and primroses.' At the south-east corner an octagonal pavilion, designed for dining, can be reached only by curving steps from the outer broad terrace through a door to the south. Four windows provide disparate views to emphasize the different stages of garden historical development. The first window looks back into the secret garden, where foliage only partly disguises the formal circles. A second view looks into the 'natural' forest to the north, a third window frames the landscape in the park beyond the gardens, where trees are now being planted in Brownian groves. The fourth window looks out on the formal terrace, where architectural frames make supports for pleached lime walks, and Irish yews accentuate the geometry.

Against the long walls which extend the main façade of the house, thickly planted herbaceous borders look out over cedars and lime trees on smooth green lawns, to focus finally on the Edwardian yew axis to the south. Some of the planting is old; glossy-leaved magnolias buttress the house between the large windows, giving a sense of maturity and continuity conveyed without intellectual effort. The more recently planted flower-beds all present typical Edwardian schemes, the influence of Robinson and Jekyll being extended by Lady Jellicoe to make use of the best plants available today. Grey- and silvery-leaved shrubs and perennials weave a pattern between tall shrub roses, under whose canopy small spring bulbs can shelter. The scale is vast; the terrace and Long Walk stretch 350 yards (320 metres) from east to west.

The western gardens, even with hidden philosophical meanings, are recognizable historical formulas; those to the east become abstract exercises, interpretation of which, like modern art, becomes individual. In a sheltered area against the house walls and under the drawing-room windows, an Impressionist garden of flowers conveys some of the atmosphere of Claude Monet's garden at Giverny. There Monet planted flowers in order later to paint them. Design depends on the artist's need to reassemble colours together on a canvas; the canvas is the work of art, not the garden, and individual colours alter and influence each other when placed together. White wisterias on tall frames back seasonal flowers in strong hues; red and crimson are toned down by browns, pinks and reds separated by white, and tall German irises with architectural leaf-spikes have purple and mauve flowers. Rather than distinguishing each colour block, the passer-by stores a colour 'impression' – a memory in the mind's eye; the artist's picture captured at a particular moment.

The eastern walled garden, reached through the gate studded with Lady Northcliffe's Tudor roses, has a central swimming-pool surrounded by flowers in the colours of moonlight. Silver santolina bushes are planted in formal rows, and 'Iceberg' roses are undercarpeted with lime-yellow-flowering alchemilla, glaucous-leaved dianthus and Jackman's rue. Romneya, white-flowered valerian, silver-leaved artemisias, and airy clouds of gypsophila make pools of light next to the shining foliage of evergreen choisya. Round the brick walls, which date from the building of the house, vines are trained to make shady tunnels reminiscent of those in the French medieval gardens which Sir Richard would have seen in 1520.

Outside these walls and further west the Surrealist or Magritte garden ends at a brick wall where a small window, framed by a pair of pencil-slim cypresses, allows restricted view of a magnolia. The five giant classical-style vases which line the terrace are in an unexpected order, sizes deliberately jumbled to cause visual confusion, accentuated by the anticlimax of the small aperture in the wall. A pathway plunges into thick woodland to emerge into sunlight where a still pool reflects the garden climax, a wall in white Carrara marble.

The gardens round the house represent man's journey through life. At the finish of his quest or struggle he arrives at the huge Ben Nicholson Wall reflected in the Dutch garden pool. Symbolizing aspiration, it lifts the spirit for a brief period out of the present into the unknown future. Thus the language of abstract art endows man's earthly experience with a further dimension. Sir Geoffrey Jellicoe and Mr Stanley Seeger have together woven a garden allegory where, beyond the immediately visual and tangible, an 'invisible' interpretation awaits comprehension.

The Tudor house at Sutton Place, the central feature of the artist's canvas, is now framed by the new complicated garden. The garden reflects the architecture of the house, and also links its contents and today's purpose with separate garden features. The planting, which implements Mr Seeger's and Sir Geoffrey Jellicoe's great conception with plants chosen by Lady Jellicoe, is not yet sufficiently mature to soften and disguise the bare 'bones' of the design. Time must pass for the 'natural' woodland to grow into thickets, trees in the landscape park must develop their broad canopies, and weeping laburnum arches and vine pergolas now give only a hint of the rich profusion of leaf and flower which will come with the passage of time. It is too early therefore to describe the 'finished' product. Nevertheless we can believe that the *real* value of artistic achievement is the creative process itself and not the completion – if indeed completion is ever possible in a garden. Each successive visit to the gardens at Sutton Place leads to new speculation as to their meaning.

The Old Rectory

Farnborough, Berkshire
(Mr and Mrs Michael Todhunter)

THE ELEGANT red-brick house, built in 1749, lies on a plateau just under the Ridgeway escarpment on the Berkshire Downs. Framed by trees which make almost encircling wings to an elliptical lawn, the south-facing front has a superb central view over a ha-ha to Beacon Hill and Highclere beyond Newbury. To east and west light woodland provides protection from wind, but the northern aspect remains exposed. A lime avenue and specimen beech to the north-east provide a canopy for snowdrops and wild garlic, and large specimen sycamores shelter the west garden. The Todhunters came in 1965 and the garden reflects not only their planting interest, but also a strong sense of what is appropriate in design. The house and garden as a unit, outward-looking in concept, retain the eighteenth-century flavour. The garden detail and specific inner garden areas are not at first visible, but are revealed successively by exploration. Thus, although the garden is divided into compartments the general impression is of a free-flowing design, where garden planting is planned to lead gently and consistently between distinct natural divisions.

The growing season in the 4-acre (1.6-hectare) garden at a height of 800 feet (240 metres) starts late and is shorter than most English gardens of comparable latitude. Nevertheless, Mrs Todhunter has discovered positions in the garden where sheltered micro-climates, formed by walls or hedging, permit success with a rather surprising range of marginally hardy plants. One suspects also that each plant is given personal attention when planted, and good drainage ensures that roots do not lie in frozen water-logged earth. Undoubtedly her own skill and interest are essential factors here, but one wonders whether the relative coldness and lateness of the garden aspect is salutary. In our temperate climate many plants from habitats where winters are colder and summers hotter are tempted into premature growth by a mild spell in winter.

Later frost-laden winds will nip these young buds.

The approach from the west lies under shady horse chestnuts. To the south of the drive a yew hedge conceals double herbaceous borders for later discovery. The lawn, its centre uncluttered by planting, but flanked with thick trees and shrubbery, slopes away from the house to the view over the ha-ha. A wellingtonia, old box trees, hollies clipped into cylinder shapes, a weeping pear and pink-flowered *Aesculus × carnea* planted at the fringes of woodland discreetly add plant interest without distracting from the prospect. Deeper in the wood are more good shrubs: *Rosa moyesii*, a seedling of *Acer pseudoplatanus* 'Brilliantissimum' (from

OPPOSITE
In the garlic wood a froth of white *Allium ursinum* flowers under the lime trees in spring.

BELOW
The old rose garden. A gravelled path, its edges softened by billowing plants, leads to the curved wooden seat.

In the courtyard behind the house are the large-leaved vine, *Vitis coignetiae*, *Hedera* 'Gold Heart' and a bush of yellow-flowered *Jasminum humile*.

Spetchley Park), and golden elder (*Sambucus racemosa* 'Plumosa Aurea'). A number of young Atlantic cedars keep the green tones in the winter landscape. This is an eighteenth-century rectory garden and as such is unlikely to have had the then fashionable park, but today's uninterrupted vista across downland to the south links the garden with the surrounding countryside. To the south-west the trees block a view to the village church, reached by a shady path.

Good planting on, against and at the foot of the walls confirms horticultural interest without hiding the proportions of the house. The mellow tones of the red brick provide a background canvas for pale flower colour, and

shapely green and grey foliage. A white wisteria, rose 'New Dawn' with semi-double shell-pink flowers, and the Chinese gooseberry (*Actinidia chinensis*) with heart-shaped leaves and reddish-hairy shoots, are tied back against the walls. *Clematis* 'Étoile Rose' is semi-herbaceous with nodding bell-shaped flowers, the colour of the silvery-pink outer petals deepening in the centre to cherry-purple. Wall-shrubs include the desirable grey-leaved *Buddleja crispa* from northern India, with lilac-pink terminal flower-panicles late in the summer, and the felted, more silvery-leaved. *Phlomis italica* with pale pink flower-spikes. Both these shrubs, perfect companion plants, can be hard-pruned after a severe winter. Blue-flowered ceanothus, daphne and a rare Persian lilac (*Syringa × persica* 'Laciniata'), with attractive dissected leaves, and shrubby salvias lean against the walls. In the bed at their feet the sun-loving navelwort (*Omphalodes linifolia*), an annual with silvery leaves and white flowers, perpetuates itself by seeding freely. Red-stemmed *Paeonia cambessedesii* from the Balearic Islands, and a group of the unusual fishbone thistle *Ptilostemon casabonae* (syn. *Cnicus c.*), with leaves veined in white, take advantage of being baked in this hot site. The long-stemmed *Nectaroscordon bulgaricum* (syn. *Allium b.*) grows up through the shrubs and stresses informality, its mauve-tinted creamy-green flowers on drooping stalks a perfect foil to the grey-leaved wallflower *Erysimum* 'Bowles' Mauve'. Mrs Todhunter has composed a border picture where mounded plant shapes give structure without distracting from the classical proportions of the house. The gently weaving flower and foliage colours strike no discordant notes.

From the house front there is a glimpse of double herbaceous or 'mixed' borders to the west of the main lawn. Almost hidden by a drooping beech, yew hedges on the north and south sides back richly planted flower-beds. At the farthest end dark yew frames a seat under an old apple tree; to the south a blue cedar (*Cedrus atlantica glauca*), is outlined against the sky. Pale-coloured flowers predominate, with plenty of grey foliage and rustling variegated grasses. Throughout the garden Mrs Todhunter's preference for gentle rather than brilliant colouring is apparent. She uses the more brilliant cerise-crimson blooms of a shrub rose, 'Cerise Bouquet', as accents in the border. A shrub with wide arching branches and attractive grey-green leaves, its repeated planting gives structure without formality. There are plenty of good plants, yet the overall effect is of unity. As with the best border designs, first impressions are more important than an analysis of method. Good plant grouping can be studied later. Decisive clumps of umbelliferous angelica, sweet Cicely and giant fennel (*Ferula communis*) from southern Europe, with mounds of dissected feathery leaves and 10-foot (3-metre) flower stems, are accompanied by the giant kale (*Crambe cordifolia*), with coarse architectural leaves and gypsophila-like airy flower-heads. Buddlejas, pruned hard in winter, flower late and keep the border going until autumn. All plants are packed tightly together to discourage weed germination, and little bare earth is visible.

Paeonia obovata alba in the border.

Variegated astrantia, with delicious cream and green leaf markings, makes a wide clump, and massed hardy geraniums include the delicate green-centred white form of *Geranium phaeum*. Although few annuals are used to give seasonal interest, space is found for unusual plants such as the dahlia-like *Cosmos atrosanguineus*, its flowers dark purple – almost black – and strongly chocolate-scented, and a dahlia species, *Dahlia merckii*, with pale pink and mauve flowers; the tubers are stored in winter.

Across the drive to the north beyond the yew hedge a shrubbery path, where species roses clamber into old trees, leads to a wall beyond which there is a view to open fields. An Indian chestnut has recently been planted in the middle distance, with native silver-leaved poplar (*Populus canescens*) and ash trees. Ground-covering woodland plants such as the large-leaved *Trachystemon orientale*, smilacina, hellebores and the relatively unknown *Meehania urticifolia* from North America reduce maintenance in island beds. Beyond, facing west on the back of the wall, roses (mainly grown for the house) are intertwined with clematis. A secret garden lies concealed beyond the doorway flanked by a pair of the shrub rose used in the main border, 'Cerise Bouquet', pruned back tightly against the wall. Inside is a swimming-pool, and at the farther end a Moorish summerhouse with a curving Gothic back window concentrates the view to the north. In this country garden every opportunity is taken to incorporate the beauty of the surrounding landscape into garden vistas, while bearing in mind the necessity of providing wind shelter. Here a hidden secret compartment looks outward but remains remote. Mood and planting are appropriately more contrived and less natural. Climbing yellow roses, including 'Golden Wings', 'Alister Stella Gray' and 'Maigold', and the more delicately tinted 'Sombreuil' cascade. The Moroccan broom, *Cytisus battandieri*, ceanothus and the purple potato *Solanum crispum* clothe the walls. The southern doorway is framed by the low foliage of hostas and a pair of herbaceous *Clematis × jouiniana*, which scramble against the stone and flower late in the summer. Lilies and the pale blue tender *Tweedia caerulia* are grouped in ornamental pots.

Following the wall east towards the back of the house, past a rare flowering honeysuckle (*Lonicera similis delavayi*), the mown path arrives at an old orchard on the other side of the tennis-court, which until now has been cleverly hidden from view by a tall conifer screen, and here is more informally disguised by a hedge of the arching branches of Rose 'Nevada'. Specimen trees planted in the last twenty years include several magnolias, *Liriodendron tulipifera*, a variegated 'wedding-cake' dogwood (*Cornus controversa* 'Variegata') and a ginkgo. A floriferous 'Kiftsgate' rose obscures an old apple tree. The planting is close but each tree is exceptionally well looked after. A beech hedge cuts this area off from the greenhouse and a kitchen garden to the north, but a wrought-iron gateway carries the eye through and away to the downs beyond.

At the back of the house the gardening, at first formal where lemon trees grow in ornamental pots in a courtyard, becomes more domestic, and planting is in luxuriant cottage-style. A central gravel path, its edges overflowing with sprawling plants, leads to a wooden seat of Chinese Chippendale design. The borders are backed by strong architectural features: great clipped cylinders of *Osmanthus delavayi* planted years ago but more recently pruned by Mrs Todhunter to a formal shape. Shrub roses scent the air and alchemilla, polemonium, white martagon lilies, euphorbia and viola spill and tumble in profusion.

To the east of the house the previous owner (Mr and Mrs Michael Todhunter came in 1965) made a new outside garden room tucked against the walls of the house. Yew hedges sweeping round from the front of the house enclose an oval pool with a central fountain, a copy of a garden area in the formal Victorian gardens at Westonbirt. A modern summerhouse has murals painted by Mollie Bishop. Near the house walls stone-edged beds support a low frame where deciduous clematis grow to make a horizontal carpet, an ingenious and novel use of space which might well be copied. In spring the beds are massed with scented hyacinths.

Beyond the kitchen garden, which may be approached through woodland to the northeast, hedges of the Hybrid Musk rose 'Buff Beauty', *Salix magnifica*, with magnolia-like leaves, the shrubby *Aesculus parviflora*, elaeagnus and forms of mountain ash are part of more good planting. A group of three cut-leaved alders (*Alnus incana* 'Laciniata') is a feature. The whole area is framed by the northern landscape, before the Ridgeway drops down and gives way to the flatter countryside near Oxford.

The garden at The Old Rectory is full of plants to stimulate, yet it is the overall economy of fussy detail which lingers in the mind's eye. Mr and Mrs Todhunter have retained, and even emphasized, the eighteenth-century atmosphere, permitting the house and landscape beyond to dominate the whole scheme. Yet each separate garden area, remote from the greater design, is a complete planting exercise in itself.

Beech shadows on the lawn in mid-summer.

OPPOSITE
Double borders face each other across a panel of green lawn.

Jenkyn Place

Bentley, Hampshire
(Mr and Mrs Gerald Coke)

IN DECIDING to come to Jenkyn Place in 1941, Mr and Mrs Gerald Coke must have been influenced by the existence of mature trees, not only around the elegant William and Mary house, but also grouped in the largely un-developed garden area which stretched to the south and west below the house. In any garden design trees fill three-dimensional space, and their volume and relationship with one another and with the mass of a house are as important as the hedges and linking paths whose lines define the structure at a lower level. Their branches frame the skyline or a distant view, and their shadows make garden patterns below, dictat-ing and modifying planting schemes. At Jen-kyn Place a vast cedar of Lebanon, dating from 1823, fills an enclosure to the east of the house, while chestnuts, a lime and a *Ginkgo biloba*

The entrance to the Dutch garden. The climbing rose 'Madame Plantier' and the golden-leaved form of bay, *Laurus nobilis* 'Aureus', grow on either side of the brick pillars.

shade the northern entrance yard and give wind protection. From the house windows a view stretching southwards over the valley of the Wey to a chalk escarpment beyond Bentley village is framed by giant ilex (*Quercus ilex*), more lime (*Tilia × europaea*) and a tulip tree (*Liriodendron tulipifera*), already of good size in 1941, in addition to trees and shrubs planted since by the Cokes. Among these the weeping silver lime (*Tilia* 'Petiolaris'), with fluttering pale leaves, already shows distinction, and a young variegated form of the tulip tree has a place. The rare Chinese yellow-wood (*Cladras-tis sinensis*), its soft green leaves glaucous beneath, started to flower in 1971 – after twenty-five years. The pale silver foliage of the weeping pear (*Pyrus salicifolia* 'Pendula') and the wedding-cake layers of variegated *Cornus alternifolia* 'Argentea' stand out among green textures. The red-brick house – strangely, and a bit awkwardly for a coherent garden plan – does not face directly to the view, but a little east of south. To compensate for this off-centre axis, the Cokes placed an eighteenth-century stone seat, framed by dark yews and woodland planting, to make a focal point on the direct line of the house. By stopping the view they have encouraged the eye to slide off down the angled green glade, following the broad mown stripes of smooth grass curving gently out of sight in the distance, and beckoning and entic-ing to further exploration.

Although Mr and Mrs Coke say that when they came to Jenkyn Place they were no gardeners, they must have appraised and ap-proved how house, trees and garden space seemed linked together, united already by classical rules of proportion and balance, and setting the stage for the creation of the garden we see today. They also discovered that every type of plant would thrive in the favourable soil, a very local form of upper greensand found in a pocket just north of the Hampshire chalk massif. The garden, later considerably

expanded, was exceptionally well protected from the east and north, and in addition sloped south, allowing not only free frost drainage, but also an opportunity to make separate garden areas on different levels, by linking flat terraces with descending architectural steps. Existing walls, to which they added patterns of wind-filtering hedges, provided shelter for 'difficult' plants.

The usual approach to Jenkyn Place is from the south, along a narrow steep-sided lane which marks the eastern perimeter of the garden area. A glimpse of the evergreen *Arbutus × andrachnoides*, with a polished trunk, and the rare *Viburnum cylindricum*, with a metallic tinge to its large evergreen leaves, quickens excitement and gives promise of the horticultural interest of the garden. The shaded entrance court, approached past cottages which were once hop-kilns, has wall beds planted with camellias and good climbers such as *Vitis coignetiae* and the lesser-known *V.* 'Pulchra', both of which blaze with scarlet in autumn. Under the trees cyclamen carpet the ground, flowering when leaves are bare, and small erythronium flourish in a raised bed at the base of the lime. In summer the area is quiet and predominantly green, a perfect prelude to the colour and interest of the succession of garden compartments and themes beyond.

From the forecourt there are three possible routes to follow. Directly south through a doorway a garden 'room', enclosed on three sides by walls, the remains of old farm buildings, is known as the Dutch garden. The southern side allows glimpses to the garden terraces below through a series of arches framed by luxuriant roses and other climbers. Plants are grown for their fragrance and foliage. A raised central bed, planted entirely with May-flowering *Daphne collina*, surrounds a lead boy and dolphin fountain. Outer wall flower-beds contain tree peonies, the primrose-yellow *Paeonia mlokosewitschii*, silver-leaved *Leptospermum lanigerum* 'Silver Spire', a fig, the loquat (*Eriobotrya japonica*) and the late-flowering *Colletia armata* 'Rosea' which scents the air in September and October. Cistus bushes with papery flowers in pink and white thrive in shelter, and a creeping mountain avens (*Dryas octopetala*) has single white flowers in May. Square eighteenth-century lead containers fitted with inner movable pots house clipped box pyramids in winter, and lemon-scented verbena (*Aloysia triphylla*, syn. *Lippia citriodora*) through the summer. Climbing roses and the variegated form of the tender *Trache-*

lospermum jasminoides, with sweetly fragrant white flowers, clothe the walls.

It is tempting to continue through the arcades, but another route just west of the forecourt allows a vista south, through iron gates and across a sundial to a lime tree far below. A directional pathway on descending levels becomes an axis linking different garden compartments. At first, enclosed by yew hedges, the view is narrow; then it opens out to traverse the wide terrace where herbaceous borders backed by high hedges face each other across a grass panel. Finally it narrows again, lined with espalier apples thickly underplanted with pink and white late-flowering crinums and amarcrinums (*Crinum × powellii* and *× Amarcrinum howardii*). To the left of the lime is Jancknes's Well, from which the site takes its name, where pilgrims after refreshment tossed a token coin on their way from Winchester to Canterbury. This pathway or vista, which continues to a formal rose garden and pond above, establishes the central framework of the upper garden; it runs at right angles to or parallel with the walls and hedges which separate areas and turn the garden into a series of linked rooms. As the path crosses each inner garden compartment a view to right or left is centred on some architectural feature – a statue, seat or gateway – often accompanied by some well-grown tree or shrub of considerable botanical interest. Everywhere flowing plant

Stone lions and a pair of staccato Italian cypresses guard the entrance to the Lion Walk.

OPPOSITE
Tall green and copper
beech hedges enclose a
green alley centred on a
reclining marble lion, a
copy of Canova's original
which decorates the tomb
of Pope Clement XII in St
Peter's, Rome.

Lead statues of the season
flank the steps leading into
the sundial garden.

shapes break and disguise the straight lines
which hold the garden design together. This
happy combination of formal design, informality of planting and rarer specimen plants
makes this garden exceptional.

The rose garden lies to the north above an
old orchard which is now a croquet-lawn,
enclosed by clipped yew hedges. It has formal
beds of Hybrid Tea roses and at the west is closed
in under a high wall by a crescent-shaped bed
of taller-growing old roses, chosen particularly
for their good heps in autumn. *Rosa moyesii, R.*

'Dupontii', and Wolley-Dod's rose are among
them. A central canal, narrowing at either end
to make the whole area seem longer, is a home
for water plants: *Pontederia cordata* with blue
spikes, sagittaria, and *Iris ensata* (syn. *I. kaempferi*) grow in the narrow rills, and water-lilies
make rafts in the wide pool. Tender wall shrubs
and climbers find protection against the warm
south-facing wall above. The most unusual is
the yellow-flowered *Caesalpinia japonica*, with
curved vicious spines and light green ferny
leaves. Usually grown successfully only in the

A fine eighteenth-century copy of Giambologna's statue of Bacchus is the central feature in the herb garden.

BELOW
The canal and fountain in the rose garden above the house.

milder counties, this plant has survived here since 1956. Near by another yellow-flowered pea, the evergreen *Piptanthus laburnifolius*, flowers in May, and the yellow Banksian rose, *R. banksiae* 'Lutea' and the Macartney rose, *R. bracteata*, respectively in April and August. A rare *Buddleja farreri* with huge felted grey leaves and occasionally fragrant rose flowers in April, and the Kew form of *B. colvilei*, with drooping tubular dark rose-red flowers in late June, also thrive against the wall. Lower-growing treasures include the suckering *Hebe* 'Fairfieldii', closely linked to the difficult *H. hulkeana* but sturdier, with pale lavender flower-panicles in early summer.

From the west end of the rose garden steps descend past mature shrubs, dominated by *Osmanthus delavayi*, grown very wide after more than forty years. Fine magnolias, deutzias, cistus and *Olearia capillaris* (one of the hardiest daisy-bushes, but seldom seen) fill in a corner bed under the west wall; further down, the bright blue *Scilla peruviana* is planted in clumps through which a vast suckering California poppy (*Romneya trichocalyx*) comes into flower in later summer. Its papery white petals with central yellow stamens crowd the woody stems among grey-green dissected leaves. Later the blue flowers of ceratostigma and perovskia mingle and give colour until autumn.

Below the yew hedge which backs on to the herbaceous border there is a view to the east of a well-shaped *Photinia serrulata*, poised beside wide gates and framed against the distant house and the magnificent old cedar behind it. The foreground borders stretching west are planned to reach their peak in mid-summer; early-flowering lupins and late Michaelmas daisies are elsewhere in the garden. Grey-leaved shrubs including lavender, hebes, santolina and perovskia give structure and body; the rest of the plants are perennial. Plants such as penstemons give colour through a long season if continually and promptly dead-headed. Plants which combine good foliage with flower contributions keep the borders looking rich over a long period. The architectural *Kniphofia caulescens*, centaureas, *Baptisia australis* and the beautiful but rare *Nepeta* 'Souvenir d'André Chaudron', with lavender-blue spikes amongst grey-green leaves, are all good plants which thrive in this fertile soil. The borders are edged with stone and plants flow over the edge, breaking the harsh line. Behind to the west a stone seat is framed in yew clipped to resemble a large and comfortable armchair.

Above the borders there is more planting leading back up to the yew-hedged enclosures and the arcades of the Dutch garden room. The cross-axial path leads downwards, through a gap in the old thorn hedge which backs the lower border, and on to the lime tree beyond. More paths go south from here: one leads to a garden of old roses; another is edged by beds of May-flowering lupins. At the western end of this walk a bronze child is framed by golden Leyland cypress (× *Cupressocyparis leylandii* 'Castlewellan'); to the east a marble lion's head is let into the wall.

As the garden stretches farther from the house, more good trees and shrubs have been planted. A new formal garden of yews in mixed foliage colours has still to mature, but a 'leaf' garden with coloured and architectural foliage plants delights both in spring when young leaves unfurl and again in autumn when leaves colour red and orange. Here there are not only shrubs and trees with golden, variegated and bronze leaves, but also, at a lower level, euphorbias, ajugas and rampant *Rubus tricolor* covering the ground.

To the east a circular raised herb garden, now surrounded by espalier-trained 'Worcester Pearmain' apple trees, looks towards a marble urn framed by the ilex trees in the long green glade south-west of the house. In the centre of the herb garden another marble statue, a copy of Giambologna's Bacchus in the Bargello in Florence, is surrounded by aromatic plants.

A tennis-court, now seldom used, is hardly noticed, for its once-harsh edges are masked by thick shrub planting which has grown to maturity over the years. Fortunately, the Cokes have always given trees and shrubs adequate space to develop. Few plantsmen exercise this discipline. Another garden, centred on an eighteenth-century armillary sphere, has brick- and stone-patterned paths dividing the area into four grass paths, each with a single tree in the centre. One is the white mulberry (*Morus alba*, the silkworm mulberry), another a medlar (*Mespilus germanica* 'Nottingham'), a third *Diospyros lotus* and the fourth *Prunus serrula* with polished brown bark. The perimeter is closed in by a low hedge of hedgehog holly cultivars (forms of *Ilex aquifolium* 'Ferox').

There are three distinct garden areas still to come before the garden tour turns and swings back up the 300 yards (275 metres) to the front of the house. There are many interesting trees, some grown as specimens, others making a canopy for groups of shrubs beneath. The eye is caught by a young golden-leaved *Catalpa bignonioides* which stands at the entrance to the Lion Walk (just in front of a paulownia it is designed to replace). The walk, an alley of clipped beech, leads to a marble lion asleep on a pedestal. Ten-foot (3-metre) tapestry walls of alternating copper and ordinary green beech rise high enough to screen all other planting, making a remote and separate world to ponder in. To the west more lions guard the entrance to free woodland planting, and to the east a sunken garden, centred on an Italian oil jar, marks the termination of the 'valley' walk, which leads down from the house. Many more good plants are glimpsed to right and left. *Aesculus indica*, a davidia, cornus in plenty, and *Acer griseum*, with peeling bark, have grown well.

On the terrace in front of the house a large old mulberry (*Morus nigra*) and a vast *Magnolia dawsoniana* commemorate the birth of the Cokes' daughter and son in 1944 and 1946 respectively, fittingly reminding one of the forty years during which the Cokes have planted and tended this garden. Against the south-facing house walls evergreen climbers *Holbœllia latifolia* and *Trachelospermum jasminoides* make green panels, and in the centre the potato plant, *Solanum sisymbrifolium*, grows in an eighteenth-century lead tank. Beyond the cedar is a small raised garden; below this, in a sheltered angle of the house, the large-leaved evergreen *Magnolia delavayi* thrives, and *Indigofera amblyantha* and *I. heterantha* (syn. *I. gerardiana*) both have attractive pinnate leaves and pink-mauve flowers in late summer.

From this description, necessarily omitting much that is botanically interesting, it must surely have become increasingly apparent that not only were Mr and Mrs Coke fortunate to find such a garden site, but that Jenkyn Place was equally fortunate in its new owners. It is not enough for the 'genius of the place' to be consulted as Pope advised; for a garden to flourish, a presiding spirit must constantly lavish it with care and interest. This garden has a personal dynamic quality: each year and each season continue to bring change. Basically Jenkyn Place is of typical English style, a happy blend of formality and exotic wilderness, but it has extra unusual qualities which spring from the enduring interest and activity of its owners. It combines being a plantsman's garden with having a well-defined and coherent design which, while stimulating the senses, satisfies the mind's desire for order.

Great Dixter

Northiam, East Sussex
(The Lloyd Family/Christopher Lloyd)

A pair of topiary coffee pots flank the path, framing the doorway and steps. An espalier pear is trained against the chimney breast.

NATHANIEL LLOYD and his wife came to Great Dixter in 1910. Then, the fifteenth-century half-timbered manor served as the farmhouse to surrounding orchards and to a group of buildings dominated by three square oast-houses situated just to the west. To help him restore and enlarge the house and design a garden Mr Lloyd sought the advice of Edwin Lutyens, and by July 1911 the plans, which are kept in the house today, were drawn for a series of semi-formal but irregular garden compartments. The new Lutyens garden scheme incorporated the traditional farm buildings and cattle yards in the overall plan, the whole fitting snugly round the house, with existing high walls and new yew hedges to enclose a series of garden rooms. To the south, where Lutyens had added a wing consisting of an-

other half-timbered fifteenth-century hall, found locally and bought for £70, the view is open, sweeping down through an orchard to the valley and lily-pond below. Just as the addition to the house seems perfectly assimilated, so Lutyens' garden scheme, with a terrace and steps to adjust levels on the south front, suggests that the garden might have existed for many centuries instead of for the mere seventy years it has had to mellow and mature. Background walls are of different heights and meet at odd angles, so that linking paths, vistas through doorways and focal points seem at first to lack symmetry and alignment. Yet effects are strong and firmly structured. Lutyens linked house and garden so that windows overlooked important viewpoints; the terrace cross-axis of wide flagstones edges the long border which extends eastwards parallel to the south front, while from the main south-facing bedroom above, the eye marks a pathway of mown grass which descends through a meadow of wild flowers. Through a gap in the east border steps lead up to another series of hedged secret 'rooms'. All through the garden the fine quality of stone and brickwork is evidence of both Mr Lloyd's and his architect's interest in local craft and materials. Lutyens' taste for oddities is evidenced by a narrow red-brick pathway, designed for wheelbarrows, which glides serpent-like through the orchard below.

Later, in 1923, the sunken garden and octagonal pool, designed by Nathaniel Lloyd himself, were added. An architectural historian and author of a book on topiary, he lived until 1954, long enough to see the yew hedges clipped as castellated battlements and the topiary specimens of birds and abstract shapes mature to make green patterns of light and shade. His wife lived on into the 1970s, until she was ninety-one. A talented plantswoman of strong character, she loved to encourage plants to grow naturally and, like Gertrude Jekyll,

enjoyed the happy accident of some chance seedling associated with stone or companion planting. She was responsible for the wild-flower gardening, at first in the northern forecourt of the approach to the house and later in the dry moat, where now early crocus are succeeded by snake's head fritillaries (*Fritillaria meleagris*) and summer snowflake (*Leucojum aestivum*). The house and garden were left in a family trust for the children, but it is Mr Christopher Lloyd, one of the sons, who lives there and looks after the garden.

Great Dixter and its five-acre (or 2-hectare) garden is situated high in the Sussex weald, about 250 feet (76 metres) above sea-level, and its hilltop situation ensures free frost drainage. This, combined with the protection of high walls and hedges, which filter wind, makes it possible to grow surprisingly tender shrubs in sheltered pockets. Rainfall is 30 inches (76 centimetres) and the fertile Wadhurst clay is almost neutral, allowing the normal lime-haters to survive. After many years of culti-vation the soil texture is workable yet moisture-retentive. Round the old horse pond to the left of the main garden entrance there are outcrops of more free-draining Tunbridge Wells sandstone.

The approach through a gate in a yew hedge is quiet. Walnuts, the tansy-leaved thorn (*Crataegus tanacetifolia*) and oriental thorn (*C. schraderiana*) with soft grey leaves, and an old pear and bay tree are planted in grass – the first of Christopher Lloyd's mother's wild-flower meadows, where naturalized bulbs thrive. Crocus, narcissi, fritillaries and anem-ones all jostle for room. Later green-winged orchids flower and the grass remains uncut until they seed, which may be the end of July. After another mow in August the small *Cycla-men hederifolium*, the true autumn crocus (*Crocus speciosus*) and colchicums start a new season. The flagged path leads to the timbered porch where ferns grow at the base of the house walls. On the left the unusual Chilean bamboo (*Chusquea culeou*) makes a dense specimen clump in the lawn, a replacement for a topiary ball-and-saucer yew planted by Nathaniel Lloyd.

Steps descend past a bed of annuals, different and experimental each year, interplanted with permanent white-flowered *Zantedeschia aeth-iopica* and for late summer white Japanese anemones, to the sunken garden where arrest-ing plants delay the garden tour. New Zealand olearias include the coveted *O. macrodonta* 'Min-or', *O. ilicifolia* with coarsely toothed leathery

leaves and fragrant white daisy-flowers in June, and an olearia garden hybrid from Tresco, *O.* × *scilloniensis*, leaves grey-green and white flower-trusses spectacular in May. The planting is thick, the plants distracting: pansies, creeping acaena, the pale Cambridge-blue form of *Salvia patens*, and the Great Dixter form of *Euphorbia griffithii* with brick-red bracts and mounded foliage. In the upper garden, east of the house, Mr Lloyd grows this euphorbia next to *Ozothamnus ledifolius*, a Tasmanian composite with almost matching orange-tinged flower-buds, which later open into small white massed daisies. In a raised bed hairy-leaved *Bergenia ciliata* has a reputation for tenderness, its leaves and flowers sometimes damaged by late frosts. *Blechnum chilense*, bam-boos, hostas and veratrum grow in shade; in the open there are eryngium in quantity and grasses with arching stems grow next to shrubs and in front of climbers which curtain walls. A twining *Schisandra grandiflora rubriflora* has crimson flowers on long hanging stalks in spring, and red berries in autumn (if you have adjacent sexes). The temperamental *Pileostegia viburnoides* against the shady wall has creamy-white flower-panicles carried in late summer, just when few other shrubs flower. Elsewhere in the garden another evergreen, a privet (*Ligustrum quihoui*), also flowers late; it deserves a place in many more gardens.

Nathaniel Lloyd's topiary birds create intricate patterns of light and shade.

To the south an archway leads past borders of magnolias and lace-cap hydrangeas. The uncommon evergreen shrub *Daphniphyllum macropodum* from Japan needs a second glance, its pale green leaves resembling a rhododendron, its petioles pink and glowing. *Drimys lanceolata* has aromatic leaves, coppery when young. The tall 20-foot (6-metre) ilex-hedged enclosure to the west remains uncluttered; the only planting is *Pinus patula* at the centre, with contrasting drooping vivid green needles. The topiary garden where Nathaniel Lloyd's geometrical yew shapes are set in grass, also keeps its own character.

In the cattle yard where Christopher Lloyd's parents had a formal rose garden, today violets, teasels and the tall *Verbena bonariensis* seed among mixed rose bushes, between which clematis grow on poles. All the roses are now established on their own roots. Bronze-leaved oxalis with yellow flowers, *Oxalis corniculata purpurea*, considered by many an invasive weed, is allowed to spread here, and on the fringes *Impatiens balfourii* seeds annually but must be controlled. In the orchard old apple trees have become hosts to vigorous cluster-flowered roses, and the meadow beneath is filled with native flowers such as ox-eye daisy and orchids (often now rare in the wild). The grass is not cut until seeding is over.

The long border of 'mixed' planting stretches east below the house. Two hundred feet (60 metres) long and 15 feet (4.5 metres) deep, it is edged with a flagged path. Mr Lloyd plants trees and shrubs with traditional herbaceous plants, and adds annuals to create the effects he seeks. In this he follows Miss Jekyll who, quite contrary to opinion, *never* advocated borders only of perennials. She used annuals, plunged pots of lilies, did anything in short to create the colour harmonies for exactly the summer season she required. Mr Lloyd quotes her in *The Adventurous Gardener*: 'I have no dogmatic views', she tells us, 'in having in the so-called hardy flower border none but hardy flowers. All flowers are welcome that are right in colour, and that make a brave show where a brave show is wanted.' 'How sensible,' comments Mr Lloyd. 'It is only the timid gardener whose mind-forged manacles constrain him to think entirely in terms of categories and compartments for different kinds of flowers in different areas of the garden.' The long border at Great Dixter contains many trees and shrubs, including shrub roses, probably in greater numbers than Miss Jekyll advised; certainly more than she

had in her own wide borders at Munstead Wood. He doesn't use dahlias, she did. He also uses early-flowering perennials as annuals, digging them up and lining them out in a nursery bed after they have made their contribution, and substituting annuals to prolong the season. This sort of gardening is difficult. As he says: 'Management factors are necessarily more complex; there are greater chances of one type of plant being swamped by another and greater vigilance therefore needs to be exercised.' Shrubs when small can so easily be swamped by 'lush encircling giants'. Also most shrubs flower early, so their form and foliage *must* contribute to the later border scene. There is no strict colour scheme at Great Dixter; instead Mr Lloyd finds that although he prefers blending hues from the same part of the spectrum, in practice clashing contrasting colours 'work' if they are isolated incidents, set among two-toned foliage. Tall Mount Etna broom towers above scarlet roses, warm bronze-flowered heleniums are grouped next to purple-spiked *Salvia* 'Superba' and the scarlet-flowered *Lychnis chalcedonica*, and orange daisy-flowered perennial *Anthemis sancti-johannis* near biennal *Reseda alba*, its flowers quiet but distinctive, with white petals and central brown anthers. Golden-leaved gleditsia is near to the glowing variegated leaves of *Ilex* × *altaclerensis* 'Golden King', with alchemilla and hosta clumped in the foreground. On a corner where steps lead up to the higher north-east garden, *Pinus mugo*, slow-growing and bushy, makes a textured shape.

In an era when 'bedding out' is thought labour-intensive and tasteless, annuals and biennials, good plants when grouped but lacking quality as single specimens, make drifts of colour between more permanent perennials or shrubs. All planting is mixed and in layers; small spring bulbs are protected under the canopies of deciduous shrubs, and taller perennials and shrubs cover the ground in the open border or under the overhanging branches of small trees (which are kept to moderate size by frequent cutting back). Foliage texture and shapes and plant structure are considered as important as more fleeting flower, fruit and leaf colours. All this information and philosophy can be absorbed by reading Christopher Lloyd's books: planting in the garden is then almost familiar, an extension of his writing, but up-to-date and extending themes already touched on. It is perfectly possible to enjoy his garden without having read a word; having read, the visit becomes an interpretation.

In the enclosures east and north of the house paths are formally edged with fuchsias, roses and Michaelmas daisies, between which vegetables and thriving nursery-garden plants are grown in rows. Formal topiary and straight lines are set off by more relaxed planting. Beyond, outside the garden proper, is the old horse pond, where large leaves of *Gunnera manicata* tower above glossy-leaved arum. The uncommon white daisy (*Senecio smithii*) relishes the rich moist soil, its puckered grey-green leaves providing another textural contrast.

Many informed visitors to Great Dixter will have already read Mr Lloyd's books, which although mainly about the garden are much more than descriptive. Of strong opinions, his writing and gardening style dominate the garden. It is impossible, as one of his disciples, with his daring colour schemes uppermost in the mind, not to look for specific plant juxtapositions. Yet in spite of his almost completely changing the original planting in each compartment, the garden subtly retains its Edwardian flavour. The blend of formal layout with exotic free planting perfectly suits the setting. In spite of thick planting and experimental colour associations – some with ephemeral bright-flowered annuals – it is the firm structure and use of plants with a good form and interesting foliage that linger in one's memory. Trained in horticulture, Mr Lloyd is a plantsman; but one who perfectly understands that, however rich in botanical interest, a haphazard collection of plants does not make a garden. At Great Dixter each plant or group of plants, even if grown experimentally, contributes to the whole effect. Plant associations are planned to seem relaxed, yet are carefully prepared many months if not years ahead. Lutyens' framework is almost hidden by profuse planting which softens and conceals masonry, and distracts the mind from architectural formality. The old walls are curtained with climbing plants and buttressed with evergreen shrubs, the carefully proportioned steps and brickwork are mellowed with seeding *Erigeron karwinskianus* and little violas. By an archway *Euphorbia amygdaloides robbiae*, with lime-green flower-bracts and almost evergreen leaves, thrives in the dry shade, spreading above Lutyens' tile-patterned paving. Mr Lloyd has written a book on *Foliage Plants*, but he does not see plants in isolation. Leaves complement flower colour, contribute to plant form, soften harsh masonry edges and blend with textured stone or brickwork. At Dixter the Lutyens/

OPPOSITE ABOVE AND BELOW
Lutyens designed a brick path to cut through the orchard below the house. In spring daffodils flower in drifts between the fruit trees; later in the season, before the grass is cut, wild flowers are encouraged to seed.

Lloyd partnership seems as impressive as any the architect forged with Gertrude Jekyll.

Is it possible to be objective about the garden if you are already one of his devoted band of readers? Probably not. Certainly the garden brings surprises. Colour schemes change, the long border is refurbished, new annuals and biennials are planted in drifts to contribute some new colour effect. Under his care the garden is dynamic, constantly growing and changing and full of interest. Nevertheless the half-timbered house and red-tiled barns and oast-houses are the frame inside which the garden lies, and together exert a strong period influence, not only as the backdrop to most garden views. A garden such as this, in which two generations have shaped development, depends on this vital link.

ABOVE
The main border which stretches east above the meadow is given structure with trees and shrubs. Hardy plants are chosen for foliage as well as flower interest.

OPPOSITE
Clipped evergreens and directional paths give a strong garden structure for all seasons. In summer, plants spill over the hard masonry lines.

LEFT
Between yew pillars a gate opens to reveal more intimate garden areas above the main border.

Saling Hall

Great Saling, Essex
(Mr and Mrs Hugh Johnson)

THE GARDEN at Saling Hall seems more like a collection of separate garden themes than one unit. Each 'garden' provides some sort of intellectual stimulus which in turn influences the mood and appreciation of the observer. There is no attempt to link the house and its surrounding gardens with the bleak and flat East Anglian landscape beyond its perimeter. Instead the garden, extending to more than 12 acres (almost 5 hectares) in all, is inward-looking, as Hugh Johnson says, designed to represent a fantasy world completely remote and private from the sugar-beet and bean fields beyond. Furthermore, each unit – whether the geometrically laid out walled garden, the small intimate yew-hedged enclosures on its northern side, the romantically exotic and partly shaded natural water garden, or the woodland and open sunlit glades of the wilderness – is envisaged as a place for privacy and seclusion. While inheriting a conventional layout near the house, Mr Johnson has deliberately introduced a series of design features in his outer garden areas. These were conceived almost as exercises in garden development and style rather than according to an 'ethic' where a dominant order imposes unity and logic to guide the visitor through a garden tour. For those who know him as the author of best-selling books on trees and on gardening principles, it is possible to trace the progression of his garden, where every trick of planting and design is used to stimulate and please.

The approach is quiet, past chestnuts and the village green and pond to a mellow brick façade, which dates mainly from the end of the seventeenth century but incorporates an earlier Elizabethan manor house. A line of giant Lombardy poplars (*Populus nigra* 'Italica') dates from 1936. Yew hedging, a row of pleached limes and a cedar of Lebanon (*Cedrus libani*) transplanted here successfully as a 30-foot (9-metre) tree in 1975, its contained root-ball with a diameter of 7 feet (over 2 metres), ensure that from the house windows the view is uncluttered by distracting flower colour. A 'Mermaid' rose and the coppery-apricot 'Albertine' curtain a brick wall to the side. Old grape vines, planted before the First World War, clothe the house walls. At their feet in a narrow border scented *Daphne odora* 'Aureomarginata' has leaves edged with creamy-white, a good form of the variable *Euphorbia characias wulfenii* has blue-green leaves and yellow flower-bracts, and the spreading orange-flowered *Alstroemeria aurantiaca* competes for space with a white-flowered Japanese anemone.

In 1971, when the Johnsons first came to Saling, fine elms stood beside the entrance drive. Behind the house in mixed woodland more elms helped provide essential wind shelter from the north and east. Since 1978, with the elms gone, a mixed planting of oak, ash, field maple, a grove of larch, another of Norway maple (*Acer platanoides*) and fast-growing evergreen Leyland cypress have strengthened the boundary screen, which still contains old English oaks of considerable girth. Within its lee Mr Johnson has established his arboretum of rare trees. Some Chilean beech, forms of nothofagus, thrive where the soil is suitably acid. Basically it is an alkaline clay with a pH of 7.5, but decomposing oak-leaf mulch on patches of sandy gravel provides unexpected and welcome acidity levels with lower readings. In East Anglia summer drought is always a problem and young trees need frequent watering in their first years; fortunately natural springs and ponds abound. In May 1985 a freak hail storm of great ferocity left a trail of damage, breaking panes of glass in the conservatory and destroying fruit blossom.

Inside the walled garden the design is geometrically strict. In the outer borders tightly clipped conifers, *Chamaecyparis lawsoniana* 'Pottenii', with feathery sea-green foliage, rise in formal rhythm above the level of the walls, in contrast to a line of apple trees with heads pruned to mounded domes. This layout owes much to the previous owner, Lady Carlyle, who lived at Saling after the Second World War, but remaining espaliered apples might almost date to the building of the walls in 1698, when the garden, equally structured in style, was primarily designed for fruit growing. Down the centre of the garden, stretching south-west from the house and the new conservatory, beds edged with low-growing box contain slim vertical Irish junipers (*Juniperus communis* 'Hibernica'), which echo Lady Carlyle's earlier planting. On the corner of each bed boxwood pyramids give extra height and interest. Within this firm architectural frame made by walls, paths and evergreens, planting is billowing and free in the best tradition of English gardening, which adapts the seventeenth-century formality appropriate to the period of the house to the wealth of hardy exotic garden plants available today. Within the walls there is a strong Mediterranean flavour, sun and heat from reflecting brick walls ripening and hardening wood and baking bulbs from southern Europe and South Africa. Shrubs with aromatic and silver and grey foliage and pale-coloured flowers jostle with perennials and herbs. Climbing and shrub roses, *Arbutus* × *andrachnoides* with cinnamon-red peeling bark, and the uncommon *Abeliophyllum distichum* with fragrant white flowers in early spring are all notable. *Koelreuteria paniculata*, whose leaves turn buff-gold in autumn, and the Mount Etna broom (*Genista aetnensis*) both have yellow flowers in July. Viburnums, hydrangeas, the graceful *Cornus alternifolia* 'Argentea' with cream and green leaves on branches held in tabulated layers, hostas and geraniums all thrive and fill the garden to overflowing with scent and soft pastel tints. A clump of bronze-leaved scarlet-flowered *Dahlia* 'Bishop of Llandaff', golden-leaved *Robinia pseudacacia* 'Frisia' and *Gleditsia triacanthos* 'Sunburst' make more sophisticated points of glowing colour, complemented later in the season with fiery oranges and reds from the large-leaved vine *Vitis coignetiae*. Against the conservatory and house wall tender plants such as *Salvia microphylla* (syn. *S. grahamii*), *Convolvulus cneorum* and *C. sabatius* (syn. *C. mauritanicus*) sprawl. The rare evergreen *Ribes laurifolium* with greenish flowers in spring, *Abutilon* × *suntense*, *Choisya ternata* and the tender scented rose 'Desprez à Fleur Jaune' with small double yellow-apricot flowers all take advantage of the shelter. At the base of the wall crimson-stalked *Paeonia cambessedesii*

spreads, attracting attention in late spring. From the Balearic Islands, this pink-flowered peony loves summer heat and dry conditions.

North of this garden area an old orchard is split up by yew hedges into compartments. A swimming-pool, a drying-green where a modern bright red rose 'Altissimo' clambers up pink granite pillars and a border of white flowers and green leaves. Beyond the valley garden, where one's feet are directed by paving stones set in grass, lie the tennis-court and 'Mount'. Pink-barked *Betula albo-sinensis septentrionalis*, a silver-leaved *Elaeagnus commutata*, a weeping pear (*Pyrus salicifolia* 'Pendula') and the Russian olive (*Elaeagnus angustifolia*), with foliage of softer grey, all enjoy sun. A collection of shrub roses is given form by a row of mop-headed *Robinia pseudacacia* 'Umbraculifera', and other trees mark the transition from the inner garden enclosures to the wilderness beyond.

Individual trees include forms of *Acer cappadocicum* with brilliant blood-red young growth, an unusual *Sorbus esserteauana* 'Flava' bearing rich lemon-yellow clustered fruits, *Pinus ayacahuite*, the late summer-flowering privet *Ligustrum quihoui* and a selection of acers. Oaks from America and southern Europe are planted in a grove, and a collection of young pine trees and another of sorbus promise future maturity and will shape the landscape and be outlined against the sky. Tree planting looks many years ahead for its effects, and many of

The seventeenth-century brick façade of the house is clothed with grape vines planted before the First World War. The line of Lombardy poplars to the left was planted in 1936.

OVERLEAF LEFT
In the walled garden box-edged beds and vertical evergreens provide a frame for soft blue flowers and silvery foliage plants.

OVERLEAF RIGHT ABOVE
In the arboretum a statue of a shepherd boy is a focal point among a fine collection of young trees.

OVERLEAF RIGHT BELOW
Hostas, kirengeshomas and ferns show their distinctive foliage shapes in the water garden.

the rarer specimens planted at Saling reflect Hugh Johnson's knowledge and the journeys from which he returns with seed from the wild, sometimes of species or forms which are new to European gardens. The planting in groves emphasizes his desire for privacy, with each separate area hidden from the next.

In the centre of the arboretum a steep bank formed by commercial gravel extraction years ago has become the site of a Japanese-type garden, where stone cascades, with water pumped from a hydraulic ram at a lower level, are in perpetual motion. Box is cut into strange shapes and the pattern of rockwork is copied from that in a Kyoto monastery. Shrubby willows grow on the bank as cover under larger trees. An oriental plane (*Platanus orientalis*), *Acer griseum*, *Alnus incana* 'Laciniata' and the beautiful *Toona sinensis* (syn. *Cedrela s.*), known as the Chinese cedar although deciduous, with pinnate leaves turning yellow in autumn, are grouped near by. The latter tree is not yet mature enough to bear its foot-long (30-centimetre) white panicles. A swamp cypress (*Taxodium distichum*), its roots in the swampy ground, is growing fast and several large specimen willows include *Salix alba vitellina*, *S.* 'Blanda' and the similar *S. × elegantissima*, known as the Thurlow weeping willow. Beyond is a further pond made in 1979, and a promontory on which stands a group of white-stemmed *Betula utilis jacquemontii*. A short avenue of black poplars is centred on a stone ball, recalling the mind to

architectural certainties.

A walk back leads through thick planting to the north-east of the house, where balustraded steps descend to an informal water garden, made by Lady Carlyle in 1959. Originally an open site with pond-side planting of large-leaved gunnera, rheums, peltiphyllums, rodgersias and rustling bamboos with blocks of chunky yellow-headed *Primula florindae*, its effects echo the teaching of William Robinson and Gertrude Jekyll. Trees such as the dawn redwood (*Metasequoia glyptostroboides*), first introduced in 1947, grow fast. The oldest known conifer *Ginkgo biloba* is much slower. Larch, parrotia, liquidambar and more taxodiums were all planted at the same time and now give a mysterious quality to the dark shaded water and surrounding foliage plants.

The clue to understanding the gardens is found in Hugh Johnson's own work. Already the extremely successful author of books on wine when he came to Saling Hall in 1971, he completed *The International Book of Trees* within two years. *The Principles of Gardening*, subtitled 'The science, practice and history of the gardener's art', followed in 1979. Hugh Johnson's own assessment of the latter book is modest in that he claims it is the distillation of his self-education as a gardener: 'I had to write it . . . while the memory of my own ignorance was still fresh.' As such it is a guide to the amateur; within its covers he explains how gardening works at a practical level. But it is far more than a garden manual: the eyes of the

BELOW LEFT
Box clipped into mounds gives an exotic effect in the outer garden.

BELOW RIGHT
The door from the formal garden to the arboretum. Paving stones set in the grass point the way.

reader are opened to gardening as a creative art, the mind is alerted to a new awareness of the conception of the 'ideal' garden – a place which not only demonstrates man's mastery over nature, but which, through stimulation of the senses, influences both mood and impulse. He describes and assesses the history of garden design not from the point of view of the scholarly historian, but in order to educate and guide the modern gardener in the search for a contemporary garden style. It is certainly one

of the best garden books of the twentieth century. Many writers are experts on design, on plants and planting or on practical horticulture. No other modern author has captured the essentials of all aspects of gardening so succinctly. In writing he identified gardening principles; at Saling he has explored their application. As a gardener he combines the plantsman/collector's instincts with the 'rules' which he has learned to expound.

Pots filled with tender plants and massed together make an architectural feature.

Hatfield House

Hertfordshire
(The Marquess and Marchioness of Salisbury)

FEW GREAT HOUSES with surrounding gardens dating back almost four hundred years are so fortunate in retaining the 'bones' of their framework. At Hatfield, although terraces have been pushed out, the basic rectangular compartments which framed the Jacobean mansion still stabilize the architecture within its landscape. The gardens are a series of terraced level enclosures where pleached lime alleys, walks in clipped ilex and rows of apple trees accentuate and emphasize the architecture. In the gardens surrounding the house on three sides – east, south and west – line echoes line in geometric symmetry, yet each separate area has so distinctive a planting pattern that there is no monotony. Each space, enclosed with stone balustrading or with living trees, relates in scale and design to the massive house in the true Renaissance style. To the north, today the main approach, a double avenue of old lime trees and inner young beech leads to the courtyard.

The building of Hatfield House and the making of the gardens surrounding it date from 1607, when Robert Cecil, Earl of Salisbury, exchanged his house at Theobalds for the old Tudor palace of the Bishops of Ely, where the young Princess Elizabeth had been held a virtual prisoner before succeeding to the throne in 1557. The site of the new house was on an eminence, so that although the front and southern approach was grand and level, at either side and to the north the ground sloped steeply away. To the east where the private apartments lay, as they do today, a series of grand flat terraces was designed. Quite different and medieval in character, the earlier palace was built in a hollow and surrounded by elaborate enclosed garden areas, each one separate and remote from the others. Simple planting of fruit trees, arbours for sitting or walking and turf banks sloping down to elaborate patterned knot gardens were inward-looking, lacking any positive link with the architecture of the house or with the landscape.

The new Renaissance gardens, directly influenced by those of Italy, became a series of interconnected spaces or 'rooms' for living in, extensions of the house, their layout closely reflecting its architecture. House and garden became integrated as a single unit. By the end of the fifteenth century Italian gardens, from being simple axial plans of tree- or topiary-fringed walks conforming to a classical concept of symmetry and proportion articulated with the house, developed a new outward-looking philosophy based on the classical love of nature and appreciation of its beauty. The building of the new palace at Hatfield coincided with an awareness of these fundamental new tenets, and in the 1980s it is the intention of the present Marchioness of Salisbury to restore this intimacy between the house, its garden and the landscape in which it sits.

In the years since the time of Robert Cecil and James I, who himself by tradition planted four mulberry trees, one of which is still to be seen in the western garden, there have been many changes, including new broader terraces around the house. The original garden design seems to have been partly by Mountain Jennings, the gardener at Theobalds who came here with Cecil, but others such as Thomas Chaundler were also involved in the formal layout of the east gardens. Even before this garden was complete it was further elaborated with fountains and waterworks of which no trace now remains. By 1611 Salomon de Caus, the French hydraulic engineer who had studied some of the complex water mechanisms introduced at the end of the sixteenth century into Italian gardens such as that of the Villa d'Este at Tivoli and Pratolino near Florence, was called in to make an elaborate water parterre under the hanging eastern terraces. These and the terraced layout above are described by a visiting Frenchman, M. de Sorbière, in 1663: 'We dined in a hall that looked into a Greenplot with two fountains in it and having espaliers on

the side ... from this Terrass you have a Prospect of the great Water Parterre ... You have also in those places where the river enters into and comes out of the parterre, open sorts of Boxes, with seats around, where you may see a vast number of fish pass to and fro in the water, which is exceeding clear and they seem to come in shoals to enjoy all the pleasures of the place.'

The grounds at Hatfield were landscaped up to the walls of the house in eighteenth-century fashion, but both house and gardens were allowed to fall into considerable disrepair, and formal beds, garden buildings and ornaments crumbled. Old lime avenues aligned on the south front and the northern court, where the main approach is now, in part survived the Landscape Movement and are being replanted. By the middle of the nineteenth century Lord Salisbury, the second Marquess, partly restored the garden to its Jacobean form, spurred on by the prospect of a visit from Queen Victoria in

In the East Gardens standard mop-headed ilex (*Quercus ilex*) line the terraces above the main lawn, where box-edged beds are filled with roses and flowering perennials.

1848. The south and north courtyards were extended, balustrades and elaborate gateways were added, in 1840 a yew labyrinth was planted above the lake and below the terraces on the east, and formal parterres in Italianate style introduced.

Today, faced with devising a practical scheme for restoration but lacking any original drawings of the exact layout in 1607–12, Lady Salisbury has an important source of information about the plants which were used to furnish the gardens. Robert Cecil's gardener was John Tradescant the Elder. Tradescant was sent out to collect plants in Holland, from where he dispatched tulips and anemones, currants, vines and fruit trees, including apricots, quinces, cherries, pears and medlars. Some of the bills for these plants still remain at Hatfield. In Paris Tradescant purchased from M. Jean Robin pomegranates, figs and other trees and was given 'manye other Rare Shrubs'. Lists include 'the Catalonian jasmine, the great rose daffodil, lilac and acacia' (*Robinia pseudacacia*, named for M. Robin and newly introduced from America), lilies from Constantinople, cistus and roses, including sweetbriars, albas and striped varieties. In a manuscript in the Bodleian Library an 'amber plum' is illustrated 'which groweth at Hatfield'. These plants were only the beginning: after he left Cecil's service Tradescant travelled in Muscovy, gathering berries in the Russian countryside, and then went on to become the royal gardener and finally in 1637 the first curator of the Botanic Garden founded at Oxford in 1625. Although Robert Cecil himself died in 1612, his son continued to make the garden, and it seems likely that most of the plants then available in England would have been planted at Hatfield.

Restoration of the gardens has followed a logical and historical pattern. Lady Salisbury, an accomplished and knowledgeable gardener, with experience gained from her re-creation of a period garden at seventeenth-century Cranborne Manor in Dorset, has made use of all available records to re-create the atmosphere of the early gardens. Now Hatfield's compartmental inner gardens, contained by strong geometric frames matching and aligned with the east and west façades of the house, all have separate planting themes which complement and soften the harsher lines of stonework and the formality of pleached trees, avenues of clipped topiary and low surrounding hedges. Against terraced walls espalier and fan-trained fruit trees alternate with climbing roses to extend the architectural form. Collections of seventeenth-century tulips, violas and dianthus stimulate interest in gardening of the period, but fit easily into the overall plans without seeming too strictly botanical at the expense of unity and beauty of design.

A visitor approaches up the lime avenue to the northern courtyard which gives access to the house. Immediately on either side and along the openwork balustrading large specimens of the evergreen tree *Phillyrea latifolia*, with olive-like small glossy leaves, make green buttresses which extend and anchor the vast house to its rather bleak eminence above the sunken garden areas to the east and west. Although they were probably planted within the last hundred years, these trees from southern Europe were already well known at the time the house was built. To the west, in front of the remaining wing of the Tudor palace of 1497 and hidden from the forecourt by a large horse chestnut, a sunken area – a rose garden in Victorian times – now contains a knot garden and a boxwood and gravel maze, where only plants known in the fifteenth, sixteenth and seventeenth centuries are grown. Steep grass banks flower with primroses, cowslips, red clover, violets and ox-eye daisies; steps lead down through a gateway in a diamond-patterned trelliswork fence. A thorn hedge (*Crataegus oxyacantha*) runs round the garden, and arbours of scented jasmine, honeysuckle and sweetbriar provide secluded seats. Clipped

OPPOSITE ABOVE
Double avenues of mop-headed standard *Quercus ilex* line the edges of the East Gardens.

OPPOSITE BELOW
The reconstruction of a Tudor knot garden and box maze lies below steep banks in front of the old palace.

FAR LEFT
Under the chestnut tree above the knot garden stands an eighteenth-century statue of a helmeted warrior.

LEFT
Eighteenth-century statues by Orazio Marinali, brought from a villa by Lake Como, face each other across the broad lawn to the east of the house.

141

box and phillyrea (the small-leaved *Phillyrea angustifolia*) give formality; almonds and plums give height where 'pinks', auriculas, double primroses and germander sprawl. Nor is the planting dull, in spite of excluding more recent introductions. The now uncommon annual *Hibiscus trionum*, with black centres and cream petals, was introduced in 1693 and finds a place here, to be envied by many gardeners. The equally rare *Periploca graeca*, the silk vine, with fragrant greenish-purple flowers in July (mentioned in Gerard's *Herbal* of 1597), grows up the palace wall. *Colchicum agrippinum*, probably a hybrid of *C. variegatum* from western Turkey, thrives in a sunny bed and flowers in August or September. Lady Salisbury has been given a collection of historic tulips and narcissi dating to the seventeenth century by the Hortus Bulborum in Holland. Spirals of variegated holly, bay trees and olives in pots stress the garden's period flavour.

The reconstructed East Gardens, the most magnificent in the original conception, can first be viewed from the windows of the house. Today a new and equally inspired design joins house, garden and landscape together as a visual unit. Italian seventeenth-century statues look down from balustrading onto a terrace flanked with avenues of 8-foot (2.4-metre) standard *Quercus ilex* clipped with dome-shaped heads. Square box-edged beds, originally introduced by the fifth Marquess of Salisbury, the present Lady Salisbury's father-in-law, are filled with roses, peonies, irises and flowering perennials, including blue- and white-flowered clumps of tradescantia, named for Hatfield's first gardener. A newly planted central yew avenue will, when mature, narrow and concentrate the view to lower terraces, the yew labyrinth of 1840 and the glint of water far below. The walls of the labyrinth make vertical and horizontal patterns, dark shadows between each row relieving paler-textured foliage shapes. Annual clipping of the 8-foot (2.4-metre) high yew takes two men three weeks. The New Pond with a 'puddled' bottom and island date to the time of the building of the house. In 1985 its setting is sylvan: tightly mown paths between rougher grass give direction through an informal planting of trees and shrubs, against a backdrop of substantial woodland. The second terrace is edged with recently planted avenues of standard apple trees of ancient varieties, and on a third terrace a pool is concealed by quince trees and backed by wings of dark yew, against which a golden-leaved *Gleditsia triacanthos* 'Sunburst' stands out.

To the south of the main East Terrace formal beech hedging encloses a newly planted orchard below the level of the main south forecourt, where the great house stands looking through ornamental gates down a broad avenue of limes to the south. Prunus dating to the 1930s weep over the balustrades and a sea of lavender surrounds a fountain. Beyond the gravelled court, soon to be reconstructed using granite setts and paving, a 'wilderness' on a lower level contains old cedars, copper beeches, oaks and robinias, and Spanish and horse chestnuts. Under the trees sheets of daffodils and bluebells carpet the ground in spring. The western garden enclosures can be reached by corner steps from the south court, or by an avenue of crab apples, *Malus* 'John Downie', which leads north through a gateway into a garden of fragrant leaves and flowers, the outer bastion of the garden 'rooms'.

Below the West Terrace of the house the gardens match the façade in width. Nearest the house and edged all round with a shady pergola of pleached limes, where shadow and sunlight make moving patterns on pale Bredon gravel which has recently replaced harsher asphalt paths, lawn surrounds an undulating yew hedge which in turn contains a formal parterre. The pattern of the beds is taken from a plan found in the archives, once part of the original gardens attached to the old palace of 1497. Its site is that of the Tudor privy garden. Roses, shrubs, hollyhocks and sun-loving perennials are undercarpeted and mixed with the hardier 'silvers' and 'greys', with bulbs to start the season in spring. At the four corners of the plot stand mulberry trees, three replacing those by tradition planted by James I on his visit in 1612, which died recently, and one an original.

A gap in the lime arbour to the west allows access to the fragrant garden, which itself contains an inner central herb bed caged with a 'fence' of scented sweetbriars. Paved paths are inset with camomile (*Chamaemelum nobile*) and thymes, fragrant underfoot, surround a sundial; lavenders, rosemaries, stone containers overflowing with the refreshingly pungent leaves of *Pelargonium tomentosum* in summer, and lemon-scented verbena at the corners, to be brushed in passing, are all arranged in patterns. Silver-leaved artichokes (forms of *Cynara scolymus*) and standard honeysuckles give extra height. Shrub roses, chosen for scent, and bulbs with fragrant flowers or leaves abound. Chimonanthus, mahonia and sarcococca flower in winter; magnolias, daphnes, and philadelphus in spring and summer. In the summer months, tobacco plants spread their evening fragrance through the garden and everywhere small scented violas seed under taller deciduous shrubs.

When the house was built, a vineyard was planted where the river Lea swept round at some distance to the north-east. The 30,000 vines were a gift to Robert Cecil from the wife of the French ambassador, Mme de la Broderie, and 500 fruit trees were also sent by the French queen, besides the loan of her own gardener to 'sett' them. By the end of the century few of the vines survived except for those in the vineyard to the north of the river (in fact the last vine died just before the Second World War) but instead, on north-facing terraces, hidden behind flint and stone walls, an elaborate radiating pattern of yew hedges was planted, seemingly to make a clipped pattern of slanting waist-high walks on the steep incline. Just as all gardens grow and inevitably change the original visual intention of their makers, so today these strange walks, where original yew specimens have grown tall and gaunt after three hundred years, provide shaded privacy. Remote from the rest of the garden, much of which is thrown open to visitors, and looking down on a broad stretch of the river, this area has a mysterious elusive quality of its own.

Gardening around a great period house demands a knowledge of the history of garden design and of plant introductions, an architect's sense of spatial balance and rhythm, and a painter's eye for composition and colour. Lady Salisbury combines these attributes with a realistic attitude to the practical side of gardening. No chemicals are employed for spraying against disease or as contact herbicides, although simazine-based weedkillers keep gravelled areas clean. She believes that healthy plants seldom need the support of modern fungicides or systemic insecticides, so plenty of organic bone- and fish-meal and calcified seaweeds, farmyard manure and leaf-mould are applied annually. Beds, borders and paths are edged with brick and paving, and granite setts and cobbling are substituted for gravel to reduce labour costs. To the north-west of the house a new kitchen garden is being made to replace the distant walled gardens now proving uneconomic to maintain. The gardens at Hatfield seem set on a fair course for their second four hundred years, each generation of Cecils making its mark and ensuring continuity and progress, as well as a strict adherence to past traditions of design and planting.

OPPOSITE ABOVE
From the terrace, statues and evergreen foliage provide architectural emphasis.

OPPOSITE BELOW
In the West Gardens formal alleys of pleached lime and inner yew hedging surround beds where planting is lavish. Roses, peonies and perennials are tightly packed together to give a long season of flowering.

Docwra's Manor

Shepreth, Cambridgeshire
(Mrs John Raven)

In 1954 the seller's agents described the gardens at Docwra's as 'One and a half acres with orchard wilderness and pigsty'. The manor house, basically a late-sixteenth-century farmhouse, had been enlarged and faced with red brick in the eighteenth century. The elegant Queen Anne façade could just be glimpsed from the village street. From wrought-iron gates a cobbled path led to the front door. Elm trees (recently replaced with *Tilia cordata*) and old yews inside the eastern boundary wall, an assorted collection of barns to the north and west and a walled kitchen garden completed the feeling of privacy. Here was a village house set so that the upper windows had a view over a park-like green, yet the garden remained secret and secluded. Today even though the surroundings are less rural the garden retains this remote quality. A housing estate lies over the wall to the north, and other new houses, built by the Ravens for letting, have gardens where a barn (burnt down in 1971) stood. Fortunately Mrs Raven was able to acquire a field to the south, part of the land belonging to the principal village manor to the south of Docwra's. Now covenanted to the National Trust, this, with the house and garden, is protected from further development.

John and Faith Raven bought Docwra's Manor in 1954, the year of their marriage; over thirty years later the garden overflows with an accumulation of plants which reflect their joint interest in collecting from the wild, Mr Raven's skill and knowledge as an amateur botanist and classical scholar, and their partnership as gifted and perceptive gardeners. Many other interesting plants have come from friends. Close planting is done in layers; trees underplanted with shrubs and roses, and lower-growing perennials and biennials sheltering a bewildering assortment of bulbs. Plants which thrive are encouraged to seed at will and many happy accidental associations give the garden a sense of great maturity and luxuriant freedom. No written description can take a reader on a conventional garden tour; instead some introduction to the Ravens and their gardening style may convey a little of their garden's interest and charm.

John Raven, although by profession a classical don at King's College, Cambridge, was rather more than an amateur botanist, and described many of his plants in *A Botanist's Garden* (1971) and in an article in *The Garden* (August 1979). He liked to assemble his collection in different ways. Some plants were grouped in botanical families as in a teaching garden, to demonstrate the strange diversity of shape and form possible between plants sharing

Looking through the old garden wall to a paved area, where a solitary plant of *Achillea grandifolia* grows in front of a feathery juniper.

essential family characteristics. In one section of the walled garden *Umbelliferae* such as sweet Cicely (*Myrrhis odorata*), many eryngium species, *Selinum tenuifolium* and fennel were planted in clumps and encouraged to seed freely. The bronze form of the culinary fennel *Foeniculum vulgare*, and the magnificent giant fennel (*Ferula communis*) from southern Europe are planted in close proximity. Every few years the latter, usually mounds of feathery lacy green, send up soaring 8-foot (2.4-metre) stems carrying graceful heads of yellow cow-parsley umbels.

Other plants from a single genus have been collected together in appropriate sites to suit the individual plant. Hellebores, particularly the 'green' forms such as *Helleborus bocconei* from Italy, *H. cyclophyllus* and the closely related *H. odorus* from Greece, *H. corsicus* and the British natives, *H. foetidus* and *H. viridis*, all thrive in shady corners. The Lenten hellebore (*H. orientalis*), with variable flower colour of speckled cream or pink, makes a carpet beneath an old Judas tree and *Prunus* 'Tai-Haku' by the kitchen back door. Among other *Ranunculaceae* is a much prized group of *Ranunculus aconitifolius* growing in a low bed in front of the greenhouse; and beneath a shady east-facing wall *Hepatica transsilvanica* and *H. nobilis* thrive beside a collection of ferns. Species peonies include *Paeonia emodi*, the European *P. mascula* in different forms, *P. mlokosewitschii*, *P. whitleyi major* and the scarce red-stemmed *P. cambessedesii* from the Balearics. A euphorbia collection shows the exciting variation in leaf, flower and habit and the widely differing cultural requirements of this genus. Some come from damp woods, others from well-drained stony banks in Greece and southern Europe. A fine amelanchier, *Amelanchier ovalis* (snowy mespilus), was brought home from Monte Grappa above Asolo, in the south-eastern foothills of the Dolomites. With large white erect racemes among pale downy leaves in spring, it deserves comparison with any of the more familiar species or hybrids of the same genus. The most treasured plant in the garden, *Cardamine enneaphyllos* (until recently still classified as *Dentaria enneaphyllos*), closely related to our native cuckoo flower, came from the lower meadows in the same region. Pale yellow racemes rise on erect stems 12 inches (30 centimetres) above deeply cut and lobed purplish-green leaves.

In 1954 parts of the site were still owned by the local council who in 1919 bought land and buildings to let out as agricultural tenancies.

The Ravens gradually managed to buy back much of the original property, increasing the total garden to well over two acres (0.8 hectares), and the compartmental scheme which evolved from this piecemeal method of acquisition adds much to the charm of today's garden. Framing and climbing plants emphasize paths and doorways which link each separate area so the whole garden design seems coherent, and everywhere roses spill and tumble to soften hard masonry lines. The light alkaline soil at Shepreth is exceptionally free-draining and the rainfall is almost the lowest in Britain. Walls and hedges provide protection from wind, and although winter temperatures are often extreme, neighbouring plants shelter each other with canopies and foliage cover. The Ravens, at first gardening near the house, gradually spread outwards, making all open spaces into a series of courtyards, each with a separate theme. Sometimes these were based on flower or foliage colour or, in equally Jekyllean style, were planned for a definite seasonal performance, usually for the earlier part of the year, as Mrs Raven has another garden at Ardtornish in Argyll where the family went for much of the university and school summer vacation. In one small enclosed yard plants mentioned in early Greek texts were originally assembled; later in this very favoured microclimate tender specimens such as blue *Salvia guaranitica*, *Carpenteria californica*, cistus in quantity, piptanthus and *Artemisia arborescens* 'Faith Raven' found a home. The latter, from high hills in Rhodes, has proved much hardier than the type species and is now in demand in commerce. Except for roses the Ravens both preferred white, yellow and blue flowers, and with their botanical interest the emphasis has always been on species rather than garden cultivars or hybrids.

The normal approach is through an entrance gate to the west, leading to a gravelled enclosure between the kitchen window and the low wall which opens onto a lawn and walled garden beyond. A tall spreading crack willow (*Salix fragilis*) planted in the early years is now a feature here above winter-flowering shrubs. Roses, clematis and honeysuckle cluster and twine in profusion, reassuring the visitor that this is not just a botanist's garden of rare plants but will delight the senses as well as stimulating the mind. To the side a stone trough, one of many filled with different soil types, catches the eye; in it in early spring *Uvularia grandiflora*, from eastern North America, bears yellow bell-flowers.

In their first year the Ravens knocked down a piece of wall opposite the kitchen windows, laid out a lawn where vegetables had grown and almost closed the vista at the far end with a tapestry hedge of green and bronze beech. A purple nut tree became a focal point on the farther side of the next walled enclosure. Today through the gap there are glimpses of a double border where blue-flowering plants and those with glaucous or silvery foliage line the central path. Height is given by tall thistles, *Onopordon arabicum* and the giant kale (*Crambe cordifolia*), while anchusas, penstemons and geraniums jostle at a lower level. In the shade of trees to the south there are more hellebores; in spring purple honesty, *Euphorbia amygdaloides robbiae* and lamium struggle for supremacy. On the south-facing wall nearer the house *Abutilon × suntense*, purple berberis, *Rosa glauca* (better known to gardeners as *R. rubrifolia*) and romneya grow between strong clumps of scarlet Greek anemones (*Anemone pavonina*), and red-stemmed *Euphorbia amygdaloides*. Against the wall the winter-flowering *Clematis cirrhosa balearica* makes an evergreen curtain, carrying its cream bell-like flowers for many months in a mild winter.

Directly behind the house, beyond the Judas tree and pale yellow-flowering prunus, a wide expanse of lawn opens out, overhung on its far side by dark yews, which partly conceal the boundary wall. A collection of ferns grows in damp shade under the sloping roof of a barn, on the tiles of which *Sedum acre* has spread like a golden carpet.

A classical temple makes a focal point on the southern part of the lawn, while to the north double curving herbaceous borders mark its limit, although a mown path invites exploration beyond. The sunny border is backed by a grey-leaved sorbus (*Sorbus aria* 'Majestica') and a weeping silver pear (*Pyrus salicifolia* 'Pendula') which disguise a sunken path and secret garden dell behind. In the border thalictrum, acanthus, delphiniums, giant kale and pink oriental poppies make a good show. In the west border, partly shaded by a horse chestnut, clumps of brilliant black-eyed magenta

Sweet Cicely (*Myrrhus odorata*), with fern-like leaves and umbelliferous white flower-heads, spreads in front of the tall variegated form of *Symphytum × uplandicum*.

OPPOSITE
In the walled garden peony species and green-flowered *Nectaroscordon bulgaricum* grow together.

A group of *Tulipa viridiflora* in the outer garden.

CENTRE
Cornus alba 'Elegantissima' in front of a hedge of purple and green beech.

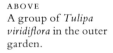

Geranium psilostemon are dominant in June, grouped round a purple-leaved birch. Sculptural leaves of hogweed (*Heracleum mantegazzianum*) and bronze rheum give architectural interest.

The old chestnut is companion to a remaining garden elm, *Ulmus carpinifolia*. The grass path, framed by a pair of topiary shapes in boxwood, passes between two rows of the modern shrub rose 'Fritz Nobis' and leads into a wild garden. Here informal planting of trees and shrubs and bulbs, naturalized in the rough grass and linked by winding paths, contrasts with the more ordered patterns in the walled enclosures. A *Robinia kelseyi*, the fine pear, *Pyrus nivalis*, a *Pterocarya fraxinifolia* kept as a bushy shrub, viburnums, hydrangeas and a young *Cornus controversa* 'Variegata' with elegant tabulated branches to contrast with more rounded forms, a *Koelreuteria paniculata*, and others grow closely together, overshadowed by a tall poplar and ash which help to screen the garden from house-building beyond. Paths mown through rough grass where Queen Anne's lace and other native flowers thrive curve round to reveal the planting, and bring the visitor back to the elm and a pathway

leading to a courtyard beyond, now used mainly as a nursery propagation area.

To the south under the house walls sun-loving cistus and tulips collected in their native habitat mingle with *Euphorbia corallioides*. *Tulipa sprengeri*, *T. bakeri* from the plain of Omalo, *T. saxatilis* and *T. cretica* from Crete enjoy the rather poor and arid soil. Standard roses including 'Iceberg' and 'Albéric Barbier' edge the cobbled path leading from the road and are underplanted with alstroemeria, both *ligtu* hybrids and the old orange-flowered *A. aurantiaca*, which come into flower in late June with blue flax (*Linum narbonense*) and madonna lilies. Among the large shrub roses placed along the railings looking over the village are *RR*. 'Nevada', *polyantha* 'Multiflora' and 'Conrad Meyer'.

During the 1970s the remaining vegetables behind the blue borders in the walled garden were pushed out to the north-western garden perimeter, and in their place in front of a south-facing greenhouse shrubs, perennials and biennials were planted. The area was crossed with diagonal paths, inside one arm of which the umbelliferous plants mentioned above were massed. Near by and at the base of a high wall,

To the left of the path in the walled garden are culinary sea kale (*Crambe maritima*) and a variegated symphytum. The yellow-flowered hemerocallis on the right is said to have come from Monet's garden at Giverny.

Aquilegia and juniper in a corner of the garden.

Lilium szovitzianum, one of the best lilies for a dry alkaline soil, St Bernard's lily (*Anthericum liliago*), *Nectaroscordon bulgaricum* with creamy-green flowers (syn. *Allium b.*), hemerocallis, and tall *Eremurus robustus* (known as the foxtail lily) all represent the *Liliaceae*. *Silybum marianum*, a giant milk-thistle with spined green-and-white leaves, echinops, achillea, including the rare *A. grandifolia*, and artemisia demonstrate how different members of the *Compositae* can be, their tiny clustered daisy-heads not easily or instantly associated with more common larger-flowered daisies. Against the west wall clumps of the sinister looking dragon plant (*Dracunculus vulgaris*) with strange plum-crimson spathes, may become a foundation plant, perhaps with some species of arisaema, in a project for a bed of 'brown' colouring which Mrs Raven hopes to establish.

To the east of the house Mrs Raven has recently rebuilt the brick boundary wall on which she has planted espalier pears. Under an old mulberry more hellebores have been planted. Sheltered by the wall, *Itea ilicifolia*, the climbing *Schizophragma hydrangeoides*, green-stemmed native dogwood, elaeagnus, *Rubus thibetanus*, mahonias and sarcococca are mainly

for winter interest. Against the wall a pale pink form of *Clematis armandii* is beginning to get away and the narrow-petalled *Camassia cusickii* flowers in early June. A pathway beside the perimeter wall leads back to the temple, through whose columns the herbaceous beds across the lawn are visible.

This short description of some of the plants gives no picture of the unusual and luxuriant planting at Docwra's Manor. Nor should it imply that to enjoy its beauty any botanical expertise is called for. The Ravens, both with a special eye for top-grade plants and an almost unique sense of appropriate plant association, quite simply made use of Mr Raven's special botanical interest and his collector's instinct, which add an extra dimension to the garden planting.

John Raven died in 1980 but his wife Faith continues to add new plants and planting schemes, so that the garden continues to live and change while preserving many of the rarities which made it of paramount interest to plantsmen. However, it is not only a collection of exotic and native plants. Each visit reveals new plant associations, new seasonal effects and a variety of new sensations.

Abbots Ripton Hall

Huntingdon, Cambridgeshire
(Lord and Lady de Ramsey)

OPPOSITE
Looking back towards the
house down the long
double borders.

BELOW
Silvery artemisias spread
in front of architectural
yuccas and a tall
eucalyptus.

GREY-LEAVED *Sorbus* 'John Mitchell' are planted as an avenue to line a rural lane which leads north-east from the village near Huntingdon. On the adjacent high wall, buttresses of green and variegated large-leaved ivy (*Hedera colchicum*) make a formal repetitive pattern. Dropping gently down, the lane leads to the formal entrance to the Hall, an elegant brick house of late Georgian appearance which lies behind and against the wall to the right, its other three sides facing into the richly planted and diverse garden areas. Through the orna-

mental wrought-iron gates, framed formally by pleached lime trees, the house sits generously protected by a sweep of mature trees. Specimens of lime, chestnut, ash and London plane, thickened with several evergreen *Quercus ilex* and a few surviving great elms, give evidence of an old garden site, where shelter from cold northerly winds will have been a primary consideration in this exposed East Anglian farmland of heavy boulder clay.

Planting on the house and around the gravel sweep is restrained. The walls are curtained with Boston ivy colouring orange and flame in October; a paulownia thrives in a sheltered corner; a high yew hedge juts out to screen the garden areas beyond from immediate view. In spring a carpet of daffodils followed by frothing Queen Anne's lace stretches up a gentle slope to a ha-ha and farmland beyond the trees; in autumn ivy-leaved cyclamen flower in shade under their canopies. A manicured lawn, cut in traditional stripes and edged with rougher textured grass, carries the eye to shrubberies on the south-east.

Through a gap in the tall yew access is gained to the farther gardens, where a landscape of water vistas is gradually and subtly revealed. At first all is formal: the river known as the Abbots Ripton brook runs canal-like through lawns parallel to the back of the house and backed by another yew hedge. Only groups of white-stemmed birch (*Betula utilis jacquemontii*), a magnolia and a playing fountain occupy the immediate foreground. A central opening in the hedge carries the eye up a long vista between herbaceous borders to a gateway and an avenue of pink-flowered chestnuts in the distance. This long view, broken only by the Gothic finials of a treillage rondel more than halfway up, hardly gives a hint of the planting interest concealed in a series of lateral and geometrically shaped garden compartments leading off its main axis. To the south of the house a fine plane tree partially conceals the water which, twisting away beyond a white-painted bridge, its reflecting surface hidden by thick planting, swings round, making a right-angled bend to emerge and spread out into a 5-acre (2-hectare) lake. Hardly visible at first from the lawns below the house, much of the lake is also concealed by shrubberies, but a broad vista opens at the end of the lawn, carrying the eye between borders towards a glint of water. Seen from the lake shore the south-east façade of the house, emphasized by its colonnaded porch, is framed by planting.

The layout of the whole area stresses the importance of elements of surprise and mystery in garden design. Few gardens, let alone one virtually conceived and made in the second half of the twentieth century, so invoke these emotions, while retaining a unity of structure which is satisfying to the orderly mind. Although Lord de Ramsey was advised by the artist and landscaper Humphrey Waterfield in the 1950s and 1960s, was helped in planting round the lake by Lanning Roper in the 1970s, and more recently has called in Peter Foster, Surveyor to Westminster Abbey, to enrich the garden with architectural features, it seems certain that it is his own sense of cohesion which, combined with a wide knowledge of good plants, has ensured overall success.

As changes of mood are stimulated, so the changes of 'style' prove provokingly confusing to the historian who likes to 'label' and date garden themes. Dominated by the fine trees, perhaps two hundred years old, a formal garden pattern, almost a grid system disguised by the rounded and billowing shapes of plants, is seventeenth-century in atmosphere. Yet, except for the long brick wall which marks the north-west boundary, some old fruit trees, and a medieval stewpond, the garden compartments and linking vistas date only to the last forty years. The wider landscape of lake, poplar-planted contoured slopes behind it and 'eye-catching' Fishing Hut, its design taken from a Constable water-colour in the Hall, could belong to an eighteenth-century park, perhaps contemporary with the building of the house. Yet the expanse of water was excavated and the land sloped and planted to deaden the noise of traffic on the road above hardly more than ten years ago. Around the garden architectural follies, Gothic in style, mark strategic spots: a thatched summerhouse for watching the evening light on water, a treillage frame with Gothic finials to make a focal point in the long stretch of the great borders; the painted Chippendale-style bridge across the water near the house. All these are modern, commissioned by Lord and Lady de Ramsey since the Second World War, yet at the end of the long south-east vista a three-arched brick bridge dates to 1740, and still carries the old driveway which was the original approach when the house was built. At Abbots Ripton the garden and the plants in it are twentieth-century in inspiration; historical traditions are not ignored but rather than being slavishly copied are employed to enrich and vary design principles.

The Hall itself dates to different periods. On its site there was originally a medieval hall, an outpost of Ramsey Abbey, of which the only remains are the monk's stewpond and the 'mound', now crowned by an oak, which may represent its excavation spoil, concealed in the formal gardens. The main part of the house is late eighteenth-century; the limes and great plane trees are probably contemporary planting. Subsequent alterations by Anthony Salvin in 1856 are now mainly disguised by more recent improvements, which with an elegant *trompe-l'oeil* trelliswork veranda give the house a Regency flavour. On the trellis facing south-west a white-flowered *Trachelospermum jasminoides* twines loosely; in summer Mediterranean olive trees and oleanders grow in pots on the warm terrace, and the air is cooled by the splashing fountain.

From the porch the view stretches south-east between thickly planted borders, mainly of white-flowered plants, to the eighteenth-century bridge near the lake shore. In the beds white forget-me-nots, cream camassias, tinted iris and white-flowered peonies perform in early spring and summer; later the season is carried on by the white Rugosa rose 'Blanc Double de Coubert', philadelphus in quantity and variety, cistus bushes and late-flowering *Spiraea veitchii*, which thrives in moist soil, bearing arching branches heavy-laden with creamy-white flower corymbs, underplanted with hosta and lamium foliage in cream and green. White martagon and madonna and regal lilies flower in summer; *Hosta* 'Royal Standard' bears its scented flowers in early September. Nearer the bridge the lawn is flanked by clumps of architectural pampas grass.

Breaks in the borders allow views through to classical urns. To the south-west one of these forms the central point in a circular lawn surrounded by June-flowering old shrub roses which thrive in the heavy alkaline clay. On the other side there is a glimpse of the lake and its farther shores. Hidden at the back a rare purple-leaved *Catalpa × erubescens* 'Purpurea', with dark bronze young shoots and leaves, is worth searching out. The elegant *Caragana arborescens* 'Lorbergii' with narrow grass-like leaves stands out in early summer, while *Koelreuteria paniculata*, spectacular in its rare flowering season and consistent in contributing bronze autumn foliage colour, is a foil to a neighbouring *Robinia pseudacacia* 'Frisia' and columnar ginkgo, with leaves turning pale yellow in October.

Near the bridge, on this side of which a dawn redwood (*Metasequoia glyptostroboides*) and beyond an *Acer pseudoplatanus* 'Brilliantissimum' stand sentinel, an urn commemorates Humphrey Waterfield who died tragically in

The sword-shaped leaves of irises are architectural, and the white seat echoes the Chinese Chippendale design of a bridge over the stream.

BELOW LEFT
A lattice-work trellis topped with Gothic finials breaks up the long vista between the double borders.

BELOW RIGHT
Looking up the long vista between the double borders towards the chestnut avenue.

Under the branches of one of the fine elm trees the white-stemmed birch and Chinese Chippendale bridge are visible.

an accident in 1971. Two maples from southern Europe *Acer tataricum* (Tartar maple) and *Acer monspessulanum*, the latter with three-lobed leaves and somewhat similar to our native field maple (*A. campestre*), fit into the more open landscape. Upstream to the south-west, a collection of willows on the opposite bank were chosen for their coloured bark in winter, and are regularly 'coppiced' in spring. The invasive *Reynoutria japonica* (formerly *Polygonum cuspidatum*) lines the near bank, and towering sea buckthorn (*Hippophae rhamnoides*), with silver leaves and orange berries in winter, makes a forest grove cutting the path along the riverside off from the rest of the garden. Narrow pathways stretch into a shrubbery wilderness surrounding island beds where large-leaved *Trachystemon orientale*, blue-flowered *Symphytum caucasicum*, epimediums and assorted herbaceous geraniums are massed in drifts beneath shrubs. Bowles' grey mint (*Mentha spicata × suaveolens*) is allowed to spread effectively, its soft colouring a foil to stronger foliage hues. The exotic *Aesculus*

neglecta 'Erythroblastos' with shrimp-pink leaves in spring, horizontal-branched forms of *Viburnum plicatum* and yellow-berried *V. opulus* 'Xanthocarpum' are all notable. Planting emphasizes foliage colours and textures.

The central herbaceous borders are reached by the Chippendale bridge, or by an alternative river-crossing tight against the roadside wall and near an old elm, where a modern grotto is set in stone. Either route reveals new garden areas which can be visited later. The border planting, backed on either side by alternating dark green Irish yews and shrubby golden-leaved philadelphus, are planned to reach perfection in mid and late summer. Shrub roses, strong-growing perennials, dahlias and annuals make a fine display. To the north-west in an old orchard spring-flowering clematis climb into pear trees, an enclosure contains a collection of tree peonies, and the rectangular stewpond, its banks planted with *Salix sachalinensis*, has white water-lilies floating on its still surface. Grey-leaved weeping pears and the uncommon *Pyrus elaeagrifolia* grow in an open area of grass. In a glade opposite, on the other side of the wide borders, small ornamental trees include *Fraxinus ornus, Crataegus prunifolia, Sorbus* 'Pearly King' and a selection of acers. The elegant trellis work, Peter Foster's design in iroko wood, makes a break in the hundred-yard (90-metre) border vista. Beyond, Hybrid Musk roses, aromatic-leaved rosemary and lavender bushes grow in front of yew hedging, now a continuous line instead of the spaced and architectural Irish yews at the bottom end of the border.

Beyond, but out of sight of the main axis, a vine-clad pergola edges a building of which part holds a hothouse, once kept to a minimum of 60°F (15.5°C). To the north-west an Edwardian-style rose pergola underplanted with silvery foliage plants is centred on a gate in the wall, its arches hiding a secret garden with curving beds where high walls shelter tender shrubs and climbers. Pineapple-scented Moroccan broom (*Cytisus battandieri*), clematis, a Banksian rose, the silver-leaved and best form of *Buddleja alternifolia*, rare glaucous-leaved *Berberis temolaica* and ghostly thistle-heads of *Eryngium giganteum* give this area a special charm.

Beyond and to the north-east along the base of the main garden wall a wide border, by some considered the *pièce de résistance* at Abbots Ripton, is filled with silvery, grey and glaucous-leaved plants. Concealed from other garden areas by a tall hedge of *Cupressus glabra* the bed is edged with a pattern of York paving, designed by Humphrey Waterfield, which allows pale carpeting plants to drift forwards, breaking the long line with gentle shapely undulations. Against the wall pollarded eucalyptus, abutilon and grey-leaved buddlejas make a backdrop for Mediterranean aromatic-leaved lavenders, santolinas, helichrysums and hairy soft-leaved phlomis species. Plants of the uncommon shrub *Shepherdia argentea* and the related *Elaeagnus commutata* give height and form. In front veronicas, acaena and the rarer *Erodium macradenum*, a gift from Lady Scott (Valerie Finnis) at Boughton, spill across stone and gravel chips, which protect these plants' crowns from standing in freezing water. Artemisias, ballota, *Dorycnium hirsutum*, othonnopsis, *Euphorbia myrsinites*, tanacetum, helianthemums and dwarf achilleas fit into pockets in different planting planes. White-flowered valerian, pink dianthus, romneyas and yuccas produce the few flowers. Silver-leaved *Salvia argentea* has its flower-stems removed to improve the leaf sheen, glaucous-leaved grasses *Festuca glauca, Helictotrichon sempervirens* and the invasive lyme grass (*Elymus arenarius*) are planted in strong groups to give textural contrast to broad leaves.

It is tempting to list all the good planting: a complete inventory for such a garden would have interest for future generations. But without the structure and planning which play such an important role at Abbots Ripton a mere catalogue conjures up just a succession of plants to fit into each garden section. In making a garden the first essential is to establish a framework; plants and planting themes then become its 'furnishing'. A description of a garden must have a similar priority: first understand the 'bones', then notice the detailed planting.

Finally a path leads between old oak trees from the painted bridge. Past iris and agapanthus beds, through a nut walk, beyond the bole of a great elm, and leaving a cleverly concealed tennis-court on the right (golden and green-leaved hops scramble over the harsh lines of its surround) the mown path leads to the waterside and the last of the follies, a summerhouse with a thatched cone-shaped roof above tall Gothic windows. It is sited to allow views across the water, where the evening light glances through the foliage of tall trees and willows which line and overhang the surface.

This garden is a brilliant mixture of formal and informal landscapes; its overall design creates unity out of a variety of separate themes. A garden visitor, his attention caught by choice plants and perfection of detail, lingers on the tour and perhaps pauses and rests where shelter or seats are provided. It is not a garden to be hurried over but one to absorb and reflect on.

A pair of ornamental urns are focal points on a cross axis on the way to the lake.

Bradenham Hall

Thetford, Norfolk
(Colonel and Mrs Richard Allhusen)

HUMPHRY REPTON (1752–1818), the great landscape gardener, found his native Norfolk countryside far from dull. Appreciating its peculiar character, where the land-shapes, 'which, though they ascend with an almost imperceptible egravity, terminate with a prospect of twenty, some thirty miles distant', he noticed also the 'prodigious softness' caused by the oak and ash planting of the hedgerows. The woodland and garden at Bradenham, 27 acres (11 hectares) in extent, cover the south-facing slopes of the highest hill in Norfolk, and reveal a gentle distant view over broad acres of an intensively worked fruit and corn farm to another low ridge in the distance above a stream valley. Colonel and Mrs Allhusen have spent thirty years developing a garden and arboretum of considerable beauty and botanical interest. Both are 'working' gardeners, not mere planners. Mrs Allhusen concentrates on shrubs and flowers, mainly in the series of inner garden compartments, but is also an expert on the daffodil cultivars suitable for naturalizing in grass in the arboretum. Colonel Allhusen has developed a considerable knowledge of trees, and his collection of more than nine hundred includes not only well-grown forest specimens and smaller ornamentals, but also rare varieties and forms.

Originally the pink-brick Queen Anne house standing just under the rim of the hill may well have been protected from the wind by curving wings of native trees, including both the common elm (*Ulmus procera*) and *U. carpinifolia*, as well as fine old oaks. Cattle and sheep grazed the parkland which sloped up to the house, in eighteenth-century style, and the walled garden enclosures behind the house were for fruit and vegetables. However by 1951, when Colonel and Mrs Allhusen acquired the property and began their extensive garden operations, much of the woodland, including the greatest oaks, had been felled by timber merchants. A succession of owners,

wartime occupation by Canadian troops, and general neglect had severely depleted remaining trees, and the courtyard and kitchen gardens to the north of the house were derelict. To the east a large oak stood in what remained of an apple orchard, a Lebanon cedar was a feature to the south-west and a copper beech had grown too large against the west wall of the house.

The soil is basically a stiff clay over chalk, with a pH reading of between 7 and 8 in uncultivated pasture. Rainfall patterns seem rather inconsistent, varying from a reading of approximately 24 inches to as high as 38 inches annually (60 to 95 centimetres). In June 1982 a freak rain and hail storm was devastating with 5 inches (12.5 centimetres) falling in an hour and a half. The winter of 1978–9 was the coldest in Norfolk for 240 years, but a 4-foot (1.2-metre) specimen Kashmir cypress (*Cupressus cashmeriana*) planted since thrives today. Its survival gives a hint of the Allhusens' skill and thoroughness in gardening technique, where every advantage is taken of pockets of favourable microclimate and each plant is given a good start. The head gardener Mr Sydney Lancaster is helped by his wife Margaret and an old age pensioner. Flowers, fruit and vegetables, as well as extensive greenhouses with pot plants for the house, are all kept to a high standard. The Lancasters have been at Bradenham for twenty-five years, arriving when the new yew enclosures had just been planted up, and have played a major role in the development of the garden.

In 1951 the first essential was to provide adequate wind protection, especially from prevailing south-west gales, in an area where only a few poor sycamores remained from the old woodland. Fortunately the Allhusens, at that time lacking experience, met Frank Knight, then Manager at Notcutts, and through him George Taylor who lived at Wisbech near by. In 1953, 2,300 trees and shrubs were planted as a shelter belt. These included belts of Scots and Austrian pine, thuja, Leyland cypress grown as specimens, beech and sycamore. *Abies grandis* did not thrive. Crataegus, hornbeam, prunus, sorbus and evergreen shrubs such as cotoneasters, escallonias and leathery-leaved *Viburnum rhytidophyllum* thickened the wood. On the exposed western perimeter a beech hedge, now 45 feet (13.5 metres) high, was established. The following year a nuttery was added to the west of the house, separated from the park by a curving hedge of copper beech which is today a mature feature. Nut trees include 'Kentish Cob' and filberts. The latter, all forms of *Corylus maxima*, include red and white varieties and 'Frizzled Filbert', as well as 'Pearson's Prolific' cob. Under them aconites, snowdrops, muscari, bluebells and cowslips have been encouraged to spread, the latter so prolifically that seed is collected here annually by Nature Conservancy groups.

To north and east woods needed thinning and replanting, but this could be done without clear felling. The kitchen and flower garden area was already protected by the curve of the hill and old brick walls, and the latter was perfectly sited for fruit growing. To this layout yew hedges were added on the north-east of the house to make firm geometrical enclosures, echoing the lines of the numerous rectangular walled courtyards which already existed directly behind and to the north-west. Each separate compartment was designed for a specific purpose. Vistas were aligned on gateways in the kitchen garden walls, on stone statues and seats, and on yew archways. Today these views are carefully framed with planting schemes which accentuate symmetry. Inside this rigid architectural frame of straight lines planting is informal and relaxed. After thirty years green alleys are hedged with well-clipped yew (cut to a precise 10 foot 9 inches or 3.07 metres, so that a tennis-court is completely hidden in one corner area). In the largest compartment a long herbaceous border, backed with good shrubs, stretches north and south. On either side panels of green lawn make cool walks, centred on statues to the north, framed with curving yew and surrounded by containers with summer annuals. On one side the eastern wall of the kitchen garden provides space for climbing roses in mixed colours, which are at their best in late June. A vista allows a view through a yew archway to lawns and trees to the south, and a series of lateral gardens leads off to the east. In one a swimming-pool, with access cleverly dis-

ABOVE
The façade of the house is framed by great cedars.

Yew wings extend to shelter the house terrace and creeping plants are encouraged to seed freely.

guised, also hides an approach to the tennis-court. A secret garden can be reached only through yew 'doorways', hidden from immediate view. Here Mrs Allhusen is making a new paved garden, with cobbled patterns surrounding raised circular beds of brick. A walk of pleached lime (*Tilia platyphyllos*) carries the eye through a gap in the yew to an eighteenth-century stone statue in shrubberies to the east; in spring selected daffodils make a sheet of yellow below the shaped limes. Another side garden is for shrub roses, old and new, where cascading climbers twine through old apple trees to add height. An old medlar (*Mespilus germanica*) and a recently planted mulberry (*Morus nigra*) grow at either end of the central lawn, where it widens to make a circle edged with low-growing roses.

The present main approach up a curving drive from the south-east hardly existed in 1951; now it reveals tempting glimpses on either side of ornamental trees planted in smooth lawn. In spring the ground is carpeted with carefully chosen daffodils, graded for massed colour and size effects and planted in solid clumps to match the shapes and canopies of overhead trees. The sloping fields leading up to the south terrace of the house have been levelled and contained with ha-has, and Colonel Allhusen's extensive arboretum is designed in firm architectural blocks which allow a central vista from the house front and selected angled views to east and west. A second cedar of Lebanon was planted in 1955 to balance the existing one, and together they flank the main south façade and raised terrace. Wings of shaped solid yew project forwards round the terrace area, anchoring and stabilizing the whole building like fortifications. Cattle still grazed behind railings near the house in 1951, but now double density rabbit netting surrounds the whole garden and ha-has control animal access, allowing unimpeded views to the countryside.

Each tree is impeccably maintained. Colonel Alhusen believes in the dictum 'a penny for the plant, a pound for the planting', and tries to ensure that holes are dug six months before planting, each one 3 feet across and 2 feet deep (90 by 60 centimetres). The top turf is laid in the base of each hole and compost, made from good loam taken from farmland topsoil, is mounded and allowed to settle. Wind is always a problem in the flat Norfolk landscape, so staking is essential for some years. The earth surrounding each tree is kept clean and its area increased as the tree's canopy extends. The Colonel does the mowing, and shallow-rooting trees are given even wider berths than those which make strong tap roots. In the east lawn conifers are well represented by a fine Bhutan pine (*Pinus wallichiana*), the Colorado white fir in its glaucous-leaved form (*Abies concolor violacea*), and spruce including *Picea omorika* and *P. smithiana* and many others to contrast with sweeping lines of low-growing Pfitzer junipers. Broad-leaved trees include *Quercus frainetto*, *Aesculus indica*, a variegated tulip tree, the Turkish hazel (*Corylus colurna*), cercidiphyllum, davidia and cut-leaved beech which have already made substantial growth; and planting continues. A Dawyck beech and a fastigiate hornbeam (*Carpinus betulus* 'Pyramidalis') face each other across the drive, and the silver variegated sweet chestnut (*Castanea sativa* 'Albo-Marginata') is eye-catching. To the west nothofagus species, the rare *Emmenopterys henryi* which has flowered in Europe only at Glasnevin and at Villa Taranto, *Sorbus megalocarpa*, and specimen betula and sorbus are memorable.

Where there are daffodils mowing is not done until the end of June, although unsightly flower-heads are always removed to help the bulbs thrive and develop. Each group of a selected cultivar, mainly of prime Dutch stock,

Flag irises enjoy the warm dry soil at the base of a brick wall.

In summer unmown grasses and wild flowers replace spring daffodils (page 158) and the pleached limes make a shady walk.

The garden is full of hidden enclosures which gradually reveal new planting themes.

consists of between 200 and 250 bulbs, and at planting time each hole is dug individually in the stiff clay to a depth of 8 inches (20 centimetres), and backfill broken up to prevent damage to bulb tips. Over the years a study of parentage has meant consistent success in choice of suitable types and careful attention is given to colour effects. Under a large English oak a cartwheel has been created, with massed flower colours separated into segments.

Behind the house a low wall separates a gravelled courtyard with a central goldfish pond from the first of the old garden compartments, where high south-facing brick walls grow peaches. In a narrow border at their base German flag irises in mixed colours flower in May. The Algerian iris (*Iris unguicularis*) flowers under the low wall through the winter months, and strong evergreens including *Cotoneaster lacteus*, garrya and pyracantha are shaped against the north walls of the house, with a large climbing *Hydrangea petiolaris*. The gateway to the courtyard is framed by good plants of *Ceanothus* 'Cascade', and against the east side of the house climbers and wall shrubs curtain the pink brick. A loquat (*Eriobotrya japonica*) nestles in a corner and the Glasnevin form of the blue potato (*Solanum crispum*) intertwines with *Ampelopsis brevipendunculata*, the claret vine (*Vitis vinifera* 'Purpurea') and the large-leaved *V. coignetiae*, which colours to vivid red and orange in autumn. Under a clock buttressed walls protect a bed of silvery-grey and purple-foliaged plants, their leaf colour linked to grey-painted window shutters and a fine copper beech which shades a shrubbery to the east. To the immediate west of the house a sheltered walled garden provides a site for climbers such as the tender *Senecio scandens*, variegated solanum, mutisia, a Banksian rose and the late-flowering *Rosa bracteata*, the Mac-artney rose introduced from China in 1793. The evergreen *Buddleja colvilei* takes advantage of wall protection, producing its drooping panicles of tubular deep rose-coloured flowers in June.

In areas of the walled kitchen garden flowers, fruit and vegetables are arranged so that views along paths or through gateways are given maximum effect. Beds of peonies and roses are arranged on a simple grid system, where lavender bushes flank paths in tradition-al style. Cordon pears, an old fig and other fruit take advantage of the warm brick. Above, up a few steps, another walled garden has a central path, linked with espalier apples underplanted with mixed bulbs and perennials, which leads to a top gateway, at the side of which white-flowered *Wisteria floribunda* 'Alba' brought back from Mme Champin's garden at Biot in the south of France partially hides a green-house. Beyond in the outer garden conifers, planted as dwarves but now grown large and effective, are backed by a semicircle of cherry laurel. A tree and shrub area extends east to back the yew garden 'rooms' added during the 1970s. New trees here include cedars, a group of 'blue'-foliaged conifers and a variegated *Cornus mas* for colour effect, *Arbutus menziesii*, *Catalpa speciosa*, a tulip tree and the rare shagbark hickory (*Carya ovata*). A line of walnut cultivars, specially grafted in Orleans, sweeps round in a curve to back the main garden and to enclose mixed borders of shrubs and perennials. Hostas, hellebores and astran-tias grow under magnolias, and a pair of standard white wisterias, *Wisteria floribunda* 'Alba' and *W. venusta*, the latter with especially long racemes, frame the eastern approach to the tennis-court.

This is only a selection of the good things at Bradenham: further planting lists would be monotonous. An undoubtedly fine arboretum and varied garden themes make it of interest. But a good collection of plants does not make a stylish garden and the Allhusens have tempered their 'collectors'' instinct with an appreciation of flower and foliage association. Few plants are grown for their botanical interest alone. In many parts of the garden the plantsman is subordinated to the artist, and textured leaves and carefully chosen flower colours make compositions pleasing to the eye as well as stimulating to the gardener in search of unusual plants.

A white wisteria drapes the upper wall of the kitchen garden.

The Dower House

Boughton House, Kettering, Northamptonshire
(Sir David and Lady Scott)

THE DOWER HOUSE at Boughton House lies tucked against an east wing of the great house itself, its architecture unaltered since 1700, and looks southwards across a wide entrance yard to two raised garden areas; the whole is enclosed and sheltered to the east and west by trees belonging to the park. There are three distinct gardens. The smallest, against the house, is partly formal but overflows with plants. A pair of variegated box pyramids flank the front door steps and a central rose-bed is still underplanted with pansies for spring, while nicotiana and the dark-flowered *Cosmos atrosanguineus*, with chocolate scent, are added in summer. When Sir David Scott and his first wife retired in 1948 to his childhood home this garden was much too small and limiting. However, beyond the yard a high retaining wall on the south enclosed two garden areas. The first walled-in section was for fruit trees and vegetables; through a gate a cold north-facing slope surrounded on three sides by park trees was the only available site for expansion.

Sir David and his first wife gradually cleared the brambles and undergrowth beyond and planting began. Stag-headed lime trees dating back to the building of the house, several elms and much later old cedars were felled to give more space. The soil is a cold alkaline clay and establishing young plants can never have been easy. The garden grew, a plantsman's collection where each tree or shrub was given a site where it could best be seen and which might suit its needs, rather than for any part it might play in an overall scheme. The areas of cultivation expanded; as young trees matured the garden took on a woodland character, making new planting more hospitable, and providing sites for treasured and more vulnerable bulbs and perennials under protective spreading canopies. Today, nearly forty years later, this almost rectangular 2 acres (0.8 hectares) has over eighty well-stocked island beds with a great variety of ornamental trees and shrubs,

the latter Sir David's special interest. Closer to the ground are drifts of tightly packed perennials through which bulbs spear their way in season. The beds are edged with mown paths; each has a name, and each plant its known location. Sir David, now in his late nineties and no longer able to move round the garden, continues to assess the quality and beauty of each individual specimen and his success in growing it.

Sir David's first wife died in 1965 and five years later he married Valerie Finnis, then working at the Waterperry School of Horticulture near Oxford, where she created its alpine nursery. In 1970 her collection of these plants was moved to Boughton. As before, in no way could the small enclosed area next to the house absorb all the plants. Instead the walled and level kitchen garden was adapted; low walls facing south and north were encased by railway sleepers to make raised beds, where with adequate drainage soil was specially prepared for growing small plants with differing cultural requirements. Today more raised beds occupy the central space, greenhouses and frames emphasize Lady Scott's interest in propagation and an alpine house has a controlled climate for the most demanding plants, while old fruit trees are a reminder of the site's original use. The wall beds, made with two sleepers one above the other, vary between 3 and 4 feet (90 to 120 centimetres) in width. The north-facing ones are peat-based for acid-loving mountain plants and ferns which thrive in cool shade; on the south-facing wall sun-loving alpines with grey and silvery foliage flourish. The collection is large, and planting is intensive and spreading out eastwards to another walled enclosure below, a yard where Sir David kept hawks when young.

In any garden which has been built up as a collection, or as Sir David has put it, is 'more a home for plants than a garden', adequate descriptions can become mere lists. Neverthe-

less the wealth and variety of plants (some very rare) in both these distinct garden areas seems so stimulating as to avoid monotony. Both Sir David and Lady Scott, working in seemingly separate garden fields, have become a source of inspiration to many. The emphasis may seem to be on collecting. Importantly in each case it is discriminating taste which determines what to grow and what to discard.

On arrival the visitor enters the enclosed front garden. What remains of formality is almost hidden by plants spilling out over path edges, crammed into generous troughs, and, if doubtfully hardy in cold Northamptonshire, placed in pots by the front door steps and removed to a warmer site in winter. On the wall *Clematis orientalis* 'Bill Mackenzie' was named by Valerie Finnis after the curator of the Chelsea Physic Garden, who still gardens in Surrey. It hangs above Mexican cuphea and green and scarlet-flowered correas from Tasmania. In a corner are the elegant pinnate-leaved *Melianthus major*, *Nicotiana langsdorfii* which although an annual in this country seeds *in situ*, yellow-flowered musk-scented *Cestrum parqui*, bronze-leaved hebes, malvastrums and othonnopsis, all underplanted with silvery tanacetum and backed by old-fashioned lad's love (*Artemisia abrotanum*). Across the garden the rare *Kniphofia triangularis* is also in flower. *Phygelius aequalis* 'Yellow Trumpet', now much in demand, flourishes and *Zauschneria* 'Dublin' produces its scarlet flowers along the edge of a bed. The latter, often wrongly called 'Glasnevin', was found by Lady Scott in a Dublin private garden.

Already excitement mounts, with an urgent desire to discover further garden areas. The garden is always hand-weeded. The soil is never forked or hoed, allowing seedlings to establish themselves where they will; even in the outer yard angelica and verbascum find cracks to grow in, setting a pattern of informality.

Across the yard and up the steep steps, where a densely branched shrubby willow, *Salix pyrenaica*, grows, the raised beds contain many treasures; at each visit in a different season new plants catch one's attention, some so rare that only experts can give precise botanical nomenclature. Identification is valuable – and many plants are labelled – but additional interest is given by Lady Scott's intimate knowledge of where each plant came from, who found or 'bred' it, and her ability by her own incisive enthusiasm to quicken duller powers of observation. In the north-facing beds a prostrate-

growing currant, the evergreen *Ribes henryi*, flowers at the end of winter with *Helleborus bocconei* from northern Italy and black-flowered *H. torquatus*. *Rhodothamnus chamaecistus* from the eastern Alps grows next to cassiope from the Arctic and northern mountains. Asiatic erythroniums, *Sanguinaria canadensis* 'Flore Pleno', flowering on 6-inch (15-centimetre) stems, trilliums, *Orchis* (or *Dactylorhiza*) *foliosa* from Madeira, a prized snowdrop, 'Lady Elphinstone', *Hepatica transsilvanica* 'Ada Scott' and both purple and white-flowered *Cardamine pentaphyllos* (syn. *Dentaria digitata*) flourish together. Later toad-lilies, with speckled mauve flowers, and a white form of *Tricyrtis stolonifera* thrive in the loamy soil, and a collection of rhodohypoxis inherited from Mrs Ruth McConnell produce pink and white star-shaped flowers. Climbing over the wall scarlet-flowered *Schisandra grandiflora* bears red fruit in autumn. Across the terrace in full sun small silver-leaved artemisias, leucanthemums, a selection of salvias which includes black-flowered *Salvia discolor*, *Teucrium polium* with yellowish inconspicuous flowers among silvery leaves and many other small plants which need a well-drained soil are found. The vigorous broad-leaved artemisia often called *Artemisia ludoviciana* 'Valerie Finnis' in nurseries and gardens is a species of *A. campestris borealis*. Among the wealth of small plants introduced by Lady Scott older shrubs, roses and climbers have long been established.

In the Hawk Yard, where a central area is a nursery for small plants, the walls provide shelter for choice shrubs and climbers, some planted by Sir David many years ago. From China a pinnate-leaved shrub, *Xanthoceras sor-*

bifolium, bears white flowers in May next to Ladham's form of *Carpenteria californica*. Fritillaries introduced by Martyn Rix, a lime-tolerant grey-leaved *Lithospermum oleifolium* from the Pyrenees, small corydalis, *Omphalodes luciliae* from Greece, variegated-leaved *Euphorbia amygdaloides*, and Christopher Lloyd's bronze-leaved celandine 'Brazen Hussy' are more recent additions. Roy Lancaster's primrose-yellow hollyhock from Russia produces seedlings.

Inside the shrubbery, entered through a wrought-iron gate designed by Sir David, a group of willows, their coloured stems regularly pollarded in spring, are silhouetted against dark yew, so placed as to be visible from the house windows during the winter. Among them are the violet-stemmed *Salix daphnoides* and the brilliant yellow-stemmed cultivar of the white willow, *S. alba vitellina*. Other trees in the collection notable for their bark are *Prunus serrula*, *Acer griseum*, slow-growing but now a fine small tree, and *A. pennsylvanicum* 'Erythrocladum' with shrimp-pink striated shoots, eye-catching when the tree is leafless in winter. There are many good evergreen shrubs which, besides giving wind-protection, provide a structure for the garden through all the seasons. One bed holds a collection of small conifers, a wedding present from Harold Hillier; others have shrubs such as *Stranvaesia davidiana* (now correctly *Photinia davidiana*) with old leaves turning vivid scarlet among the fresh green of the current year's growth, *Phillyrea decora* (now *Osmanthus decorus*), a large bush of the slow-growing variegated Portugal laurel, tall cotoneasters which filter wind, and *Sycopsis sinensis*, a member of the *Hamameli-*

ABOVE LEFT
Trilliums and other acid-loving woodlanders thrive in the raised beds.

ABOVE RIGHT
In the woodland garden paths wind round island beds, where trees and shrubs overhang thick plantings of perennials and bulbs.

OPPOSITE ABOVE
Imperial lilies (*Fritillaria imperialis*) are clumped between shrubs in the woodland beds.

OPPOSITE BELOW
Canopies of trees and shrubs shelter low-growing plants in the woodland garden.

daceae with petalless yellow and red-anthered flowers in early spring. This, *Viburnum rhytidophyllum* with rough, almost corrugated, foliage, and *Viburnum henryi*, a contrast with glossy leaves and more elegant form, were all introduced in the early 1900s when E.H. Wilson travelled to China for Veitch's nursery, although the latter had earlier been discovered by and named for Augustine Henry. Near by the rare *Lonicera maackii podocarpa*, also brought from China by Wilson, is a graceful spreading small tree with scented yellowish-white flowers, followed by red berries. It is often assumed that many of Wilson's plants will thrive only in acid soil conditions, but at the Dower House they are growing well in the alkaline soil which in places has pH 7.5 or even 8.

In a garden coloured foliage needs to be used with care; too much in eye-catching sites gives a restless effect. Here, where forest trees make a dark background to form the eastern, southern and western boundaries, coloured, variegated and golden leaves bring contrast and make pockets of light in dark corners. Immediately above the orchard wall a specimen *Acer pseudoplatanus* 'Brilliantissimum' is a focus from the house, its young leaves almost pink in April; the variegated form of the cornelian cherry (*Cornus mas* 'Variegata') stands to the north-west. A group of *Cornus alba* 'Spaethii' and golden-leaved *Sambucus racemosa* 'Plumosa Aurea', a young tree of *Robinia pseudacacia* 'Frisia' raised in Holland before the last war but which has still to flower, golden-leaved berberis and *Physocarpus opulifolius* 'Luteus', the leaves of which retain their pale gold through the whole summer, are all placed discreetly. A variegated silver elm grows near shrub roses in the south-east corner. The variegated elder, *Sambucus nigra* 'Pulverulenta', has leaves mottled and striped in cream. In October a hawthorn becomes draped with a curtain of buttercup-yellow, the twisting climber *Celastrus orbiculatus* reaching high into its branches. A place has been found for *Berberis temolaica*, a shrub so difficult to propagate that it is rarely seen in gardens; the glaucous young leaves, ageing in late summer to purplish-brown, are beautiful and unusual.

Island beds allow trees and shrubs to be seen from different angles, and drifts of perennials carpet the ground. In spring Lenten hellebores, anemones and hepaticas, *Hacquetia epipactis* with golden flowers, dentarias and the perennial honesty (*Lunaria rediviva*) make strong clumps; later hostas, double-flowered

herbaceous geraniums, *Calamintha nepetoides* and tall cimicifuga prolong interest when many flowering shrubs are over. In early autumn the leaves of small euphorbias turn bronze and golden-yellow, blending with the scarlet autumn colouring of euonymus and maple. In such a garden there is always space for more good plants. Sir David and Lady Scott's gardening partnership ensures new development. Lady Scott has further enriched this garden area with uncommon smaller 'woodlanders', which thrive and spread in the soil, where after forty years of organic and natural mulches from falling leaves there is a top-layer of hospitable loam. Against the south-facing wall plants seem to have escaped from the alpine beds beyond. Lady Scott's own *Helleborus lividus* hybrid 'Boughton Beauty' and Ken Aslet's more tender form find a place here.

For forty years Sir David has assembled the 'best' woody plants; for as long Lady Scott, at first as Valerie Finnis, well-known throughout the horticultural world, has developed her judgement of 'quality' smaller plants. Today at the Dower House both the gardens and the packed area in front of the house reflect the disciplined choices these two experienced and knowledgeable gardeners constantly make.

OPPOSITE
A close planting of bronze-flowered fritillaries, golden feverfew and Lenten hellebores in spring.

Acid-loving *Rhodohypoxis baurii* from South Africa thrive in a stone trough and flower for many weeks.

Stone Cottage

Hambleton, Leicestershire
(Mr John Codrington)

THE GARDEN at Stone Cottage is far from conventional. It differs from many others in three compelling ways. Firstly the design, imposed on a basic rectangle stretching north at the back of the house, is intricate and deliberately confusing. What seems at first to be a compartmental system, with paths meeting at right-angles and axial vistas stretching the length of the garden, has been contrived to mislead; off parallel alleys, their ends blocked by hedging, entrances lead to inner secret gardens; sometimes these are completely hidden behind head-high planting screens and at other times they have open views, but movement between areas is restricted by the path layout. John Codrington is a garden designer who studies both linear and aerial perspectives to increase or diminish dimensions and distance – the garden has a maze-like quality, with a difference. Exploration of a traditional labyrinth leads to dead-ends and disappointment; at Stone Cottage, although each corridor or entrance has been planned deliberately to disorientate, each new distraction leads to some concealed enchanted garden area.

Secondly, Mr Codrington is an artist who allows abundant planting to dominate and dictate the design. Flower and foliage colour and texture make patterns; the garden is composed of a series of pictures, revealed successively on any garden tour. One path is edged with flowers of blue and mauve, in another area pale yellows predominate, softly enriched by golden and variegated foliage plants, and another is for white flowers, set off with grey and silvery leaves. It is the growing plants and not the pathways which seem to delineate separate garden 'rooms', and their control and discipline is so subtly done that even an important vista, such as that at the north of the garden overlooking Rutland Water, seems completely natural and uncontrived. A seat is placed so that, where a gap in the thick woodland allows, the view is caught and framed by spreading branches. This is the only place in the garden where outer defences are breached; elsewhere the garden looks inwards – a green jungle remote from the countryside and the world beyond its boundaries.

Thirdly, and this is quickly apparent, many of the plants at Stone Cottage are far from ordinary. Mr Codrington, an army officer for twenty years, travelled widely and collected seeds, bulbs and plants as he journeyed. An amateur botanist, he has a keen and perceptive eye for an unusual plant; he gives each individual specimen the conditions it enjoys and then allows it to spread and, he hopes, multiply. At the same time many of the plants are British natives: Queen Anne's lace (*Anthriscus sylvestris*), Welsh poppy, leucojum – plants which the tidy gardener might call weeds, but which he uses as 'natural' ground cover between exotic shrubs. His knowledge and enthusiasm are unusual; he notices the detail of each plant and can speak of it intimately.

Mr Codrington's sister, the late Mrs Doyne, first came to Stone Cottage in 1952. The garden, except for the front area which faces the village street, was very exposed; an old lonicera hedge on the boundary was the only protection from the north-east winds. Mr Codrington helped her to plant trees for shelter: willows, poplars and evergreen Monterey cypress (*Cupressus macrocarpa*) were planted round the perimeter. Austrian pine (*Pinus nigra*) and Scots pine, some Lawson cypress (named cultivars of *Chamaecyparis lawsoniana*) followed, and later some Italian cypresses were planted, grandchildren of some grown from seed originally brought back from the Garden of Gethsemane in 1925. The soil is a heavy limy clay, rich in nutrients but difficult to cultivate. At the bottom or north end of the garden, beyond an oval farm pond, quick-growing deciduous trees were used to create a woodland canopy under which sweet wood-

ruff, wood anemones, bluebells, cyclamen and hellebores would thrive. Round its edge grow moisture-loving ligularias. When purchased, the garden behind the house consisted of a rectangle of grass with parallel borders round the edges. Now, although some of the inner paths run parallel, the outer perimeter is disguised by curves and promontories of planting. Open lawns merge into narrow shady alleys tightly hemmed in with overhanging trees and luxuriant undergrowth.

The front garden at Stone Cottage faces south; abundant planting in the narrow border at the base of the house walls takes advantage of the warmest site in the garden. An olive brought back from Malta, aromatic-leaved

ABOVE
The view over Rutland Water.

A clump of variegated ground-elder (*Aegopodium podograria* 'Variegata') is surrounded by comfrey (*Symphytum grandiflorum*).

OPPOSITE
Euphorbia polychroma, blue-flowered *Brunnera macrophylla* and pink tulips in spring.

The cottage-garden style seems deceptively simple. Beside a young Chusan palm with distinctive fan-shaped leaves, the Californian poppy, *Romneya trichocalyx*, thrusts its papery white flowers through an undergrowth of dense planting.

Mediterranean myrtle (*Myrtus communis*) and South African bulbs such as amaryllis and nerine, which love to be baked, are packed together. Plants spill out over the path edge, and climbing roses, honeysuckles and vines, and bright-yellow-flowered *Fremontodendron californicum* enjoy the heat. In spring tulips 'White Triumphator' and pink 'Queen of the Bartigons' flower between bushes of 'Hidcote' lavender flanking the central path. The native field geranium (*Geranium pratense*) with pale blue flowers has seeded here to flower later in summer. Purple-flowered honesty and golden-leaved feverfew seed haphazardly near a fence over which ivy grows. Through the handsome wrought-iron gate to the east an overgrown path winds through an old orchard, where spring narcissus, aquilegias, cow-parsley and ox-eye daisies thrive in rough grass which is not cut until July. Under old apple trees, up which a huge species rose has clambered, arching stems of Solomon's seal (*Polygonatum* × *hybridum*) bear dangling white flowers, next to the soft lilac of *Cardamine pentaphyllos* (syn. *Dentaria digitata*). Elsewhere in the garden *Cardamine enneaphyllos* (syn. *Dentaria enneaphyllos*), brought back from the slopes of the Abruzzi in Italy, has creamy flowers and bronze foliage. The uncommon *Smilacina stellata*, the biennial *Smyrnium perfoliatum*, which seeds itself here and elsewhere in the garden, cowslips (*Primula veris*) and *Luzula albida*, a white-flowered windrush, all flourish. Clumps of hellebores include

Oriental poppies and delphiniums.

Beyond are a golden privet and feathery Pfitzer juniper, and round the corner *Acer pseudoplatanus* 'Brilliantissimum', with shrimp-pink leaves in spring, is set off by ground-cover of blue-flowered *Brunnera macrophylla*. Just out of sight is a surprise, a group of orange- and vermilion-flowered roses, the sun-loving brick-red Maltese cross (*Lychnis chalcedonica*), orange *Geum* 'Mrs Bradshaw' and scarlet phlox, all from the 'hot' side of the colour spectrum, in contrast to the cooler greens and yellows which came before. Rose 'Dusky Maiden' has flowers of crimson, but beyond flower colours fade away to misty mauve and purple, increasing the feeling of distance. *Prunus × cistena* has dark purple leaves, and those of *Sambucus nigra* 'Purpurea' are bronze to tone with the greyer foliage of *Rosa glauca*. More pale yellow flowers, a favourite flower colour for Mr Codrington, are contributed by *Aconitum vulparia* (syn. *A. lycoctonum*) and giant cephalaria. *Trifolium pannonicum*, with pinnate green leaves and clover-heads of creamy-white, was brought back from Romania.

Across the garden is a vista to a single jet fountain and an architectural grey-leaved yucca, set in an inner garden where the flowers are white or black. The view back to the house is framed by a pair of evergreen *Osmanthus × burkwoodii* clipped into symmetrical spheres. The path which is almost central to the garden runs down towards the pond and opens out a view across it. The borders by the water are richly planted with moisture-loving large-leaved plants. Rodgersias, rheums, rustling miscanthus, luzulas and bamboos grow luxuriantly; tall umbrellas of giant hogweed (*Heracleum mantegazzianum*) tower above the paths. Pockets of peaty soil make beds for primulas and astilbes. Mr Codrington allows many native flowers to seed: sedge (*Carex pendula*), kingcups (*Caltha palustris*), meadow-sweet (*Filipendula ulmaria*) and purple and yellow loosestrife (*Lythrum salicaria* and *Lysimachia vulgaris*).

Paths lead off at right angles, one paved with diamond-shaped stones, another, narrowing between pale foliage which makes the path seem longer, leading to a statue of St Fiacre. Purple-leaved nut is trained to make an archway, and beyond, the golden foliage of *Philadelphus coronarius* 'Aureus' and a sprinkling of Welsh poppies glow among the greener leaves of comfrey. A return path ends theatrically at a mirror on the wall of a shed, framed by a pair of golden yews, the glass thickly framed in green foliage. Pools of autumn-flowering

H. corsicus, the native *H. viridis*, with green flowers, and *H. foetidus*. The yellow-flowered form of *Iris foetidissima* makes a clump next to brick-red flowers of *Euphorbia griffithii*, and the little annual spurge *E. stricta* seeds everywhere, its foliage golden in autumn. Past a snake-bark maple the path curves northward to emerge onto an open lawn, dominated by *Pinus nigra*. On the corner which juts out *Magnolia × soulangiana* 'Alba Superba' is being invaded by rose 'Maigold', a vigorous climber with bronze-yellow fragrant flowers. More climbing roses clamber into the pine, both 'Crimson Conquest' and the vivid 'Scarlet Fire'. Silver-leaved artichokes are architectural and more good shrubs, including *Prunus laurocerasus* 'Zabeliana' with horizontal-branched growth, are underplanted with lime-green-flowered *Euphorbia amygdaloides robbiae* and a carpet of feathery *E. cyparissias*.

Cyclamen hederifolium and spring *C. repandum* appear under deciduous bushes to right and left, and in one corner are a patch of variegated ground-elder and a clump of perennial honesty (*Lunaria rediviva*). The white and grey garden seems mislaid between the hedges joining the first area of sunny lawn, but is linked to the long axial path, where tall *Juniperus virginiana* 'Skyrocket' introduces formality. Silvery-leaved *Artemisia arborescens*, a form brought back from Crete, feathery *A. canescens*, ballotas, senecios, superb *Lysimachia ephemerum* with translucent spring foliage and creamy-white flower-spikes, white-flowered forms of *Geranium phaeum* and sprawling *Epilobium glabellum* all mingle here; but while the planting is informal, a rectangular pond and low surrounding hedge hold the structure together.

Near the back door an area is screened off for herbs, their running roots contained in a chequerboard pattern of paving stones. Not all are for culinary use: warning labels identify plants with poisonous properties. Monkshood (*Aconitum napellus*), thorn-apple (*Datura stramonium*) and henbane (*Hyoscyamus niger*) grow close by. To the west of the house a gravelled area, once concealing a way to the garage and a turning place, has become a bed where seedlings of wild and garden flowers grow haphazardly between grasses such as *Briza maxima*. Pink-flowered corn-cockle (*Agrostemma githago*) now rarely seen in corn-fields, and the blue cornflower (*Centaurea cyanus*), with granny's mop (the common

Aquilegia vulgaris) are all happy here. The bright red native field poppy (*Papaver rhoeas*) springs up annually beside the Californian eschscholzia, *E. californica*, which also self-seeds in the dry, sunny conditions, producing its papery poppy-flowers in tones of orange and yellow. Neither of these poppies will 'naturalize' in grass. The annual *Nigella damascena* perpetuates itself, its inflated pale brown seed pods almost as decorative as the bright love-in-the-mist blue flowers of the summer months. Many of the hardy geraniums seed and spread here, carpeting the ground next to the annual larkspur (*Consolida regalis regalis*), yellow perennial foxgloves (*Digitalis lutea*) and the poached-egg flower (the little quick-growing annual *Limnanthes douglasii*). Nor is the gravel dull earlier in the season, as both the mauve-lilac *Crocus tommasinianus* and golden-flowered *C. chrysanthus* open in February to make patches of colour in the pale gravel. Perhaps this gravel 'bed' where wild and introduced plants jostle each other in unplanned abandon best represents Mr Codrington's garden philosophy: he allows plants to create the natural effects he wants rather than disciplining them to a predetermined pattern. Certainly Stone Cottage garden expresses his enjoyment in making all his plants seem perfectly acclimatized. He also makes his type of gardening seem simple; this is far from the case. Its success depends on his deep knowledge of both native flora and the conditions in which they and his introduced 'rarities' will thrive.

BELOW LEFT
White ox-eye daisies and meadow crane's-bills have sown themselves in the lavender hedges which line the path to the front door.

BELOW RIGHT
In the white garden fan-shaped leaves of the hardy Chusan palm (*Trachycarpus fortunei*) look exotic beside native Scotch briar (*Rosa pimpinellifolia*).

Renishaw Hall

Derbyshire
(Mr and Mrs Reresby Sitwell)

BEFORE Sir George Sitwell set about completely redesigning the gardens at Renishaw, a task which he never completed, there was just a sloping lawn to the south of the house which carried the eye to the river valley below and on to Bolsover on a high distant ridge. Today hanging terraces and white statues frame a view over an eighteenth-century-style landscape lake, its limits obscured by woodland planting in Brownian style. These gardens are Sir George's enduring artistic creation and today, in the care of his grandson, Mr Reresby Sitwell, remain almost exactly as he left them.

Other ambitious details, long pursued in abstract and in practice, were never achieved. From wooden towers constructed for the purpose in the lake and on the hill, he would measure and survey. Schemes to introduce glass fountains, aqueducts in rubble, gigantic figures, cascades through the woods, stone boats and dragons in the water of lake and pool, and blue-stencilled white cows 'to give distinction to the landscape' were never realized. The water garden itself was completed by his grandson and a high fountain jet in the centrally placed swimming-pool was added only in 1967.

Sir George Sitwell's book *On the Making of Gardens* (1909) was recently reprinted in *Hortus Sitwellianus* (Michael Russell, 1984), together with a foreword by his son Sacheverell and a description of the gardens at Renishaw today by his grandson Reresby. Sir George's book is necessary reading for any garden designer. There is nothing amateurish about his decisive advice. His words echo those of Leon Battista Alberti in the fifteenth century; what he writes is an experience of the greatest Italian gardens, seen through the eyes of a cultivated Englishman of the Edwardian era.

Sir George wrote of 'the great secret of success in garden-making, the profound platitude that we should abandon the struggle to make nature beautiful round the house and should rather move the house to where nature is beautiful ... The garden must be considered not as a thing by itself, but as a gallery of foregrounds designed to set off the soft hues of the distance; it is nature which should call the tune, and the melody is to be found in the prospect of blue hill or shimmering lake, or mystery-haunted plain, in the aerial perspective of great trees beyond the boundary, in the green cliffs of leafy woodland which wall us in on either hand.'

Other senses besides sight — hearing, smell and touch — should be in harmony with surroundings. 'Straight lines, according to Ruskin, are valuable because they suggest restraint and set off by their monotony the freedom and variety of natural curves: it follows that the flowers will be fairer in formal beds, wild foliage when opposed to massive masonry.'

Renishaw stands 250 feet (76 metres) above sea-level, with commanding views to the south over the Rother valley, and beyond as far as Bolsover. Built originally in the early seventeenth century as a gabled and battlemented manor house for the Sitwell family, the house was extended to east and west at the end of the eighteenth century and, since the final ballroom addition of 1808, has seen little change. Classical stables of 1795 hide a walled garden area to the west, but the only real pleasure grounds which existed before the early years of this century were on raised ground to the south-west, where a lime avenue ran southwards at right-angles to the house. Sir George Sitwell made his terraced garden overlooking the valley on a southern slope of lawn and parkland, engaging unemployed local labourers to dig out a lake of 17 acres (6.9 hectares). Renishaw perhaps owes more to the true spirit of the Italian Renaissance than any other garden in England today. Quite different from the monumental Italianate gardens of Barry and Nesfield, the formal area, almost symmetrically aligned, depends for its success

OPPOSITE
The Gothic Eagle House and flowering magnolia in the upper garden.

175

on careful restraint in stonework, good statues (imported by Sir George from Italy), the framework of yew hedges with openings flanked by grouped pyramids of yew, and glimpses of quiet reflecting water. The garden terraces are essentially a foreground frame to the idealized landscape beyond, itself enhanced by its Brownian lake where water disappears behind clumped trees. Two main pairs of statues – those of Diana and Neptune on the first level (said to be the work of the eighteenth-century sculptor Caligari), and the lower 'giants' – face outwards towards the view, and by their positioning narrow and contain the vista.

In *On the Making of Gardens* Sir George Sitwell attaches so much importance to the actual setting of the garden that he considers one should be sited only where there is a beautiful prospect. In this he followed the teachings of Alberti. In imitation of classical authors, Alberti recommended a hillside site for a villa, for the views 'that overlook the city, the owner's land, the sea or a great plain and familiar hills and mountains ... in the foreground there should be the delicacy of gardens.' It was Alberti who in his treatise *De Re Aedificatoria* first stressed the importance of the relationship of house, garden and landscape, which should form an integrated unit. The main layout at Renishaw seems partly early Renaissance in character, with flat or slightly sloping enclosures divided up into square or rectangular divisions by green walls of yew and terraced stonework, with axial and cross-axial vistas and a central circular pool. But as well as seeming to be a series of architectural rooms excluding the house, the garden encompassed the view. In this it anticipated the essential linking of house to landscape which epitomized the later Baroque garden designs, where eventually the garden merged into the countryside beyond. During the early years of this century Sir George visited most of the old garden sites in Italy; Renishaw seems to be a happy blend of their developing garden style, spanning the fifteenth, sixteenth and seventeenth centuries. One has only to turn to his descriptions of whole gardens or of their architectural detail to trace some of the inspiration behind Renishaw: the Villa d'Este with hanging terraces and play of water; the Isolotto

and lemon garden in the Boboli gardens; the great statues representing the cities of Lucca and Florence reclining at the feet of Fame blowing into a shell, which preside over the steep hillside garden at Garzoni; the soaring cypress avenue and steps at Crivelli; Gamberaia with formal parterre and green high-sided bowling alley framing a view across the valley of the Arno and Florence to the Apennines beyond – all show something of relevance.

But Sir George absorbed more than Italian architectural detail. Some quotations from his book express his vision. In his age, as he points out in the introduction, Sedding, Blomfield and Inigo Thomas preached a return to a formal framework for a garden, based on the Italian ideal as formulated during the high Renaissance. 'You can't hope to persuade us that nature built the house; why insult our understanding by pretending that nature made the garden?' A new style of gardening attempted to reconcile the formal design of the architect with the rival merits of natural planting. Sir George planted a strictly architectural garden framework especially to relate his house in the foreground to the idealized eighteenth-century landscape he created beyond.

Today, although pylons march across the valley beyond the terraces at Renishaw, the southern view remains almost as he left it. Fortunately when still a young man (he inherited in 1860 at the age of two) Sir George employed Henry Milner, author of *Art and Practice of Landscape Gardening* (1890) to plant a screen of woodland to disguise two main

railway lines, an ironworks and a colliery, and today this woodland is an essential part of the modern landscape.

To the north of the park, Sheffield housing estates creep over the summit of the hill, but a grove of beech trees near the house gives privacy as well as wind protection. On the main approach chestnuts have been planted to form an avenue and partly to screen the 'landscape' golf course which covers the hill

TOP
Beyond a pink-flowering chestnut statues of an Amazon and a warrior guard the entrance to the holly walk.

ABOVE
Acanthus spirosus and solid clipped yews flank entrances to the upper garden compartments.

177

sloping northwards below the house. The bleak, austere house has a romantic appeal which turns to something more contained and domestic on the south. Here, using Sir George's frame of yew hedges for dark background, borders are filled with mixed planting. The terraced gardens lie between a protective wing of dark woodland to the east, where oaks, sweet chestnuts and beech make a canopy for snowdrops, bluebells and seeding balsam. An avenue of hollies, watched over by a pair of statues of an Amazon and a warrior, penetrates eastwards into the dark wood.

To the west, a steep bank forms the boundary to Sir George's formal garden. Here a lime avenue tops the ridge, running southwards to a statue of an angel, originally from a Genoese garden. Beyond, the top lawn is planted informally with shrubs and trees. John Evelyn is known to have advised 'Mr Justice' Sitwell, another George, on the planting of avenues in the last quarter of the seventeenth century. A Gothic temple, once glassed in as an aviary, makes a focal point with a centrally placed Italian well-head. An English oak planted in 1815 to commemorate Waterloo towers above more recent planting of maples, a dawn redwood (*Metasequoia glyptostroboides*) and *Ginkgo biloba*, a tulip tree, a davidia, a mulberry and assorted rhododendrons, which can grow in the slightly acidic soil. Old robinias and laburnum make a shelter for a newly placed armillary sphere, and several good shrubs such as the late-flowering *Aesculus parviflora*, deutzias, white-stemmed rubus and philadelphus will mature into good groups.

From the terrace the main features of the great Italian garden design are visible. On the level lawn where herbaceous borders are backed by dividing yew there are further lateral enclosures to west and east, known respectively as the First and Second Candles from the three-tiered fountains of pink Verona marble which are placed at their central points. A cross-view between pyramids of yew includes the fountains and terminates to the east with the holly walk deep into the wood. Below, the second terrace with wide ornamental pool, glimpsed between Neptune and Diana standing as sentinels on the main staircase, is also split into three yew-hedged enclosures, with cross-vistas edged with giant yew pyramids arranged in threes. To the west the buttressed terraced garden has a raised walk, a long bed supported by sandstone walls against the bank above. To the east the water garden, where a moat almost surrounds the simple and effective planting of

Eucryphia glutinosa which flowers in August, is sheltered by lilacs on the far side. The final vista, between the statues of giants placed as a pair above steep semicircular steps, allows a glimpse of the lake shining below.

On the top terrace the grey Gothic-style house is softened with a curtain of plants. *Magnolia grandiflora, Cytisus battandieri*, jasmine and camellias are pruned back against the walls. Great cylinders of holly make buttresses guarding the French windows and, with domes of skimmia, *Osmanthus decorus* and choisya, anchor the great house on to the terrace.

In the First Candle box-edged beds contain varied planting, planned by Mr Reresby Sitwell and his wife for interest through the summer. In fact, Sir George – although cautious about flowers which might distract from an overall appreciation and himself totally uninterested to the point of disliking them – recognized their contribution. His son Sir Osbert described Sir George's belief that a garden was 'a place of rest and peace, and in no way intended for a display of blossoms . . . such flowers as might be permitted had . . . not to draw attention to themselves . . . but to form vague pointillist masses of colour that could never detract from the view, and to infuse into the air a general sweetness never to be identified.' He did commission drawings from Gertrude Jekyll for flower-bed planting. She, perhaps remembering how the Italian gardens she visited in her youth were often bedded out with bright annuals which never appeared too garish in the strong Italian sunlight, designed beds of orange marigolds for Sir George, but probably never visited Renishaw to see this grand Italian conception in the grey Derbyshire landscape. Her plans were never executed. Today the planting round the fountain includes shrub roses such as the modern 'Constance Spry' and 'Nevada', pink 'Complicata', regal lilies, ceanothus and grey-leaved tamarisks; grey-toned foliage and pale flower colours.

To the east, the design is more complicated, with the Second Candle forming a focus to a rose garden (once with box-edged beds, but now these are less formally placed in the grass). A spreading pink chestnut stands to the north and behind it a fine fern-leaved beech (*Fagus sylvatica* 'Asplenifolia') makes a background at the eastern end of the house, beyond the ballroom. An oak tree on a mound was planted in memory of Clinker, a famous racehorse from Sir Sitwell Sitwell's stud at the end of the eighteenth century. Sir George's original design for this area includes a series of sunken

On the lower terrace a vertical jet of water is framed by the solid yew pyramids which flank each entrance to the central pool garden.

gardens, but for ease and economy of maintenance the arrangement has been simplified. A secret garden remains, now dominated by tall shrubs, and hidden steps lead down to the lower level.

A grass walk stretches across the whole garden from east to west, a wall bed under the supporting walls. Cotoneasters flank steps, and iris and peonies grow in profusion as a foreground to wall-shrubs and roses. Round the central pool more beds of mixed shrubs and perennials match the water's shape, and planting remains below the horizontal line of yew hedging. In the buttress garden pink and crimson roses mingle with purple-leaved berberis and trail on different levels. To describe the effect, we can quote Sir George himself: 'So, if it is to be a rose garden, do not choose these stunted, unnatural, earth-loving strains, which have nothing of vigour and wildness in them, nor banish other flowers which may do homage to the beauty of a rose as courtiers to a queen. Let climbing roses drop in a veil from the terrace and smother with flower-spangled embroidery the garden walls ...'

Sir George thought and wrote about the importance of water in the garden. He studied the whole art of shadowed water, pointing out the value of dark evergreens as a background. Equally, he realized that by cutting off the lateral rays of the sun round a water-surface the water appears deeper and darker. The moated garden at Renishaw, not completed until after he had moved to Italy in the 1920s, is unique. An 'island' (actually a peninsula) surrounded by thick yew on the inner rim demonstrates his theories.

In every well-planned garden there are many harmonies of appropriateness – in relation, convenience, proportion or scale, form, colour and historic style – so subtle as to escape individual notice; being fused together, they rise above the threshold of consciousness in a vague and general sense of ordered beauty.

Hodnet Hall

Hodnet, Market Drayton, Shropshire
(Mr and Mrs Algernon Heber-Percy)

UNTIL 1870 the family lived in a fine half-timbered Elizabethan house in the valley, already their second substantial residence on land owned by unbroken inheritance since the Norman Conquest. Salvin was employed to build the third house, the House on the Hill, from designs based on the great Elizabethan mansion at nearby Condover. The old Tudor house now forms the nucleus for tea-rooms and gardens below.

The approach to Hodnet carries the visitor along a well-kept entrance drive from the east and passes the churchyard (near which, under the shade of the beech avenue, Bishop Heber composed his hymns before his appointment to the See of Calcutta, where he died prematurely three years later at the age of forty-three). Massed *Rhododendron* 'Cunningham's White', *R. ponticum* and hydrangeas give colour in spring and late summer respectively, but the entrance seems almost secret, with no hint of the extensively planted water gardens and steeply descending open terraces beyond. Southwards, towards the car-park, a beech avenue still stands which marked the approach to the old house in the lower valley. A tall weeping beech to the east deserves notice.

The present owner is Mr Algernon Heber-Percy, and the garden itself was mainly made by his father. Since taking over he has completely remodelled the Hall, drastically reducing it in size for more convenient living by cutting off the original roof and top floor. A vast west wing projecting northwards now makes an attractive open-roofed garden, where an Italian well-head is surrounded by plants which twine and clamber on the old walls, and the formal gardens in the yew enclosure now form the site of a family swimming-pool and recreation area.

A lime avenue stretches north from the grand front entrance; a circular stone-edged bed and fountain of Victorian style placed there in 1955 is formal. Today the view is enhanced by part of a free-standing classical portico, brought from Apley Castle and erected in 1966 in memory of Brigadier Heber-Percy by his family and friends. It stands in open parkland silhouetted against the northern sky.

From the south terrace of the great house the ground falls very steeply to the lake, itself part of a series of hanging ponds to the west of the house. From inside the drawing-room the main garden planting is almost invisible, but the eye is carried instead to the 1656 dovecote of stone and brick, standing on the steep slope of parkland beyond the river valley, and beyond to Long Mynd and the Shropshire hills around Church Stretton to the south of Shrewsbury.

Ferns, grasses and sculptured gunnera leaves reflected in the stream offer contrasts of texture and colour.

Until 1921 a single broad terrace ran along this south front, and a formal rose garden entirely enclosed by a yew hedge lay on flat terrain to the west. Today more terraces with traditional herbaceous borders of peonies and perennials and interesting wall-shrubs such as *Illicium floridanum* and the Moroccan broom (*Cytisus battandieri*) are backed by balustrades with tumbling wisteria and honeysuckle. Rose-beds of the scarlet floribunda 'Lilli Marlene' are framed with lavender bushes. A large *Halesia monticola* and a hamamelis dominate the top of the steeply falling terrace, leading the eye from the formal theme, appropriate to a flat terrace on which a great house sits, to the more informal planting which links the terraces to the water landscape and countryside.

In 1923 a lake was made below the house by throwing a curved dam across the end of the valley, and the water – now canalized – flows on to a deep pool known as the Horse Wash near the stables beyond. From there a further series of pools became the foundation for an area of natural garden compartments, which lie in the lowest part of the valley near the remaining black and white timber buildings of the old Tudor farmhouse. Steep steps descend to the water's edge from the broad terraces to the south of the house, but the planting at the sides remains informal, leading the eye into the natural landscape across the lake, and to the west into an open meadow lying under hanging woodland on the northern slope. Oaks, beech, lime and sycamores predominate, and on the skyline Scots pines and larch give protection. Up the valley, where a water garden has been developed, much of the planting around the water remains hidden from afar, so that the whole effect is natural, and wild flowers flourish at the wood edge;

Giant leaves of *Gunnera manicata*, water-lilies and willows in the foreground frame a view across the lake to the house and steeply falling terraces.

campion and speedwell are succeeded by fox-gloves, rose-bay willow herb and bracken, and there is no evidence of the selective chemicals so often used today. All the more credit goes to the management of this extensive garden, where four gardeners (helped by the owner) maintain 60 acres (some 24 hectares) to a high standard. Groups of grey poplar (*Populus canescens*) and silver birch are planted along the water's edge. Many published photographs of Hodnet gardens stress the rioting colours of assorted rhododendrons and azaleas, but the reality is much more subtle. The most vivid colours are hidden from immediate view and a preponderance of soft primrose, pink and white flowers – the preference of the present owner – softly blend into a natural landscape, where even the introduction of foreign tree exotics such as nothofagus remains discreet.

A series of three broad pools on rising levels takes the visitor to the western limit and a return pathway on the south leads through a beech wood, carpeted with bluebells in late spring. Between each pool bridges or stepping stones allow access to either side, and planting becomes more elaborate. Water cascades and small tributaries provide moisture, and in the acid soil low-growing rhododendrons and candelabra primula, trilliums and giant king-cups are succeeded by summer-flowering hostas, astilbes, *Iris ensata* (syn. *I. kaempferi*) and mimulus. Ferns grow in shady corners, and giant rhubarb and *Gunnera manicata* give interesting foliage texture, form and colour. Small ornamental maples and cherries add height and form and, with more domestic shrubs such as spiraea and potentilla, are reflected in the water. A raised bed of hardy

agapanthus makes a sheet of blue in late summer. All the planting is on a grand scale, with sweeps and drifts of each different flower or foliage colour.

To the south of the main stretch of water below the house willows are grouped with suckering native dogwood. The main planting of the terraces on the northern steep bank is most easily seen from here, and to the west the sloping meadows are covered with daffodils in spring. On the terraces Japanese maples, rhododendrons with attractive foliage such as *R. yakushimanum*, yellow-flowered *RR*. 'Remo', 'Tortoiseshell Champagne' and 'Tortoiseshell Wonder', are mixed informally with berberis, heathers, kalmias and pieris, all of which thrive in this acid soil, but summer-flowering shrubs have been added in order to keep interest and colour. Many of the early-flowering deciduous azaleas later contribute fiery autumn leaf colours.

Towards the east small pools are lined with iris, rodgersia, candelabra primula, astilbes, ferns and lysichitons and dominated by giant gunnera leaves. The Horse Wash pool is overhung with laburnum trees and a large English walnut, and on its banks *Primula* 'Postford White' and white astilbe follow each other in flowering succession. Completely changing the garden theme, a nearby bed is planted with delphiniums and philadelphus for late June. Above, on the south slope, shrub roses grow in a garden enclosure sheltered by oak trees, which include a group of American oaks, forms of *Quercus rubra* which colour scarlet in autumn. Trees and shrubs are under-planted with the creeping North American dogwood (*Cornus canadensis*). Elegant rustling

bamboos include *Arundinaria murielae* with bright green canes and arching stems, one of the best species in cultivation, introduced from China by Ernest Wilson in 1913. Near by the more erect *A. viridistriata* from Japan has striking leaf-blades striped in gold and dark green.

Beyond and up steps behind the tea-rooms in the old Tudor house another wooded area is planted with good shrubs and low-growing foliage plants. Groves of Canadian Preston hybrid lilacs, the mahogany-barked *Prunus serrula*, *Magnolia obovata*, sorbus and acers are lightened by the pale foliage of golden philadelphus (*Philadelphus coronarius* 'Aureus') and variegated Asian dogwoods, including both *Cornus controversa* 'Variegata' and *C. alternifolia* 'Argentea' with delicate green and silver leaves. A recently planted group of bronze-green *Mahonia nervosa* catches the eye, and everywhere trilliums, meconopsis and hostas continue this woodland theme.

From here the garden visitor returns northwards along the eastern edge of the garden, and wide steps lead gradually down to more pools and shrubbery planting near the tea-rooms. This pathway, the oldest part of the garden, is lined with gnarled robinia trees and has a good collection of magnolias, planted in 1956–7 and only now beginning to flower freely. Davidias, cercidiphyllum, *Parrotia persica* and cornus are outstanding for autumn colour. Several specimens of *Acer griseum*, with glowing peeling bark, grow near ornamental prunus and malus trees, which contribute spring flowers and good autumn leaf tints.

On the return to the house, before the steep slope, a rose garden of circular shape and formal design has been planned to include other plants which ensure a long flowering season. The outer circle of May-flowering peonies surrounds beds of *Rosa* 'Korresia', with yellow flowers carried freely in June and through much of the summer. The central circular bed of *Hydrangea paniculata* 'Grandiflora' is edged with grey-leaved lavender and *Caryopteris* × *clandonensis*, which has pale blue flowers in later summer. The hydrangea carries its massive panicles of sterile florets, white at first but fading to pinkish, through September and into the autumn. Above, on the slope east of the house, more interesting planting includes a large flowering specimen of the rare Asiatic evergreen *Trochodendron aralioides* and the fragrant white-flowered *Lonicera maackii*, a shrubby honeysuckle from Manchuria.

In the terrible winter of 1981–2 temperatures at Hodnet were the lowest on record. During a prolonged period night temperatures fell very low, temperatures reaching −18.5°F (−28.5°C) on 13 December 1981 and −15°F (−26.8°C) on 10 January 1982.

Many rhododendrons were killed outright, including a number which were part of Mr Heber-Percy's father's original planting. Several specimens of *Magnolia grandiflora* and many other evergreen shrubs were lost, particularly in the valley region, into which frost drained and where it remained. The following year one thousand replacement rhododendrons and other plants were obtained from Reuthe's in Kent, and much new planting has been done since. In a new area below the car-park leading up to the beech avenue Mr Heber-Percy has planted mainly species rhododendrons. Yellow-flowered bushes include *Rhododendron campylocarpum*, *R. cinnabarinum xanthocodon concatenans* group with waxy apricot-yellow bells, and *R. wardii*, from China and named for Kingdon Ward, who first introduced it. Large-leaved Himalayan *R. falconeri eximium* has bell-shaped rose-pink flowers, and *R. falconeri* waxy creamy-yellow flowers with purple blotches, and both have rust- to orange-coloured leaf tomentum to add distinction. Forms of *R. augustinii* with bluish flowers, *R. russatum* with vivid purple-blue clustered flowers and *R. thomsonii* with blood-red flower trusses give colour depth and contrast. This area will take some years to develop its full flower potential, but like the rest of the garden is carefully planned for its maturity.

Roses and lavender surround a central bed of *Hydrangea paniculata* 'Grandiflora'.

Holker Hall

Cark-in-Cartmel, Cumbria
(Mr and Mrs Hugh Cavendish)

HOLKER HALL has been the site of a house since the Prestons owned the land around it and built the first recorded house in about 1604. The present approach follows a gently curving drive through a deer-park, revealing views to Morecambe Bay on the south and west and the misty outlines of Lake District hills to the north, to arrive at a shady south courtyard, where yew and ilex hang over balustrades and the massive west wing completely dominates the prospect. Built just after a disastrous fire of 1871, in deep rose-coloured sandstone, its style is Elizabethan in inspiration, its architectural composition and detail representative of Victorian prosperity. To the east are attached Georgian buildings, but the main wings of the previous houses lay to the north, jutting out at right angles to partly enclose the formal gardens. The north block, refaced in the 1840s, now contains Mr and Mrs Cavendish's private apartments, and has in its fabric traces of the earlier architecture.

The garden, like the house, has passed through many different stages of development. A formal garden was laid out by Sir Thomas Lowther after house improvements of 1720. It is tempting to believe that Sir Thomas may have been influenced by the developing topiary gardens at nearby Levens Hall, which were begun in the last years of the seventeenth century. Formal and compartmental in style, the geometric garden enclosures at Levens fitted round the house, providing sites for parterres and topiary features. Certainly when working on the new gardens at Holker in 1729, Mr Richardson seemed to have aspirations towards being a gentleman and not a working gardener, perhaps considering himself equal in status to Guillaume Beaumont, the Frenchman who was then designing the Levens park and gardens for Colonel Grahme. Bitter complaints from Sir Thomas's steward were relayed to him in London, even over the extra expense incurred by the gardener's eating

habits: 'We shall go to Board wages on Munday next, but if Mr Richardson eats at Holker, yr honr shou'd allow more than 3s p. Week for him, being as he pushes a good knife and Fork.' Started in 1729, the garden was embellished with statues sent by sea from London. All traces of this garden were later swept away as the Landscape fashion decreed that parkland should reach to the windows of the house, matching in style the period and 'modern' Gothic of the east wing introduced by John Carr of York for Lord George Cavendish, Sir Thomas's nephew, in the last quarter of the eighteenth century. Carr also designed a classical temple to ornament the new park, but this was never built. A fine cedar of Lebanon, one of five grown from seed sent home from the Middle East by a friend of Lord George, still survives in the garden.

In the 1840s Holker, now owned by Lord George's grandson, the 7th Duke of Devonshire, was again remodelled, a conservatory added, and the gardens redesigned and enriched by Joseph Paxton, the Duke's gardener and friend. At some stage a lead statue of Inigo Jones, originally at Chiswick House and inherited by the Devonshires with Lord Burlington's title, was placed in the garden. The Italian fountain, a new walled garden to the north of the main road to Barrow-in-Furness, and balustraded terraces (later further altered by Mawson) round the house were part of Paxton's development. He also sent some of the first seeds of monkey puzzle (*Araucaria araucana*), brought back from Chile by William Lobb in 1844. One tree near the house remains from the original planting; the mild climate and very high rainfall, an annual 70 inches (175 centimetres), has proved very suitable for this conifer. Towards the end of the nineteenth century, after fifty years' growth, it was blown over in a gale, and was reinstated with the help of a team of seven shire horses. Later a grove of monkey puzzles was established on the higher slopes near a tall wellingtonia or giant redwood (*Sequoiadendron giganteum*) to bring an exotic touch to the woodland. The latter tree, a native of California, was first introduced in 1853 and may well have been planted at Holker soon after, as the arboretum developed under Paxton's influence.

The already developing woodland at Holker – set against the intensely romantic Lakeland hills as a backdrop, and with rolling pasture stretching to the sea – contained Paxton's rare conifers and, by the end of the nineteenth

century, groves of rhododendrons from Hooker's first journeys to the Himalayas.

Protected from the full force of prevailing south-westerly gales by the farther shore of Morecambe Bay, Holker has a mild climate, with very high rainfall and acid peaty soil, which provides ideal growing conditions not only for conifers, but also for the tender exotics which were being introduced in such numbers from Asia and the southern hemisphere.

Formal gardens round the house must have been altered again after the fire of 1871 and rebuilding of the west wing, but later, after the death of the 8th Duke in 1908, his heir Lord Richard Cavendish and his wife Lady Moyra employed the successful Windermere landscape architect Thomas Mawson to design a rose garden with curving pergola in the outer woodland. Mawson almost certainly was also responsible for alterations to the terraces and gardens between the north and west wings, where high hedges of English yew make a pattern of small enclosures and Irish yews flank steps and entrances, in typical Mawson style; but no definite plans survive in confirmation. However, it seems certain that he was engaged in alterations at Holker when Paxton's orangery was demolished. Already with clients all over the British Isles, and soon to extend his practice abroad, he worked in what he called a 'composite' style, a combination of formal and informal, natural and artificial: 'He could always see where formality should cease and nature hold sway.' At the bottom of a woodland slope, backed by ancient oaks, he set low terraces and a balustraded boundary wall to contain curving south-facing rose-beds. Today Mawson's rose garden survives, its pergola draped with wisteria and a twining Chinese *Schisandra chinensis*. The pergola, overhung by a large strawberry tree (*Arbutus unedo*), hides a *Celastrus orbiculatus* at the back, which has found its way upwards into an old oak, where its curtain of leaves turn golden in autumn.

Both Lord Richard and Lady Moyra were keen gardeners, and although the gardens round the house retained a Victorian flavour, much good planting went on in the woodland setting both before and after the First World War. Lady Moyra, a friend of the Rothschilds

ABOVE LEFT AND RIGHT
The formal summer garden is a contrast to the naturalistic woodland beyond.

OPPOSITE ABOVE
Irish yew, clipped hedges of English yew and groups of hebes give a firm structure.

OPPOSITE BELOW
Standard specimens of *Hydrangea paniculata* 'Grandiflora' mark corners of the formal beds.

at Exbury, planted rhododendrons and camellias, and tender shrubs along the wall on the north-eastern boundary were partly of her choosing, although planting continued after the Second World War when the present Mr Cavendish's mother ran the gardens. The latter added several interesting trees, including the rare Asiatic *Lindera obtusiloba*, and introduced shrub roses such as *Rosa californica* 'Plena' to the formal bedding schemes in front of the north wing. Weeping prunus arranged symmetrically softened the harsh lines of the heavy balustrading and architectural yew shapes. The house – with its park of 120 acres (48.5 hectares) where fallow deer have grazed for two hundred years, and formal and woodland gardens together comprising 22 acres (9 hectares) – was thrown open to the public.

Mr Hugh Cavendish inherited in 1972. He and his wife Grania have greatly extended the woodland planting and completely altered much of the more formal inner gardens. Nevertheless one of the charms of the Holker landscape lies in the recognizably 'period' garden features which are retained. During the four hundred years of occupancy the appearance of the house has radically altered; nevertheless to the expert earlier features are identifiable. Similarly in the two gardens the historian traces developments of style flowing side by side with the history of plant introductions, and observes their intermingling elements.

Circumstances change. Holker Hall now has a large visiting public, who come not only in spring, when flowering rhododendron groves and other shrubs drench the woodland with colour above sloping banks of early crocus and bluebells, but also in the summer holiday months. A new formal garden now lies on an open plat to the north-west, so placed as to be on an axis with the garden entrance from the main southern courtyard. Passing between yew-buttressed beds, now overflowing with mixed plantings of shrub roses, perennials and annuals, the visitor drops down steps to a garden where four grass panels edged by pale limestone are surrounded by beds of carefully graded summer flower colour. Height is given by weeping silver-leaved pears arranged in a central bed of massed lavender, edged with box with an outer circle of germander (*Teucrium chamaedrys*).

Plants around the edge are chosen mainly to flower in summer, when the woodland garden beyond is quiet with green leaf tones; small evergreen shrubs give foliage interest through-

out the year and spring bulbs such as tulip, allium and iris extend the strict colour schemes. To the north-west the view through ornamental gates is to the sea and open sky; here flowers of misty blues and mauves fade into the distance. At the opposite end yellow and white-flowered plants are cool, with blocks of silver santolina and fresh apple-green leaves of *Hebe rakaiensis*. Pale pastel colours in the west border are partly shaded by a hornbeam hedge, where busts of Roman emperors rest in niches, while to the north-east, where a new beech hedge marks the boundary, flowers in 'hot' yellow, red, purple and crimson are graded in sequence. Blocks of box surround sorbus – both *Sorbus* 'Joseph Rock' and *S. cuspidata* 'Sessilifolia' – and grey-leaved thorn, *Crataegus schraderiana*, growing in the borders. The trees are arranged in regular order. Bushes of Portugal laurel to be clipped into topiary umbrella shapes now flank the gravel paths. Seventeenth-century in inspiration, and in its formality perhaps close to the garden which Sir Thomas Lowther made to complement his building

stairway at Shrublands, this feature at Holker provides a Victorian focus. Moisture-loving exotics, kalmias, clethras and other evergreens thicken the dense planting and provide flower colour and scent in season. A row of fastigiate Italian cypresses, specimens of *Cupressus sempervirens*, bay, and a fine specimen of *Ilex latifolia* add to the mystery. At the top the view opens out, woodland glades stretch east and north on gently sloping ground, and an old sycamore avenue gives direction to informal planting. A bank has recently been planted with specimens of dogwood, even the American hybrids of *Cornus florida* thriving here in the mild climate. Sorbus species and cultivars, *Tilia henryana* (a Wilson introduction from his 1901 expedition to China), the shagbark hickory from eastern North America (*Carya ovata*), and birch with coloured barks all thrive among old oak trees and beech. Grass is cut at informal levels and wild flowers are being encouraged to seed and join existing naturalized daffodils and martagon lilies. Planting is in groves so that as trees mature contrasting areas of shade and open sunlight will allow long views and distant vistas. Above, by the roadside wall, new planting is designed to complement earlier and well-established plants. Fine magnolias, evergreen *Umbellularia californica* with aromatic leaves, scented clethra, *Osmanthus yunnanensis* with olive-green leaves and introduced by George Forrest from China in 1923, hoherias from New Zealand, and winter-flowering scented honeysuckle thrive in the shelter. Near the group of monkey puzzles a large-leaved *Cornus controversa* introduces tabulated architectural form.

Descending again past Mawson's rose garden on the lower slopes there is a wealth of exotic planting, some mature specimens and some newly placed. Stewartias, styrax, zelkova, fine cercidiphyllums, catalpa and rhododendron species and hybrids are more thickly planted in the lower garden, and island beds allow planting of smaller shrubs and bulbs. Knowledgeable and enthusiastic owners give a new spirit to old planting, and thinning, pruning and feeding gives new life to established groves, where planting must now be more than a hundred years old. The gardens at Holker are full of contrast but do not stand still. The formal gardens near the house and the arboretum beyond seem equally well in hand, all set for new centuries of progress to be shared with an increasingly interested and informed visiting public.

White *Lavatera* 'Mont Blanc' and ornamental cabbages provide colour and interest in the annual borders.

alterations of 1720, the garden design makes use of modern plants to enhance its attraction without losing its historical flavour. Its placing, conception and execution all seem perfectly attuned to the house and inner terraces, and mark Mr and Mrs Cavendish's developing interest in gardening detail. Mr Vernon Russell-Smith and Miss Jane Fearnley-Whittingstall also helped with the planting plan. Through a trellised archway beyond the beech hedge, roses grow on tetrapods round a croquet-lawn. More formal planting in blocks of pale colour frames the windows and doorways of the north wing, and a smaller garden beyond for sitting in. A veranda is draped with *Vitis coignetiae*, wisteria and summer jasmine, and more trelliswork arches painted in slate-grey establish a formal rhythm.

Beyond, in total contrast and hidden by the old monkey puzzle, dark ilex and *Rhododendron arboreum*, steep cobbled and stone steps lead up to the Italian fountain and the statue of Inigo Jones at a higher level. Italianate in architectural style, with hints of Barry's masterly

Levens Hall

Kendal, Cumbria
(Mr and Mrs C.H. Bagot)

No other park or garden in England except perhaps Hampton Court has retained its original features from 1690 until the present day. For three hundred years the famous topiary gardens, where nine miles (14.5 kilometres) of trim boxwood edge the flower-beds surrounding 'bushes cut into globes and cones, or even judges' wigs and grotesque birds' in green and golden yew, have remained virtually as designed by M. Guillaume Beaumont. He lived on until 1741, in failing health, so towards the end of his life he will have experienced much of the strange beauty which these textured shapes display – the enchanting accidents of light and shade we experience today. Colonel James Grahme, the keeper of James II's Privy Purse, bought (or received in settlement of a gambling debt) the estate from his kinsman Alan Bellingham in 1688. Letters dated 1864 show that Colonel Grahme was a keen gardener and friend of John Evelyn, and that he and M. Beaumont were already involved in developing the gardens at Bagshot for the King before he fled into exile. Together the Colonel and Beaumont, as much a friend as an employee, devoted the next few years to making Levens into one of the finest examples of late-seventeenth-century garden architecture. Not only are the garden and park preserved today, but letters and garden accounts from 1689 to 1729 exist to give a vivid picture of how they were envisaged and completed.

The grey stone house of Levens Hall, built during successive periods around the central thirteenth-century pele tower, lies along the western side of the main A6 leading north from Lancaster to Kendal. Inside the garden a high wall hides any view to the deer park to the east. Described by West in 1790, in his *Guide to the Lakes*, as 'the sweetest spot that Fancy can imagine', the park was laid out at the same period. It is dominated by the avenue of oaks, which stand on a steep escarpment overlooking the winding valley of the river Kent, but groves of Scots pine and Spanish chestnut strengthen and broaden the linear effect, and groups of sycamores soften the contours of the parkland. Later William Sawrey Gilpin, the great advocate of the Picturesque, described Levens Park as 'A happy combination of everything that is lovely and great in landskip'; and perhaps we can see why Gilpin compares this remote landscape to the wooded cliff high above the river Wye at Persefield, described in his *Essay on the Picturesque* (1782): 'Wild, rugged, gloomy and precipitous, an example of untamed nature to epitomize the sublime, only the straight line of trees shows evidence of man's mastery over the wild landscape and distant lakeland hills.' The avenue stretches east and then turns sharply northwards to dominate

The gardens are famous for the fantastic topiary shapes in yew and box, some of which are nearly three hundred years old.

FAR LEFT
In the north-east garden a spiralling boxwood shape marks a corner of a flower-bed, part of a group centred round a maidenhair tree (*Ginkgo biloba*).

LEFT
Dark shapes cast shadows on the lawn beyond the cedar.

the shape and contours of the immediate foreground in this bleak northern countryside. Although it is separated from the house and garden by the road, the historical unity of the estate, apart from its romantic setting, makes it imperative to ensure its preservation. In 1969 the park and avenue were threatened by a motorway link road, but largely owing to the efforts of Mr Robin Bagot, the father of the present owner, the line of the four-lane highway was successfully diverted to leave the trees unharmed, and the final viewing point over the river valley remains unspoilt.

Unfortunately the archives reveal nothing of Beaumont's French origins or of his early life before his work with Colonel Grahme began. Since he was French it has often been inferred that if not a pupil of Le Nôtre, he must at the very least have been a gardener in his style. In the intimacy of the Levens garden, however, there is no hint of the vast dramas of Vaux-le-Vicomte or Versailles, where avenues radiate from flat parterres and march across the landscape, making alleys in the thick French woodland. Kip's engravings show us many English estates adapted to the French fashion, of which but a handful remain recognizable today. Wrest and Bramham, the water canals at the recently restored Westbury Court, avenues remaining at Boughton and the form outlines at St Paul's Waldenbury all date from this period and display the French influence. The more domestic Melbourne, with cross-axes of yew walks and fine statuary, relates more closely to Beaumont's plans for Levens. In this northern garden broad terraces, linked by paths and cross-vistas, mark a horizontal pattern. Hedges of yew and box further com-

partmentalize the garden, and a beech alley, now 15 feet (4.5 metres) high and wide, stretches down the centre, framing an old cedar to the north and opening out to a central rondel where arches allow views to east and west, the latter extending over the semicircular look-out above the bastion. Under the beech a spring-flowering carpet of wild garlic suppresses weeds. Originally a holly hedge extended east along the edge of a sunken bowling green, but here today double herbaceous borders line the broad grass path and separate the lower garden from the old orchard to the north. To the west of the great beech rondel a new line of cordon apples makes a screen behind a border of tree peonies. Here *Rosa sericea omeiensis* with translucent red thorns, tradescantia (already introduced in the seventeenth century) and bergamot, and further south shrubs with pale and golden foliage, contrast with thrusting Irish yews. In Beaumont's day each geometric separate garden had its function: in layout it was almost a replica of Lawson's garden plan in *New Orchard and Garden* (1618) for a typical seventeenth-century manor house. Topiary, parterres, orchards and herbs all have their compartments; their construction and the building of the protecting outer walls are fully documented by the contemporary correspondence and accounts. Against the high west-facing boundary wall, the siting of which called for rerouting of the main road, Beaumont planted espalier fruit, and trained pears and apples still make an architectural and leafy background to a modern planting of shrubs and hardy perennials.

To the north the boundary of the forecourt

is a stone palisade, first planned with a pattern approved by Grahme: the 'Pedystool' for it was cut from stone in 1694. Today modern tree planting inside the court includes a cedar, a variegated tulip tree and *Cercidiphyllum japonicum*, while an old twisted mulberry standing near a west gate and a line of robinias (*Robinia pseudacacia*) on the east are from an earlier period. Once elms stood between the carriage entrance beyond the palisade and the river, and the mixed planting of ornamental trees made over the last twenty years needs time to mature. Limes and fine sycamores shelter the house from prevailing south-west winds, and under their canopies a public car park is unobtrusive.

After 1692, until his old age when he suffered from over-indulgence in alcohol, Beaumont spent much of his time away from the estate, advising at other great properties including Longleat, Drayton, Stoneyhurst, Edenhall and Ashton Park. At Levens from 1692 the work went on, often held up by weather, including snowstorms and gales which ripped out newly planted trees. Money for wages and for materials was always short but gradually the

ABOVE
The flame creeper, *Tropaeolum speciosum*, a scarlet-flowered perennial nasturtium, clambers over the topiary shapes.

OPPOSITE AND LEFT
Topiary cut in boxwood and in darker yew gives textural and colour variations without more ephemeral flowers. Beds surrounding the clipped shapes are filled with massed annuals such as *Verbena venosa*.

195

The beech alley, now fifteen feet (4.5 metres) high and wide, is carpeted with wild garlic.

great bastion, as it is called today – perhaps the first ha-ha to be constructed in England (some twenty years before Bridgeman first used one at Stowe) – was constructed on the western perimeter of the garden. This innovation as an architectural device is normally linked with Walpole's description of Kent's use of it. 'He leaped the garden fence, and saw that all nature was a garden' introduces us to the whole conception of the great eighteenth-century landscape park. The ha-ha seems to have been of French origin and was probably first employed as at Levens. A deep ditch and high retaining wall, as its modern name suggests, was proabably used partly as a fortification to prevent the entry of sheep or cattle, but also to allow an unimpeded outward view, 'to take off the odious appearance of confinement and limitation to the eye'. At Levens today, as in 1692, the formal garden layout contrasts and is not intended to blend with the landscape; rather the eye is carried west through an equally regulated avenue of dark sycamores, which during much of the year obscures the vista to Whitbarrow Scar at the edge of the Lakes. A row of sombre Irish yews marks the inner edge of the broad path above the bastion, more reminiscent in style of the raised terraces and walks of an Elizabethan manor than of the eighteenth-century Landscape ideal where gar-

den and countryside would merge as one. Beside the eastern perimeter wall, a wide gravelled terrace reaches for 150 yards (137 metres) to allow a view of topiary shapes near to the house. Although the whole garden area at Levens is only 5 acres (just over 2 hectares), the lavish width and scale of paths and hedges balance with the house and the old cedar (could it have been planted in the 1690s?) which fills a space against its northern gable.

Above all, Levens is world-famous for the beauty and ingenuity of its topiary in both yew and box. Spirals, umbrellas, turned chessmen, cottage loaves, squat and mushroom-like shapes (some like hats on high trunks), appear to be arranged in a haphazard pattern. Other more symmetrical blocks are solid cubes with straight tops and sides. Angles, curves and flat planes of textured foliage reflect light from different angles. Through most of the seasons the densely set yew and box foliage makes a tapestry pattern where young leaves contrast with those that are darker and more mature, so that even the most solid and almost ungainly shapes yield an ever-changing diversity. Some are clipped to take the form of human figures, and one seems to wear a crown. Queen Elizabeth is surrounded by a group of her Maids of Honour, and topiary jugs are said to allude to a local Levens brew called 'Morocco'. Under a mounded yew shape resembling a judge's wig, a comfortable seat provides a resting place. In autumn streamers of scarlet-flowered nasturtium, *Tropaeolum speciosum*, fling themselves over the highest yew hedges, and the native form of Solomon's seal, *Polygonatum multiflorum*, has seeded itself in the gravel paths to give an unplanned air. This sort of gardening, strictly formal and regimented as it must be, may seem to leave little scope for the present-day owner's ingenuity.

In fact the box-edged flower-beds which surround many of the sculptured shapes are carefully planted with massed winter and summer bedding, and different colour effects allow for experiment. In winter lily-flowered tulips, dark red and yellow wallflowers and forget-me-nots are massed in separate flower-beds to make blocks of colour. At the end of May, after the last frosts, new colourful annuals are fitted in to the box-edged beds. Most effective, and now traditional at Levens, are violet-blue *Verbena rigida* (syn. *V. venosa*) and, surrounding the golden yew shapes, a complementary sea of pale blue-flowered cynoglossum. Elsewhere silver-leaved cineraria are interplanted with single plants of

The view westward over the bastion to an avenue of sycamores.

bronze-red-leaved *Lobelia cardinalis* with vivid scarlet flowers. Petunias in deep violet and red shades, pink impatiens and lime-yellow pansies give contrast, and in stone urns more grey-leaved tender bedding plants and fuchsias intermingle. In the north-east corner of the garden, where Beaumont had his own house, planting in his day was probably of herbs or kitchen stuff. Today two maidenhair trees (*Ginkgo biloba*) and the dawn redwood (*Metasequoia glyptostroboides*) dominate a series of diamond- and rectangular-shaped beds, and more cushiony box shapes mark edges and corners. Around one tree a formal rose garden extends colour and interest; around another, the base of its trunk carpeted with variegated lamium, spring tulips are later replaced by fuchsias; and variegated hostas are more permanent planting in nearby borders.

Fortunately lack of money, collateral inheritance and perhaps the remote situation ensured that the park and garden at Levens retained over the years the period flavour which so perfectly suit the gaunt fortress-like house. Neither Capability Brown nor Repton advised here to break the symmetry of avenues or garden enclosures. Instead, successive generations have maintained and replanted the basic frame, trimmed the yew and box shapes and adapted the garden to a modern age, with visiting public, a garden centre, a play area for children in the outer 'wilderness', and other amenities which will help defray the heavy cost of upkeep. Three gardeners on 6-foot-high (1.8-metre) trestles spend three autumn months clipping yew shapes, arches and battlemented edges, as well as the vast pleached beech alley and its curving archways. Electric cutters powered from a generator speed the work, but the box topiary and hedging is still tackled by hand. Inheriting an historic garden is a great responsibility.

Newby Hall

Ripon, North Yorkshire
(Mr and Mrs Robin Compton)

ALL the greatest English gardens have a unity of design which integrates them with the house itself and the landscape in which they are set. Newby is no exception. Today the eastern drive winds through parkland, but as it nears the brick house one avenue of white-flowered chestnut (*Aesculus hippocastanum* 'Baumannii') and another, wider, of hornbeam (*Carpinus betulus*) carry the eye to the oval courtyard where a hornbeam hedge and dark Irish yews formalize the final approach. Originally the entrance of the house, which dates mainly to the last decade of the seventeenth century but has many later features, lay to the west, and a Knyff/Kip engraving of 1720 shows the double avenues which stretched east and west, and the conventional *patte d'oie* radiating from the western façade. When Celia Fiennes visited in 1697 the house can barely have been completed, but already a walled courtyard enclosed a formal garden on the entrance side, laid out with gravel walks between grass plots, 'with brass statues great and small in each Square', borders of flowers and 'green banks with flower potts'. On the other side of the house she writes of 'just such a garden', but with grass paths and 'Squares full of dwarfe trees both fruites and green'. Today the west view over the river is framed by cedars and Pfitzer juniper and reaches across green lawn and fields to the

OPPOSITE
Double herbaceous borders, forming the main axis of the garden, stretch from the river Ure to the south façade of the seventeenth-century house.

RIGHT
Near the house, terraces outlined by stone balustrading and urns are planted with formal evergreens. At Newby contrasts of foliage colour and texture combine with architectural shapes to unite the design of the garden.

ABOVE LEFT
Stone paths lead through
the woodland west of the
main garden.

ABOVE RIGHT
A grove of white-
stemmed birch (*Betula
jacquemontii*) is
underplanted with *Hosta
undulata*, its cream leaves
margined in dark green.

woods of Studley Royal and Fountains Abbey
beyond. A hedge of white Rugosa roses lies
under the line of the terrrace.

The 25-acre (10-hectare) garden lying on the
slope to the south is bounded by the valley of
the river Ure. Always a pleasure ground, and
planted in the eighteenth century with good
trees such as Turkey oak (*Quercus cerris*), white
oak from easten America (*Quercus alba*), and
oriental plane (*Platanus orientalis*), the garden
we see today dates mainly from the late 1920s,
when Major Edward Compton was given the
estate by his mother. Situated on the brow of
the gentle incline, the house was already
stabilized by a balustraded terrace to the south
and a broad cross-axial walk where Irish yews
framed fine eighteenth-century Venetian
statues. The balustrades were designed by
William Burges, who at the same time built the
church surrounded by weeping beeches, which
is a feature near the main gates of the park to
the east. They contained an elaborate Italianate
parterre of box-edged beds set among gravelled paths, one of which extended as a central
feature across the Statue Walk down to the
distant river valley. In 1925 a grass tennis-court
lay to the east and a croquet lawn to the west;
farther on circular beds of *Cotoneaster horizontalis* and rectangular rose borders preceded the
final stretch, where yew hedges backed
herbaceous borders facing each other across the
path, terminating at a stone palisade above a
landing place at the river's edge. Winding
walks led through Victorian shrubberies of
aucuba, punctuated with baskets of ivy filled
with pelargoniums in summer. On the west the
garden boundary was marked by informal

woodland, in which was concealed the rem-
nant planting of one of the original lime
avenues in the French style radiating from the
west façade of the house. Sometime in the first
few years of this century Miss Ellen Willmott
helped plan a rock garden just within this
perimeter, and planted alpines in specially
constructed moraines and screes; elaborate
waterworks carried across Gothic-type rock
archways provided suitable sites for moisture-
loving plants. Very much on the same line as
her own rock garden at Warley Place in Essex,
constructed in 1882, it was almost certainly laid
out by the same firm, James Backhouse of
York. A winding pergola for different ivies
was also designed by Miss Willmott. To the
south-east lay a large walled kitchen garden.

Major Compton flagged the terrace, remov-
ing the parterres and replacing them with a lily
pond, its outline relating to the curves of the
stone balustrades. On the next and lower level
great bastions of clipped yew, backed by
groups of soaring *Chamaecyparis lawsoniana*
'Erecta Viridis', were planted to mark the
boundaries of a flat lawn, from which broad
steps descended to the axial pathway where
smooth lawn replaced the original gravel. The
yew hedging and herbaceous borders at the
southern extremity were extended in blocks
northwards to the Statue Walk; at each point
where the hedging was discontinued cross-
axial vistas penetrated into lateral and almost
geometric compartments. This layout, thus
'formalized' in seventeenth-century fashion,
provided inner garden 'rooms'. From the
Statue Walk, which runs exactly east and west,
further entrances and steps to upper and lower

garden areas completed the grid system. Paved paths and a new rose pergola joined Miss Willmott's curving pergola and informal rock garden to this new structured design.

Planting followed the Hidcote pattern; a wide range of interesting plants 'furnished' these garden rooms. Inside the precise framework there were separate areas of seasonal and colour interest. To the north of the Statue Walk an architectural sunken area, now known as Sylvia's garden, with raised stone and brick beds, echoed a ceiling design by Robert Adam, who decorated the interior of the house in the middle of the eighteenth century. Another section, once the croquet ground, was enclosed with a copper beech hedge to become a shrub rose garden. In the woodland Major Compton planted groves of *Acer griseum* with translucent peeling bark and, near by, a specimen of the varnish tree (*Rhus verniciflua*). Davidias and magnolias grow well in the deep acid to neutral soil. Now mature, these plantings reflect Major Compton's plantsman's interest and knowledge, which he developed side by side with his already keen sense of architectural balance. The 'new' gardens at Newby with which he 'framed' his fine house were filled with plants covering a wide range of botanical interest. Inside the geometric formula of the design, once hedges could protect plants from the prevailing southwest winds, he was able to plant lavishly.

Fortunately for Newby Hall, Major Compton's son, Mr Robin Compton and his wife are as keenly interested in the garden as he was. Even in Major Compton's time the garden was visited regularly by the public; now the house, too, with its rare collections and Adam ceilings, has been restored by Mrs Compton and thrown open. Major Compton worked at Newby from 1921 until 1977; much of his planting is satisfyingly mature, but after a half-century borders have needed replanning and replanting, woodland glades and important vistas need opening out, and trees and shrubs need constant attention to maintain the garden 'pictures'.

From contemporary accounts and from his own description of the gardens towards the end of his life, Major Edward Compton was more than a plantsman and designer. He seems to have had a painter's skill in placing colours and textures of flower and foliage so that they would together make a pictorial composition, with carefully graded tints and shades matching and blending, and light foliage and pale flower colours balancing with dark, heavy and

more structural shapes. A garden can be well maintained yet lose some further elusive quality which depended on the aesthetic understanding of the original designer. At Newby, this colour awareness is if anything more strongly conveyed today than in the past. Mr and Mrs Compton do no random planting; each plant must be perfectly suited to enhance the whole scheme. A progress through the garden and each of its compartments reveals a series of static pictures, each one complete and perfect in itself. Sometimes a particular plant or colour association dates from Mr Compton's father's time although it is often a subtle adaptation of the earlier ideas. A row of purple-leaved *Prunus cerasifera* 'Pissardii' backs the Irish yews on the south edge of the Statue Walk, and fan-shaped *Cotoneaster horizontalis* make skirts framing yews and statues. A copper beech hedge surrounds the sunken garden to blend with the purples, mauves and blush-pinks of the older shrub roses. Groups of purple-leaved cotinus to the east act as a foil to grey-leaved pears and the pale foliage of variegated *Cornus alba* 'Elegantissima'. In a pair of rectangular beds behind the top ends of the yew hedges and just below the Statue Walk, suckering *Amelanchier canadensis* makes a flowering thicket in May and leaves assume rich tints in autumn. Major Compton replanted Miss Willmott's pergola to make an arbour of *Laburnum* 'Vossii' and twining wisteria, now one of the glories of late spring at Newby.

In Sylvia's garden Mrs Compton has recently made a formal pattern of grey and silver foliage plants. Placed on corners and outlining paths, these act as a frame to flowers with pale colouring. The Byzantine stone corn-grinder at the centre rises from a sea of *Calamintha nepetoides*. Uncommon and tender lavenders such as *Lavandula canariensis*, *L. lanata* and *L. stoechas*, a half-hardy annual, the blue lace flower (*Didiscus caeruleus*), and others reflect the Compton's shared gardening interest.

The approach to Sylvia's garden is through a planting of 'Wars of the Roses', where Mr Compton has planted the white rose of York ('Alba Semiplena') with the red rose of Lancaster (*R. gallica officinalis*), and near by a low hedge of the striped Rosa Mundi. Past a specimen *Staphylea holocarpa rosea* and a large cedar to the north, steps descend to the open and sunlit sunken garden.

Beyond, a bank of philadelphus and cistus contributes flower and scent in June and *Cupressus arizonica* is architectural. To the south, towards Burges's stone seat which terminates the west end of the Statue Walk, a tall *Sorbus intermedia* planted at the time Miss Willmott advised in the garden is now 70 feet (21 metres) tall, perhaps the tallest in the country. The rose pergola running south from the Statue Walk has recently been redone with iron hoops and replanted with roses chosen for fragrance and gentle pale colouring to match and blend with the flavour of the rose garden.

While maintenance has been made labour-saving with stone edging to borders and, when necessary, contact herbicides reduce the burdens of hand-weeding, history and continuity are not ignored. The July garden planned by Mr Compton's father is now heavily shaded by a notable variegated sycamore, but planting continues and includes the seldom seen white-flowered *Crinodendron patagua*, *Correa backhousiana* and the tender *Azara lanceolata*, which grow near established groups of *Cornus kousa*. Farther west in the rock garden old specimens of *Pinus mugo* and acers have been augmented by evergreens such as *Olearia virgata lineata*, the small *Ilex crenata*, clethra species and the variegated buckthorn (*Rhamnus alaterna* 'Argenteovariegata'). A *Styrax japonica* flowers above creeping *Alchemilla alpina*, with a ground-covering of the curse of Corsica, (*Soleirolia soleirolii*, syn. *Helxine soleirolii*) which thrives in the moist shade. Recently the original aqueduct has been repaired and the continuous sound of dripping water is soothing. In the more open pergola area hostas thrive beside prostrate *Ceanothus thyrsiflorus repens*.

Down towards the river new specimens of *Idesia polycarpa* and the early spring-flowering *Stachyurus praecox* add interest near a monument to a drowning tragedy. The present Comptons have extended the grove of *Acer griseum*: a plantation of white-stemmed birch (*Betula utilis jacquemontii*) underplanted with *Aconogonum campanulatum* (syn. *Polygonum c.*) is luminous in shade. A well-grown *Magnolia sargentiana robusta*, *Davidia involucrata*, *Prunus serrula* with polished mahogany bark, *Acer ginnala* – more of a shrub than a tree, and with vivid autumn colouring – and *Populus lasiocarpa* are all E.H. Wilson's introductions from western China and thrive here in the deep acid soil. Rhododendrons, corylopsis, camellias, *Aesculus parviflora* and the shuttlecock fern *Matteuccia struthiopteris* all draw attention.

Across the bottom of the famous double borders, several more garden compartments have their separate themes. In one, the tropical garden, all the plants, such as aralia, *Eryngium pandanifolium*, *Kniphofia caulescens*, phor-

miums, ligularia and rodgersia, have large or sculptured leaves to give a jungle effect. *Magnolia dawsoniana*, also one of Wilson's introductions, flowers against a south-facing wall above. An orchard area above is planted formally with espalier fruit and hedges of *Philadelphus* 'Dame Blanche' to flower in June and scent the air; each wall is covered with good and often unusual climbers, some of which seem too tender for such a northerly garden. Loquats, trachelospermum and *Viburnum henryi* grow well, reflecting skilled garden care, whereby plants are given adequate winter protection when young and vulnerable. *Solanum crispum* 'Glasnevin' and white-flowered *S. jasminoides* 'Album', *Carpenteria californica* and abutilon species clothe the walls with flower and foliage.

There are still more garden compartments on the east of the main axis formed by the herbaceous borders against their dark yew hedges. Above the orchard a new white garden has been planted by Mrs Compton; there are other areas where foliage plants weave textured patterns, and taller trees and shrubs create patterns of light and shade. Across the central view the rose garden is still full of subtle pink and mauve-flowered roses; salmon and apricot tints of modern rose hybrids are not allowed. Under the roses violas, herbaceous geranium, *Parahebe perfoliata* and the spreading silver-leaved *Convolvulus althaeoides* from the Mediterranean survive the cold of winter. Blue-flowered *Baptisia australis*, cynoglossum, and *Clematis integrifolia* with nodding flowers of indigo-violet intermingle, all perfect complements to sprawling rose shapes.

Back across the central border path another garden 'room' is planned for late-summer flowering: indigoferas, perovskias, purple-flowered hebes, *Desmodium tiliifolium* and deciduous autumn-flowering ceanothus. Mr Compton has collected together a fine number of tender salvias, which include the late-flowering bright blue *Salvia uliginosa* and darker *S. guaranitica*, and the pineapple sage (*S. rutilans*) with scarlet flower-spikes.

Today, with only five gardeners, the Comptons use few annuals to enhance the colour schemes, but are constantly refurbishing and extending with plants only recently available. Fortunately a garden evolves and changes and provides the opportunity for a new generation to contribute more planting interest. Development continues side by side with maintenance, as a second generation tends this fine twentieth-century garden.

OPPOSITE ABOVE LEFT
Near the house tall Irish yews, statues and stone masonry give the house an architectural frame.

RIGHT
Stone urns, soaring *Chamaecyparis lawsoniana* 'Erecta Viridis' and bastions of clipped yew on the terrace below the south front make a strong framework.

BELOW
A curving stone seat at the end of the broad Statue Walk which makes a cross terrace dates to the period when William Burges advised in the garden.

Howick Hall

near Alnwick, Northumberland
(Lord Howick)

THE TWO almost distinct gardens at Howick together cover perhaps 15 acres (some 6 hectares) in all; about a quarter of this area lies on acid soil which overlays a whinstone outcrop to the east of the house. Today it seems exciting that Lord Howick, grandson of Lord Grey, who really started the woodland garden during the 1920s, and son of Lady Mary Howick, who has developed and supervised the two gardens to a high pitch of perfection during the years since, talks now of further expansion. Particularly interested in trees and recognizing the unique and favourable climate at Howick, he intends to take in more woodland to provide a site for a new arboretum to the west. In days when many great gardens are spiralling into decay through lack of funds for maintenance or

The vivid orange flowers of *Kniphofia* 'Lord Roberts', growing in an enclosed garden under the tall Atlas cedar (*Cedrus atlantica* 'Glauca'), can be glimpsed above the top of the yew hedge.

A stone urn is silhouetted against the lavender hedge.

are losing their impetus through a new generation's lack of horticultural interest, these plans for the future are exceptional. At Howick five gardeners maintain the area impeccably.

The Northumberland coast is swept by strong north-easterly gales but the gardens at Howick, although hardly more than a mile from the sea, lie in a wooded valley where old oaks, Spanish chestnut and beech (and still a few elm survivors) make a protective wind-break and help provide a canopy for the east garden. From the eighteenth-century sand-stone house the ground slopes downwards to a stream and then rises again to the level plateau of parkland beyond. In this part of the garden the soil is alkaline, and terraced levels provide perfect conditions for sun-loving plants. The top terrace dates from the building of the house in 1776, while the balustrading and lower levels were added in 1812 and completed in the 1840s. Descriptions in *The Gardener's Chronicle* of 1884 detail formal box-edged beds set in gravel, some in an elaborate Greek key pattern, and mainly filled with annual bedding plants in the contemporary fashion. To east and west in front of the wings of the house, however, less conventional planting seems to have been ahead of its time: 'Hardy heaths, aubrietas, kalmias, lilies, phloxes, *Anemone japonica*, *Pyrus coccinea*, roses and such-like hardy things, the general effect of these being quite unique.' These gardens are still planted with permanent shrubs, perennials and bulbs. A hedge of lavender lines the lower terrace, while a planting of agapanthus forms the outer edging of the higher level, and is a glorious sight towards the end of August. To the east a blue Atlantic cedar faces the clock-tower on the sweeping eastern wing of the house, and a small yew-hedged enclosure is planted with lavender and massed *Kniphofia* 'Lord Roberts', with bright orange-red pokers late in the season. Against the wing tender shrubs thrive. A *Buddleja farreri* flowers in spring, before the large grey felted leaves develop, the fragrant panicles rosy-lilac. Evergreen *Osmanthus yunnanensis* bears scented flowers towards the end of winter. Tall bay trees, clerodendrum, *Deutzia setchuenensis* and potentillas are informally grouped. Below the upper terrace, where *Dryas octopetala* has made a spreading mat and watsonias flower in late summer, the mixed planting of roses, shrubs and perennials includes *Carpenteria californica*, *Choisya ternata* and dark-flowered penstemons. Stonework is softened with prostrate junipers, and a hedge of white Rugosa roses makes another horizontal line across the slope. In the valley below, the stream – dammed in the 1930s by Lady Mary's parents – has gunnera and willows planted along the banks, while mown paths wind through rougher grass where ornamental trees include acer species such as *Acer griseum* and a large *A. saccharinum*, sorbus, and birch with ornamental barks. A distant view to the north-west reveals an uncommon golden-leaved Scots pine (*Pinus sylvestris* 'Aurea'). A garden enclosed by a yew hedge fills a space to the west of the house, the dark yew making a perfect foil and background to flowers in pale colours and plants with silvery and grey foliage.

Back to the east the grass is filled with naturalized daffodils, whose flowering is followed by a scattering of mixed tulips and doronicums, happy under a copper beech and a fine specimen of the southern beech, *Nothofagus procera* from Chile. Later, meadow grass waves with ox-eye daisies, clover and poppies. Mowing is delayed until July and colchicums, forms of *Colchicum speciosum*, carpet the ground from late August until October. This is one of the fine sights at Howick.

Most visitors come up the drive, past a specimen *Sorbus* 'John Mitchell' and groups of *Cercidiphyllum japonicum*, which are a feature here, their leaves becoming scented as the pigment breaks down in autumn. A pathway turns immediately into the wood, leaving the more formal garden until later. In this area of acid soil Lord Grey planted further shelter-belts among the trees, using yew, the Monterey cypress (*Cupressus macrocarpa*) and bushes of shining green-leaved *Griselinia littoralis* from New Zealand which have since grown to tree size. Although rainfall is only an annual 27 inches (67 centimetres), humidity is high and sea 'frets' blow in from the coast. Deep humus-laden soil is further enriched by frequent mulches of bracken, which helps retain moisture, and frosts are seldom severe or long-lasting.

Any description of the gardens may lose a clear definition between the planting contribution of Lady Mary and that of her father, who died in 1963. Many of the great Asiatic rhododendrons, magnolias and acers, and the eucryphias, hoherias and senecios from the southern hemisphere, will have been first planted by Lord Grey – some established with seed obtained from the great Forrest and Kindgon Ward expeditions of the 1920s and 1930s, and others introduced earlier from Westonbirt or Wakehurst. Planting of this scale and quality takes time to mature and some of the plants are perhaps now at their best. Fortunately planting has continued under Lady Mary and many more of the same genera have been added over the years, with additions of olearias, *Drimys winteri* and *D. lanceolata*, embothriums, and a rare *Lindera obtusiloba* which greets the visitor at the entrance. Today in spring *Magnolia campbellii* opens early, its pink tulips carried high on a 40-foot (12-metre) tree. A pair of *M. wilsonii* flowers later, the pendent cupped flowers overhanging a winding woodland path. Now *Eucryphia cordifolia* makes a tall pyramidal shape, in August and September covered in translucent creamy-white blossom, and the deciduous *Hoheria lyallii* and evergreen *H. sexstylosa* carry their white flowers in July and September respectively. *Clethra delavayi* also flowers in July, carrying white lily-of-the-valley racemes very freely. Large-leaved rhododendrons grow to tree proportions beside acers and cercidiphyllum. *Rhododendron johnstoneanum*, with long elliptical leaves, densely scaled and brown beneath, has yellow clustered flowers marked conspicuously with red spots. The elegant *R. williamsianum*, introduced by Wilson in 1908, has round heart-shaped translucent foliage and bears pink bell-

A winding path between trunks of old oaks is flanked by blue-flowered *Rhododendron augustinii* and bamboo.

OPPOSITE ABOVE
In late summer white colchicums, naturalized in grass, are a feature in the garden.

OPPOSITE BELOW
Spring-flowering dentarias, bergenias and trilliums grow under *Rhododendron litiense* with soft yellow and *R. williamsianum* with shell-pink flowers.

flowers in early May. Although emphasis has been mainly on making a collection of species rhododendrons, there are good hybrids of the smaller-leaved *R. triflorum* (syn. *R. augustinii*), which include *RR*. 'Bluebird', 'Blue Diamond' and 'Blue Tit', and these, with startling blue flowers in May, contrast in scale with the more statuesque giants. A Loderi rhododendron 'King George' makes a vast bush near bronze-leaved *R. fictolacteum*. Everywhere the greens of rhododendron leaves, many with felted brown beneath, contrast with other leaf colours and textures – the shining surface of Portugal laurel and griselinia, or the more delicate translucency of *Cercidiphyllum japonicum*, specimens of which are planted in groves throughout the wood – and with the

darker outlines of eucryphia, cupressus and yew. In the favourable microclimate at Howick the tender June-flowering rhododendrons do well, their flowers white or faintly flushed pink and very fragrant.

But this is not all. What makes Howick remarkable as a woodland garden is the planting at all visual levels. The earlier trees which shelter the garden date from the eighteenth century; two hundred years later their maturity was exploited to provide sites for more demanding and tender exotics below their spreading heads. In turn shrubs, both evergreen and deciduous, make a sheltering canopy for drifts of smaller ground-hugging plants – stately lilies and flowering perennials which add a wealth of botanical interest throughout

the garden. Between groves of rhododendrons there are planted 'valleys' of blue omphalodes; mauve and white-flowered dentaria rise above a dense mat of *Blechnum penna-marina*; trilliums from North America, the pale primrose-flowered *Paeonia mlokosewitschii* and seedlings from *P. wittmanniana*, hellebores and variegated ground-elder cover a wide range. The hybrid azalea 'Palestrina' bears its greenish-white flowers above an underplanting of *Erythronium tuolumnense*. Later *Glaucidium palmatum* carries lilac flowers and the orchis (now correctly *Dactylorhiza elata*) glows with vivid colouring in a shady corner. The elegant *Dodecatheon meadia* and *Ourisia elegans* thrive where soil is moist. Giant lilies (*Cardiocrinum giganteum*) are spectacular in July; in September auratum lilies scent the air and clumps of blue-flowered agapanthus are luminous in the dark wood, in front of *Eucryphia glutinosa*, covered with creamy single flowers.

Few woodland gardens reflect such careful planning of colour and form. Each bend in a path reveals some new composition where leaf and flower association seems to have been carefully planned many years before, calling not only for the eye of a painter in perfecting a composition still only in his imagination, but also for the skill and knowledge of the gardener who knows how to ensure that plants will grow to maturity and perform as expected. It is not possible to list all the plants, nor perhaps to convey adequately their arrangement. Island beds of dense planting are followed by open sunlit glades where only the brownish-red trunks of *Pinus sylvestris* distract with colour; the plantsman's instinct to collect at the expense of a coherent garden design has been resisted. Howick is a great woodland garden because it is much more than a collection of exotics. Each separate garden view seems to give evidence of Lady Mary's and her father's sense of scale and colour. Spring and summer effects are equally good, and in autumn there is a final burst of foliage colour. The peeling flakes of *Acer griseum* bark are seen where the sun filters through them. Near by in an opening in the darker wood *Hydrangea aspera villosa* flowers above textured hosta leaves, and drifts of lemon-flowered *Hemerocallis citrina* are complementary to a late pale blue poppy, a form or seedling of *Meconopsis napaulensis*, perhaps a cross with *M. regia*, also from the Himalayas.

Botanical interest and beauty are equally matched in both gardens, and the future seems well assured.

General Index

Index of Plants

Figures in *italics* refer to illustration captions

artichoke: Cynara scolymus
Arum 129
    A. italicum 'Pictum' 45
arum, bog 89
Arundinaria
    A. murielae 185
    A. viridistriata 40, 185
ash: Fraxinus
Astelia
    A. cunninghamii 18
    A. nervosa 18
Aster (Michaelmas daisy) 124, 129
    A. acris: A. sedifolius
    A. divaricatus 28
    A. × frikartii 56
        A. × f. 'Mönch' 45, 106
    A. sedifolius (A. acris) 56
Astilbe 28, 40, 77, 105, 172, *182*, 184
Astrantia 117, 161
    A. major (masterwort) 53
Aubrieta 207
Aucuba 76, 200
auricula: *Primula auricula*
azalea *12*, 184
    Ghent 94
    Japanese 16, 41
    'Palestrina' 209
Azara 27, 70
    A. dentata 45
    A. lanceolata 202
    A. microphylla 45

Ballota 155, 173
balsam: *Impatiens parviflora*
bamboo 18, 29, 76, 77, 89, 127, 136, 172,
    208; *see also* Arundinaria *etc*
bamboo, Chilean: *Chusquea culeou*
Banksia
    B. coccinea 22
    B. grandis 22
    B. serrata 20
Baptisia
    B. australis 105, 124, 202
bay: *Laurus nobilis*
beech: Fagus
beech, Chilean: Nothofagus
beech, southern: Nothofagus
Berberidopsis 16
Berberis 45, 146, 167, 179, 184
    B. temolaica 155, 167
bergamot: Monarda
Bergenia *209*
    B. ciliata 127
Beschorneria
    B. yuccoides 23, 76
Betula (birch) 13, 36, 40, 45, 76, 147, *154*,
    184, 191, 207
    B. albo-sinensis 133
    B. utilis jacquemontii 136, *152*, 200, 202
birch: Betula
Blechnum
    B. chilense 18, 40, 127
    B. penna-marina 209
bluebell 95, 112, 143, 157, 169, 178, 184,
    190, *208*

Bomarea
    B. caldasii 23
    B. × cantabrigiensis 23
box: Buxus
Brachyglottis repanda (rangiora) 20
Briza
    B. maxima 173
broom: Cytisus
broom, Moroccan: *Cytisus battandieri*
broom, Mount Etna: *Genista aetnensis*
Brunnera 43, 77
    B. macrophylla 107, 171, 172
buckthorn: *Rhamnus alaternus*
Buddleja 117, 155
    B. alternifolia 42, 45, 59, 80, 155
    B. colvilei 124, 161
    B. crispa 106, 116
    B. farreri 124, 207
    B. 'Harlequin' 65
Bupleurum
    B. fruticosum 27
Bursaria
    B. spinosa 23
Buxus (box) 32, 62, 63, 64, 65, 69, 70, 78
    et passim

cabbage tree: *Cordyline australis*
Caesalpinia
    C. japonica 23, 122
Calamintha
    C. nepetoides 48, 81, 167, 201
Calendula (marigold) 53
Callistemon 23
Calodendron
    C. capense (cape chestnut) 18
Caltha
    C. palustris (kingcup) 172
Camassia 153
    C. cusickii 149
Camellia 26, 28, 31, 32, 33, 94, 178, 190,
    202
    C. 'Donation' *15*, 16
    C. japonica 16
    C. saluenensis 16
    C. × williamsii hybrids 16
camomile: *Chamaemelum nobile*
Campanula 44, 63
    C. betulifolia 59
    C. lactiflora 77
campion 184
Caragana
    C. arborescens 'Lorbergii' 153
Cardamine
    C. enneaphyllos (*Dentaria enneaphyllos*)
    145, 170
    C. pentaphyllos (*Dentaria digitata*) 165
Cardiocrinum
    C. giganteum 209
cardoon: Cynara
Carex
    C. pendula (sedge) 172
Carpentaria
    C. californica 80, 145, 165, 202, 207
Carpinus (hornbeam) 45, 78, 80, 157,
    190

    C. betulus 198
    C. b. 'Pendulus' (weeping hornbeam) 77
    C. b. 'Pyramidalis' (fastigiate hornbeam)
    159
Carya
    C. ovata (shagbark hickory) 161, 191
Caryopteris 48, 105
    C. × clandonensis 185
Cassia
    C. corymbosa 59, 76
Cassiope 165
Castanea (sweet chestnut, Spanish chestnut)
    143, 178, 192, 206
    C. sativa 'Albo-Marginata' 159
Catalpa 69, 105, 191
    C. bignonioides 125
    C. × erubescens 'Purpurea' 153
    C. speciosa 161
catmint: Nepeta
Ceanothus 26, *38*, 48, 70, 88, 117, 118, 178,
    202
    C. arboreus 'Trewithen Blue' 16, 107
    C. 'Cascade' 161
    C. 'Gloire de Versailles' 48, 106
    C. impressus 107
        C. i. 'Puget Blue' 40
    C. thyrsiflorus repens 202
cedar: Cedrus
cedar, Chinese: *Toona sinensis*
Cedrela
    C. sinensis: Toona sinensis
Cedrus (cedar) 43, 45, *61*, 65, 77, 84, 88, 113
    et passim
    C. atlantica 26, 69, 96, 116, 207
        C. a. glauca 117, *206*
    C. deodara 47, 93
    C. libani (cedar of Lebanon) 63, 72, 73,
        84, 93, 104, 105, 120 *et passim*
celandine 'Brazen Hussy' 165
Celastrus
    C. orbiculatus 167, 189
Celmisia 40
Centaurea 124
    C. cyanus (cornflower) 173
Centranthus (valerian) 24, 113, 155
Cephalaria 52, 172
Ceratostigma 33, 124
Cercidiphyllum 77, 159, 185, 191, 207
    C. japonicum 29, 105, 195, 207, 208
Cercis
    C. siliquastrum (Judas tree) 59, 95, 145,
    146
Cestrum 40
    C. 'Newellii' 76
    C. parqui 27, 164
Chaenomeles 88
Chamaecyparis (cypress) 105
    C. lawsoniana (Lawson cypress) 168, 200
        C. l. 'Ellwoodii' 66, 67
        C. l. 'Erecta Viridis' *203*
        C. l. 'Pottenii' 132
        C. l. 'Triompf van Boskoop' 43
    C. pisifera 'Filifera Aurea' 94
    C. pisifera 'Sulphurea' *92*
Chamaemelum